THE SUBJECT IS
ʃtorY

THE SUBJECT IS
Story

Essays for Writers and Readers

Edited by
Wendy Bishop
and
Hans Ostrom

BOYNTON/COOK
HEINEMANN
Portsmouth, NH

Boynton/Cook Publishers, Inc.
A subsidiary of Reed Elsevier Inc.
361 Hanover Street
Portsmouth, NH 03801–3912
www.boyntoncook.com

Offices and agents throughout the world.

Library of Congress Cataloging-in-Publication Data
The subject is story : essays for writers and readers / edited by Wendy Bishop and Hans Ostrom.
    p. cm.
    Includes bibliographical references.
    ISBN 0-86709-534-2 (alk. paper)
    1. English language—Rhetoric. 2. Narration (Rhetoric). 3. Creative writing.
    4. Report writing. 5. Storytelling. I. Bishop, Wendy, 1953– II. Ostrom, Hans A.

    PE1408 .S83 2003
    808' .042—dc21

                                         2003007332

Editor: Lisa Luedeke
Production: Sonja S. Chapman
Cover Design: Catherine Hawkes, Cat & Mouse
Compositor: Laura Proietti, Argosy
Manufacturing: Steve Bernier

Printed in the United States of America on acid-free paper
07 06 05 04 03 DA 1 2 3 4 5

To story-tellers everywhere.

Contents

Preface and Introduction

With students in mind—

Aunt Sue has a head full of stories.

This is the first line of Langston Hughes' poem "Aunt Sue's Stories," which tells a story about how important Aunt Sue's stories were in helping one person get a sense of the past, understand the world, and explore the pleasures of listening to stories. Aunt Sue is not alone; each of us has "a head full of stories," and stories about stories, and stories about telling, listening to, writing, and reading stories, and . . .

The collection of essays gathered here provides a way for you to talk with each other, your teachers, and yourself (your head full of stories) about *story*. In this book, *story* does not refer exclusively or even mainly to literature—novels, short stories, narrative poems. In this book, the word encompasses more than that and is applied to folktales and gossip, your particular essays and general cultural narratives, ways you talk about how you write, ways others talk about how you should write, tales told in school, about school, and out of school.

Our decision to work with a wide-open definition of story seems to be supported by the *Oxford Dictionary of the English Language* (the online version). The first definition of the word not considered obsolete reads as follows:

> 4. a. A recital of events that have or are alleged to have happened; a series of events that are or might be narrated.

In other words, judging by this definition, story, as a concept and as a practice, is portable, flexible, and durable. (Incidentally, and as you might have guessed, the history of the word *story* can be traced back through French words like *histoire, estoire,* and *estorie,* to a Latin word, *storia.*)

We wanted the writers who helped make this book to focus first on story as it relates to *your writing and reading* and second on story as it relates to *your lives,* with an awareness of how a person's life outside college overlaps with that person's life inside college—and of how the outside/inside distinction is indeed more of a false story (a tall tale) than a true one.

Also, the fact that our heads are full of stories, the fact that story can apply to any "recital of [any] events" in any form, and the fact that story can show up almost anywhere in your writing and reading—these circumstances, precisely because they *are* potentially so confusing, seemed to be one good reason to gather essays that discuss story and the different ways it relates to you, your writing, and your education. To the extent that education means becoming more aware, the book aims to educate by offering us ways to become more aware of story and get more perspective on how it functions in our lives.

With students and teachers in mind—

Briefly, and much more specifically, we'll now tell the story of what you're in for when you read this book. Part I—The Persistence of Story—is the most panoramic section of the book, taking broad views of story in the history of rhetoric, in different educational and cultural settings, and in our everyday lives. To begin, Hans Ostrom's "Story, Stories, and You" connects everyday stories, including those you share just before class begins, to broader cultural narratives and the sheer abundance of story in our culture(s). Ostrom also discusses an issue common to several chapters in the book: namely, the apparent conflict between the fact that narration is one of the main ways we all put language to use and the fact that, in college writing, narration is often looked upon with suspicion while argumentation is exalted—and often (the history of rhetoric notwithstanding) portrayed as excluding story. What role has narration played in oral and written argument, in speeches and writings whose main purpose is to persuade someone of something? James Herrick's chapter, "Narration and Argument," answers this question, locates narration for us in the twenty-five-hundred-year history of rhetoric, and reminds us why types of storytelling have always been important to argumentation. In "Looking for Dr. Fuller," Douglas Hesse adds to Herrick's historical perspective and puts story in its place, or at least one place, within the tradition of the essay, a tradition that can be traced back to the sixteenth century. At the same time, Hesse discusses ways we do and ways we can deploy narrative in the most contemporary of essays, the ones we are writing right now.

Although the chapters in this panoramic section are full of specific examples, Part II—Story, Discovery, and Recovery—is even more insistent about getting down to cases. John Boe's refreshing "Storytelling, Writing, and Finding Yourself" indirectly reminds us that the depiction of self-discovery in writing as touchy-feely is a stereotype begging to be discarded, and that telling stories, writing, and self-discovery remain a productive, challenging, and highly practical trio. Stuart Ching connects self-discovery with recovery—as in retrieval in his chapter "Remembering Great Ancestors: Story as Recovery, Story as Quest." In "The Stories We Are," Michael Spooner continues the work of situating the individual in the culture and tells a subtle, enchanting story-within-a-story along the way. David Wallace concludes Part II with "The Poems Came Late: Literacy as Cultural Dialogue." Wallace's chapter addresses questions of *voice*, definition of self, asserting one's self, and sexual identity.

Indirectly, then, Part II explores discovery of self within circumstances of storytelling, cultural identity, sexuality, gender, and ancestry. Part III—Story in Context: Responsibility, Community, Heritage—is even more expressly concerned with story in such contexts.

When we write personal narratives, in college settings and elsewhere, *what are our responsibilities?* What do we owe to ourselves, our readers, and conventions of the personal narrative? In their chapter, Robert Brooke, Rochelle Harris, and Jeannine Nyangira answer these questions in specific, attentive ways. The next authors by no means abandon the question of responsibility, but they nonetheless concentrate forcefully on questions of community and heritage, even more so than authors of earlier chapters, like Ching and Spooner. Carolyn Alessio explores stories as modes of knowing that are vitally connected to "multicultural identity in the writing classroom." In "Necessary Confessions," Joseph Eng deftly examines how the categories of "the personal" (including the *writer*) and "the communal" (including the *audience*) are permeable. In an exploration running parallel to Eng's, Gayle Duskin concludes this section by asking questions about the categories "oral" and "written," specifically but not exclusively within contexts of African American cultural identity, in her chapter, "Ancient Tradition and Contemporary Storytelling."

The fourth and concluding section—Persuasion, Product, Process, and Story—to some extent mimics the first section in that the chapters here offer rather broad views of story. Paul Heilker develops an intricate, illuminating analogy between travel and writing and deepens our understanding of the essay genre. Stephanie Dyer and Dana Elder take up the question of story and argument by opening a category that combines both for the contemporary writer: the suasive essay, which melds *persuasion* and *reflection*. Wendy Bishop concludes the book by examining writing process stories, or the tales we tell and are told about that mythic beast, "the writing process." She also takes a fresh look at the question of processes (what we *do* as we write) and products (what we *have* after we have written) in connection with story.

With teachers in mind—

Thought is not merely expressed in words; it comes into existence through them.

—Lev Vygotsky

Teachers like you and like us know there are so many demands on classroom time. Why, you might ask, should we spend time there telling stories? We argue here that stories are not merely personal but instead are crucial. They provide ways to see and examine our thinking as we introduce ourselves on the first day of class, as we tell the stories of our lives in the contexts of others' lives, as we narrate our classroom and authoring experiences.

We think that you and your students will enjoy these essays because they are intentionally filled with stories; the authors here enact possible pedagogies, asking you and your students to consider your own histories with and reliance on story as a major mode of making meaning . Some of the authors in this collection offer invitations to write within their chapters and others offer additional hint sheets at the end of the book to help elaborate possible assignments for your classes.

Still, we realize that you teach courses from a variety of perspectives that focus on different mixtures of the personal and the public, the private and the political. There are essays and invitations that support your own particular mixture. If you choose the rhetorical turn, start with Herrick's, Ostrom's, and Dyer and Elder's chapters. If you focus on the essay, consider pairing Hesse's and Heilker's essays as your classroom turns to narrative designs. If you prefer a cross-cultural approach, there are many chapters to draw from, including those by Ching, Wallace, Eng, Spooner, and Duskin. Issues of the personal can be framed by Brooke, Harris, and Nyangira's chapter as well as by Bishop's chapter. That is to say, while we have arranged these chapters in sections and followed each section with questions on pages titled "Sharing Ideas," which help you put essayists in dialogue with essayists, we think you will find that these chapters are adaptable for distinctly differently themed courses. We make such a claim because some of the strengths and joys of story are, of course, flexibility, diversity, and compelling detail. Story will help you forge a strong classroom community even as storytelling allows your writing students to produce texts that go on beyond the classroom, making their rich thoughts manifest through words.

Acknowledgments

While we won't keep you from the rest of the book by telling the story of how it came into being, we do want briefly to thank all those who matter most to this version of our writing lives. Lisa Luedeke keeps believing in books like this one, by teachers and students *for* students and teachers. All our thanks to her and to the production staff at Boynton/Cook Heinemann. Thanks also to the students in our classes, the contributors to this collection, and to our families; whenever we meet at writing conferences, we tell and retell fond tales of Jackie and Spencer, of Dean and Morgan and Tait.

—Tallahassee, Florida, and Puget Sound, Washington, winter 2003

Part I
The Persistence of Story

The universe is made of stories, not of atoms.

—Muriel Rukeyser

1

Story, Stories, and You

Hans Ostrom

I.

I'm an English professor, and I like to get to class early—by at least seven minutes. I'd prefer ten, but that would mean encroaching on the buffer between the previous class and mine. Five is too few, not to mention too conventional.

Early arrival appeals to me in several ways. Some of these are connected to work habits I absorbed long ago, some to a bit of anxiety that persists despite my years of experience. Another appeal is that class members who show up during this interval tell stories to each other. As I write on the blackboard, shuffle through papers, look at notes, or stare out the window, I listen to the stories you tell. (In place of the words *student* and *students*, meaning people who have taken English classes from me, I'm chiefly going to use the word *you* in this essay. I mean by it "you, the reader," but I also mean to imply that I think you're enough like people who have taken my classes to stand in for them during this chapter.)

When you catch on that I almost always arrive early, more of you arrive early. Also, the further along in the semester we go, the more invisible I seem to get during those seven minutes. Maybe I'm not officially "the prof" until the top of the hour. Maybe familiarity breeds invisibility. Maybe you rather like paying me little attention up until the time you must appear to pay me a lot of attention. Of course, if you have an urgent question for me about the class (another reason I arrive early), I seem to become instantly visible, but that's another story. Anyway, you seem to talk more freely to each other, with less self-censoring, the further along the semester goes.

Self-censoring doesn't disappear altogether. All stories are, at some level, disclosure—an opening of doors or windows onto something previously concealed. But there are some things, many things, I would rather not know about you, that you would rather I not know, and that you would rather not disclose to a class member a few minutes before class. I'd rather not hear stories most properly told to close friends, a parent, a sibling, a mental health counselor, a medical doctor, or a spiritual confidante. (You can think of examples as easily as I.) Few, if any, of the stories I overhear during early arrival fall into these categories.

What *have* I overheard? Your tales of broken plumbing, campus radio shows on which you play death metal, parties, horrid roommates, bizarre neighbors, mythic struggles with term papers, deaths in the family, concerts, raves, road trips, rock climbing, awful jobs, good jobs, bad internships, good internships, wicked professors, wondrous professors, unfair grades, surprisingly easy tests, memories of high school, weather, automobiles, stray cats taken in, a flasher whom campus security and the police department can't seem to nab, auditions, tryouts, victories, losses, visits to the emergency room, favorite television series, fire alarms, calculus equations, fevers, nausea, body piercings, unjust university policies, job interviews, money woes, all-nighters, food poisoning, national crises, local customs, and so on.

What's the use of these stories you tell? What do they have to do with story in its more academic or literary sense? What do they have to do with your writing and reading? Why do you tell them, why do I like overhearing them, and why am I writing about them here? The rest of the essay will, more or less, try to address such questions.

II.

The banter I overhear during the seven minutes tells me more about who you are. In general, of course, the stories, anecdotes, gossip, inside jokes, narrative asides, and news people exchange—and people exchange these things almost constantly during waking hours—express and define who we are. Most of the time such expression and definition do not occur in any explicit, melodramatic, or even dramatic way. We're not dealing here with Hamlet's "To Be" monologue or an intense scene from a film like *Chasing Amy*. No, the daily talk expresses, defines, and changes us cumulatively, bit by bit. Bit by bit, I learn about you as I listen to you talk to each other.

I get not just news (your printer broke, you aced a quiz) but how you tell the news—with anger? Whimsy? Melodrama? Weariness? Stoicism? Fatalism? Do you portray yourself as a loner, a victim, a hero, a comic survivor, a player, a spectator, a genius, a dummy, a lucky gambler, somebody special, or just one of the crowd? What roles do you assign others? Sometimes you develop serial narratives (your printer broke—again; you're about to begin a long struggle with organic chemistry—again). Themes emerge; one of you tells an anecdote that triggers an anecdote from someone else, and a chorus of voices coalesces.

I learn about the plural you, the student body and mind—what "you all" care about at this moment on this campus, how you report and shape what you care about, how you talk about us professors, at least with one temporarily invisible professor in earshot. I get a sense of your unvarnished attitudes toward the college, a sense of your music, movies, and books, a sense of our shared material conditions: work, money, buildings, roads, weather, disease. I get a sense of how our experiences overlap (perhaps we've seen the same films) and, just as importantly, of how different you are from me and why I cannot and should not want to try to erase such difference or try to pretend it isn't there.

Isn't it awfully tempting at times to think of education as something that happens only in our minds, on some intellectual plane or collegiate plain, a realm of ideas that is *elsewhere*? In this temptation lurks a possibility of escape, as well as an offer to leave the crowd behind and join an exclusive club. It's awfully good to recall that such a realm doesn't exist, that body and mind, college and world are inseparable. When I listen to you talk to one another before class, I'm more easily able to remember that the class is attached to, is a part of, a web of experiences, lives, and physical, chemical material. When we turn to ideas, texts, and arguments at the top of the hour, we don't travel to a different realm; we are still in our lives, at a moment, in a place; we're breathing, seeing, hearing, scratching, sniffling. We're always grounded; your stories before class reassert this fact for me and maybe also for you.

Nonetheless, a devil's advocate might ask how this overheard casual conversation before class amounts to story in any way that resembles the stories and narratives other essays in this book discuss. The conversation is casual, the stories are sometimes only a sentence or two long, and they are often interrupted, abandoned, or confused—all this I grant the devil's advocate. Still, whenever conversation recounts events, whenever it arranges and represents a piece of the past, or whenever it invokes, reflects, refers to, or improvises upon other stories, it is, officially, *story*—narrative.

A patient devil's advocate might press the issue, pointing out that, given such a broad definition of story—one that may include, for instance, a sentence of gossip—almost all the talking (listening) and writing (reading) in which we engage amounts to, or at least includes, narration. What *isn't* narration, for heaven's sake?! To the devil's advocate, who may not prefer the expression "for heaven's sake," I have to say, "Indeed." Indeed, most conversation is narrative. Indeed, I think the broad definition is justified. Such an inclusive definition does not, however, prevent us from moving ahead to distinguish some kinds of stories from others, to categorize narratives, to value some stories more than others, and so on.

This view—that narration is ever-present in and crucial to our experience—is not new. For instance, in a book called *Human Communication as Narration: Toward a Philosophy of Reason, Value, and Action,* Walter Fisher (1987) argues that narration is the primary form of our communication. Or, as one of his readers puts it, "Walter Fisher makes narrative the set of which all human communication is a subset. Thus, to understand story is to understand human communication and, by implication, human thought" (Herrick 2001, 241).

A fellow named Kenneth Burke (1945) argued that almost all human expression could be viewed, if not as story, per se, then as drama. He suggested that one productive way to analyze what we hear and read is always to look for five elements: the act, the scene, the agent, the agency, and the purpose. Put another way, we might look for *what* is being described, what happened, or what someone is suggesting should be done (act). When we look for scene, we're looking for location—*where* the *what* takes place, the context, the circumstances. Then we look for *who* is acting (agent), *how* he or she is acting (agency), and *why* he, she, or they are doing what they're doing (purpose). Look for these elements anywhere you like—in a casual story a friend tells you, in a lecture by a professor, in an editorial you read in your newspaper. Plays and movies are overtly dramatic. Burke argues that almost all human communication is implicitly dramatic, that people constantly play rhetorical roles, and that they express their motives through language all the time. Try out his analysis. Can you detect any or all of these five elements in written or spoken communication that, on the surface, may not seem dramatic?

Other people who have analyzed communication focus on archetypes, deep patterns, and myths, suggesting that even when we tell a friend a story about what happened to us when we went to get our driver's license renewed, we may unconsciously structure the story according to an ancient pattern. For example, Ernest Bormann (1983) has identified basic plots in stories that groups of people (organizations, friends, nations, etc.) repeat to one another. Americans, for instance, tend to be drawn to the "rags to riches" plot; many Americans tell each other stories that suggest that "if you work hard and never give up, you can do anything." Perhaps they repeat the stories automatically, or to cement a position in the society, or to account in some way for one person's success and another's failure. Other Americans tell stories with basic plots that run counter to the "rags to riches" theme, arguing implicitly that hard work and persistence often don't pay off, that "the system is rigged." Bormann isn't so much interested in whether these basic plots and themes are true but rather in what they tell us about the groups that repeat the plots and themes in stories they tell. What basic plots do you see in stories your friends tell—about parents or work, for instance? In stories you hear on talk shows or in television drama and comedy or in news stories? What seem to you to be other basic American plots?

Because narration is everywhere, because our senses of reality are composed largely of narrative, we may not notice or analyze story as much as we should. People like Fisher, Burke, and Bormann show that often there's pleasure, understanding, or both to be gained from being alert to how we structure reality with narrative. Such structuring of reality occurs in novels, movies, myths, national histories, and ongoing reporting of national crises, but it also occurs in the microstories contained in casual conversations. So as I write here about stories you tell before class, I mean to imply that casual does not mean unimportant or unproductive. I mean to say that just listening to stories somewhat more consciously and critically can tell you a lot about your world.

If we tend to overlook and underanalyze narrative because it is ever-present in our lives, it's also true that because narrative is so commonplace, many people in the academic world look upon it with suspicion. Narrative writing is often portrayed as too personal, merely anecdotal, insufficiently rigorous, or all of the above. Academic writing tends to be organized according to topic, theme, main points, abstract ideas, generalizations, or process, in contrast to writing organized according to time, place, plot, and person or character—story. When we find narrative in academic writing, it tends to have been "treated" so as to appear more objective, formal, or rigorous. For example, write-ups of scientific experiments are essentially narrative, but there is not supposed to be drama, and there is not supposed to be a person, or a character. We are supposed to learn that a certain chemical "was added" to the solution at a certain time in a certain amount. We are not supposed to learn that "in the afternoon, Angela wearily added salt to the solution." We are supposed to learn the results of the experiment, but we are not supposed to learn that "ironically, the blue liquid exploded."

Similarly, social scientists constantly struggle to present data, all gathered by living, breathing humans, as if the data existed independently of the gatherers. Political scientists, anthropologists, and psychologists have all developed protocols—rules—for gathering data that are meant to ensure that the gatherer does not influence the data. (Samples of opinion, for instance, are supposed to be random.) The data-filled stories they present, such as case studies, are supposed to be objective, representing a reality that is freestanding.

Whether human agency can truly be removed from any human activity, including science, and how objective science and social sciences are—these remain debatable questions. I don't want to get into them here, at least not directly. Instead I want to highlight the tension between how *commonplace* narrative is in our lives and language and how *the status of narrative in academics is shaky*. I also want to ask you to look for narrative outside of literature and history classes. Where does narrative exist in the science, social science, business, and math classes you take? To what extent do the writing and the conversation (lectures, discussion) in these fields still try to tell stories of some kind? In what way has story been changed so as to look different from literary and historical narrative? Do these changes make sense to you? To what extent do you find the reading and writing you do in these fields pleasurable?

You might also reflect on instances when a teacher has viewed your academic writing as inappropriately narrative. Maybe this has happened in an English literature class, where the teacher has indicated that your paper contains too much plot summary. The teacher thinks your paper has, in its own words, retold the story of the novel or the play but not interpreted the plot enough. Assuming you want to adapt your papers to the teacher's guidelines, you might ask yourself what particular part of the plot drew you in—and why? That is, as you work toward a first draft of a paper, you might still want to write a plot summary; apparently there's some comfort and use in that for you.

Instead of transporting that plot summary to the paper itself, however, use it as a starting place for further analysis.

Or perhaps a teacher regards your paper for political science as too personal. You've used the pronoun *I*, and the teacher doesn't like this. You've included personal anecdotes related to the political issue in question. Again, think of adapting. How can you get around using *I* but still get across the points you're interested in? How do other people write in this supposedly less personal way without sounding pompous or artificial? Take a look at their writing and see what sort of moves they make, what sort of phrasing they employ. As for the personal anecdote: ask yourself what point you were hoping the anecdote would get across? If you still want to make that point, ask yourself how you might do so by different means—maybe by referring to a passage in a textbook that makes a similar point, maybe by referring to some data that support your personal view. Especially if you find the teacher approachable, you might raise the issue of genre with her or him. (*Genre* means a type of essay, with specific rules.) Why does your teacher frown upon personal anecdote? What's the rationale behind a wariness toward the pronoun *I*?

There's a good chance some of you might be very comfortable with the writing required in science and social science classes and uncomfortable with the narrative writing required in English and history classes. You, too, might think of adaptation. If the process write-up in a lab report comes easily to you, how might you transfer elements of that writing to a history paper? If you've successfully written for social science classes but are taking your first creative writing course, you may feel uncomfortable. Luckily, creative writing has the capacity to absorb other writing. For instance, you might create a character in a short story who is a social scientist. This would allow you to write about something you know and to use some of the language of the social scientist.

Learning to get comfortable with different modes, genres, phrasings, and lingo is a huge part of education—in and after college. You probably already know that certain jobs and professions want you to communicate in certain ways, to write and speak in certain forms and modes. Negotiating the tension between narrative and other ways of writing and speaking in college is good practice. Such adaptation is just one more avenue by which we all have to make our ways in the world. If at some point we take a principled stand and refuse to adapt, that's fine; at least it will have been a conscious decision, not the result of being unaware.

III.

I taught a rhetoric class for seniors recently. Part of the course included work on rhetoric in popular culture, so sometimes we talked about television shows. One member of the class had viewed many recent, old, and ancient situation comedies. (She regarded *Family Ties* from the 1980s as old, so I was forced to create an "ancient" category to include such shows as *The Honeymooners*, which I had previously regarded as merely old.) She was an extremely shrewd, well-informed reader of situation comedies, their rhetoric, and their functions in popular culture. However, when I mentioned that almost all American situation comedies depend upon sets with three "doors" (entries, exits) and three cameras, the information took her completely by surprise. She seemed to know immediately how to use the information, how to blend it into other ways of reading the shows.

Narrative is a bit like this in our lives. It is as common to our communication as three doors and three cameras are to American television comedy, and it's so common as to be invisible. Once visible, however, narrative can be enormously instructive, can help us break down and understand our worlds. That's been one main point of this essay.

The world of college can interpret the commonness of narrative to mean insufficiently refined, too personal, merely anecdotal, or not abstract, not conceptual, enough. Nonetheless, story still finds its way into all sorts of academic writing, even if it's undergone some serious mutation. Recognizing the tension between narrative and other modes of organizing material is part of a college education. So is adapting one's speaking and writing to the modes preferred in humanities, social science, and science classes. And so is identifying and analyzing narrative wherever you find it and in whatever disguise it assumes. This has been a second main topic of the essay, which began by discussing the stories you tell before class, stories I listen to carefully for what they have to say, what they might imply, how you tell them, and why you tell them.

Now I'll finish up by suggesting a few more ways to think about story, stories, and you. On your own or as part of a class, you could easily turn these suggestions into prompts for writing everything from journal entries to formal papers. But you don't need to see them as writing assignments, and you may improvise upon them as you see fit.

First I'd suggest that as you go through what is for you a usual day, be alert to the ubiquity of stories, how they're part of conversations, of what you overhear, pass by, write, and read. Analyze these stories by any means that seem productive to you. Begin, if you like, simply by asking *how* exactly a certain story is being told and *why* the teller is telling it. Listen to—and for—stories. When someone complains to you about a third party, notice how this individual structures the complaint. What's the plot of the complaint? Is the complainer self-portrayed as a hero, a victim, a witness, a judge—or what? What position are you meant to occupy as you listen? Do you find yourself responding to the story in the way the complainer desires you to? Ask questions of stories you read in newspapers and on websites. Ask questions of stories in the shape of rumors, e-mails, letters, advice, reminiscences, secrets, speeches, excuses, and rules. Such stories don't just surround your life. In some ways they constitute it.

Next I'd suggest that you look for implicit or slightly disguised stories in what you read, view, and hear in college. Sometimes I begin a course by having students deconstruct (take apart) the syllabus I've just handed out. One way to take it apart is to ask what familiar stories it echoes—stories about education, about how truly important this class (and every class, of course, according to the teacher of the class) is, about progress, personal responsibility, punishment, authority, and power. You might look for such echoed stories in syllabi you receive, in your college's bulletin, its mission statement, and its official history.

Of course, look for stories and narrative structures in all the material that comes your way in your studies. Look in the textbooks, the course packets, the assignments, and the lectures. Look for the stories people tell during class discussions. Try to find the basic plots reflected in business, exercise science, accounting, literary criticism, sociology, mass communication, art history, chemistry, biology, or whatever other courses you take. Analyze the stories told by coaches, orchestra conductors, theatre directors, and academic advisors.

Finally, I'll say this: Think of your own education as a kind of story with a plot. Are you satisfied with the plot? How would you change it? To what extent have others written the plot for you? How might you revise it? What roles do you occupy, what characters do you find yourself playing, in this story, "education"?

Works Cited

Bormann, Ernest. 1983. "Symbolic Convergence: Organizational Communication and Culture." In *Communication and Organizations: An Interpretive Approach,* 99–122. Edited by L. L. Putnam and M. E. Pacanowsky. Newbury Park, CA: Sage.

Burke, Kenneth. 1945. *A Grammar of Motives.* Berkeley: University of California Press.

Fisher, Walter. 1987. *Human Communication as Narration: Toward a Philosophy of Reason, Value, and Action.* Columbia: University of South Carolina Press.

Herrick, James. 2001. *The History and Theory of Rhetoric: An Introduction.* 2nd ed. Boston: Allyn and Bacon.

2

Narration and Argument

James A. Herrick

It is a somewhat surprising fact that C. S. Lewis, among the most prominent British literary scholars of the twentieth century, spent a good deal of his time writing popular fiction. His seven Chronicles of Narnia are still among the most widely read children's stories, and his science fiction works, known as the Perelandra trilogy, maintain a readership even though the first book in the series was published in 1939. Why would a great scholar of Renaissance literature turn to storytelling, a decision for which Lewis received a good deal of criticism from his colleagues at Oxford and Cambridge?

The answer to this question is likely discovered in two facts. First, in addition to being a literary scholar, Lewis was a Christian apologist. That is, he saw one of his purposes in life as being the defense and propagation of the Christian faith. Second, Lewis recognized something about stories that other great writers before him had also recognized: they can be highly persuasive. Thus, Lewis set about to write fiction that conveyed his case for Christianity, his argument that the basic tenets of the Christian faith were worthy of his readers' consideration, and even acceptance. In a letter to one of his readers, Lewis responded to a question about the first of his science fiction books, *Out of the Silent Planet*. One line in that letter stands out as particularly revealing of Lewis' understanding of the persuasive nature of stories. "Any amount of theology can now be smuggled into the people's minds without his knowing it under cover of romance," by which Lewis meant a story set in a fanciful place (1966, 167).

We usually categorize stories or narratives as something other than persuasive arguments, and rightly so. We see them as entertainment, or works of the imagination, or as vehicles for expressing deep emotions. And stories are all of these things. However, scholars in the fields of rhetoric, argument, and persuasion have increasingly recognized the persuasive power of stories.

In this essay I want to explore briefly the relationship between stories and arguments, whether they be stories that are themselves arguments or argu-

10

ments that include stories. I hope to show how narrative can be a resource for the writer wishing to advance an argument or persuade an audience. Understanding the relationship between stories and arguments may enhance your own efforts toward building a strong case for views you wish to advocate.

Narrative Brings Arguments to Life

The connection between argument and storytelling is actually not new; it has been recognized and exploited for millennia. For example, the great philosopher Plato (427?–347 B.C.E.) presented his philosophy in dialogue or narrative form. Plato, himself once a playwright, let his philosophy emerge from the pages of stories about great debates among famous contemporary figures living in ancient Athens. His use of narrative allows us to consider two important qualities associated with narratives as arguments.

First, Plato's use of stories rather than propositional arguments rendered his philosophical works lively and interesting to read. Let's face it: philosophical arguments can be hard to trudge through, as anyone who has ever tried to read Kant can attest. By presenting his philosophy in narrative form, Plato imbued his ideas with a vitality often lacking in straightforward philosophical argument. It will be helpful to consider an example of how Plato used characters in a story to make a philosophical discussion more interesting to read.

Individuals who believe in something called the rule of nature think that the strong should govern the weak. It is one thing to simply present an argumentative case for this view. But to have a character in a narrative actually make the case for this view draws the reader into the argument almost irresistibly. Plato's dialogue *Gorgias* was originally written as an argument against the Sophists, a group of professional speech makers who were paid to persuade. In this intriguing story, an evil character named Callicles promotes the rule of nature. Rather than just telling you what the rule of nature is, Plato has Callicles make an impassioned defense of the idea in *Gorgias*. Callicles says: "This is, in fact, how justice is determined: the stronger shall rule and have advantage of the inferior. By what principle of justice did Xerxes invade Greece, or his father Scythia?" He adds, "to my mind men are acting in accordance with natural justice when they perform such acts, and, by heaven, it is in accordance with law, too, the law of nature" (1952, 483e). There can be no doubt what Callicles believes; Plato has brought this dangerous political philosophy to life in his story by making it the principle by which a character in his story lives.

Narrative Sets Ideas in Contrast

A second quality of narrative as argument is also evident in Plato's dialogues. Plato's use of narrative allows him to pit one idea against another by placing characters in a debate. That is, his philosophical stories bring several voices to life at once, placing these voices in conversation with one another. Here is a famous exchange from the same dialogue, *Gorgias*. In this section, Socrates and Callicles clash over the question of what constitutes the good life. Callicles believes that the good life involves getting as much for yourself as possible, whereas Socrates argues that this view is morally corrupt. For him (as for Plato), the good life means pursuing what is both just and beautiful. Callicles is incensed by this idea and responds that "what is beautiful and just by nature" is for the strong individual "to allow his desires to become as mighty as may be and never repress them . . . and gratify every fleeting desire as it comes into his heart" (492–493). Only an individual who lives in this way is truly free.

Socrates answers Callicles' argument for hedonism by affirming that Callicles is not actually free in his pursuit of pleasure. Rather, he is a slave both to his own desires and to whatever audience he has to persuade in order to get what he wants. This fact is evident any time Callicles is seen in public with his lover, as well as any time he steps before the legislative assembly in Athens to make a speech. Socrates retorts that when Callicles speaks before the Athenian Assembly, he changes his views to fit the audience's expectations. "If you are making a speech in the Assembly and the Athenian Demos [people] disagrees, you change and say what it desires." Socrates adds, "And in the presence of this beautiful young son of Pyrilampes, your experience is precisely similar. You are unable to resist the plans or assertions of your favorite" (481d–e). Thus, despite his great rhetorical skill, Callicles is actually a slave, both to public opinion and to his own desires. Socrates concludes that "the best way to spend one's days is to live and die in the pursuit of justice and the other virtues" (527e).

Plato's *Gorgias* is a lively and interesting narrative about several fundamental moral issues. In this narrative, vividly portrayed characters flatter, ridicule, interrogate, and argue. Plato's main points are clear throughout, but so are the views of his opponents. Of course, there is a risk involved in taking this narrative approach in which characters are allowed to "speak for themselves." In order for the opponent's point of view to have any credibility whatsoever, it must be presented as something an intelligent person might actually believe. Thus, as readers, we hear the opposing point of view presented strongly and even persuasively. Consequently, we have to make up our own minds—and we might make what in Plato's opinion is the wrong choice.

What if Plato's readers were actually persuaded by Callicles? This was a risk Plato was willing to take in order to make his own argument as compelling as possible, by placing it in the mouth of a tenacious and engaging character involved in a debate against intelligent rivals.

Narrative Allows Marginalized Voices to Speak

The fact that stories allow varying voices to be heard has been appreciated in modern times as well. For instance, the Russian linguist Mikhail Bakhtin

(1895–1975) noted that, though various voices are always heard in our social world, not all are heard equally (1973, 86). He noted that stories provide an opportunity for making marginalized voices heard, for giving them a persuasive weight that they might not have in ordinary argumentative settings such as debates and speeches. Bakhtin was interested in the novel's capacity for allowing many voices to be heard at once and to be heard in such a way that no voice was superior to another. He thus elevated the possibility of full voices for many perspectives in order that, as part of what he termed the Great Dialogue that is human existence, we might discover "the best possible avenues to truth" (1984, xxv).

Bakhtin admired what he termed the "polyphonic" nature of Fyodor Dostoevsky's novels, that is, the fact that each character was fully developed and presented his or her perspective on the world robustly (1984, 3). Bakhtin wrote that "a plurality of independent and unmerged voices and consciousness, a genuine polyphony of fully valid voices is in fact the chief characteristic of Dostoevsky's novels" (6). Bakhtin, then, saw in Dostoevsky's stories a model for allowing equal voice to various perspectives in the ongoing conversation among people about their experiences and the truths by which they live. Bakhtin points out that allowing arguments to transpire in narratives may be one means of helping us to manage our differences and to appreciate people who are different from us.

Humorous Narratives Can Win Over the Audience

We discover another reason for considering stories as a component of persuasive writing in the works of the greatest public advocate of the Roman era, Marcus Tullius Cicero. Cicero wrote several influential books on how to plead cases effectively in public settings, and in one of these books, *De Oratore*, he turned his attention to an especially elusive subject: humor. As might be expected, stories are important to his discussion of humor.

Humorous stories come with both benefits and liabilities, and the public advocate needs to be aware of both. Cicero points out that there is "great and frequent utility" in humor, while at the same time noting that it is an "absolute impossibility" to learn wit by studying it (1976, II lvi 228). (This comment reminds me of a college roommate of mine who, having been stung by the accusation that he did not have a sense of humor, checked out a book of jokes and set about memorizing them!) Perhaps the most difficult aspect of humor in public settings is knowing when to use it and when to avoid it. Cicero lamented the fact that we have no theory to guide us in such cases.

Humorous stories incorporated into an argument carry with them several benefits but also certain dangers. Humor's greatest risk lies in its potential for making the advocate look foolish by ridiculing things the audience reveres. A public advocate must maintain dignity even when relating an amusing story, says Cicero (II lvi 367). Funny stories should be avoided if they deal with "outstanding wickedness, such as involves crime," as well as real human suffering. The advocate wants to make a serious point even when using humor, otherwise she will be seen as simply "a buffoon," Cicero cautions (II lx 247). It is imperative that writers and speakers possess a good sense of what their audiences consider appropriate matter for humor. Nothing is more disastrous for an advocate than to tell a funny story about something the audience considers a serious matter.

If the advocate can maintain appropriate respect for the audience's sensibilities, the humorous narrative carries with it several distinct benefits. Cicero noted first that humor "wins goodwill for its author." This is because audiences admire someone who is humorous, attributing intelligence and quick-wittedness to the advocate. For instance, though Mark Twain's stories sometimes place clueless characters in ridiculous situations, we attribute intelligence and wit to Twain himself. Cicero also believed that a humorous narrative well told makes a writer appear to be a person of "finish, accomplishment and taste" (II lxvi 373).

But, the greatest benefit of a humorous narrative in a speech or essay is that it "relieves dullness" (II lxvi 373). Anyone who has slogged through a long, tedious argument or been forced to sit through an overlong and dry speech can appreciate Cicero's point. Cicero suggests that the humorous story, while making the audience laugh, must also seem plausible. That is, the story must relate to experiences the audience members have had or can imagine actually occurring. Cicero writes that the humorous narrative must "present to the mind's eye, such things as bear the semblance of truth," or the audience will dismiss the story and perhaps the advocate as well (II lxvi 266).

For the accomplished orator, a humorous story demonstrates mental agility while at the same time attracting and holding audience interest and winning goodwill. However, Cicero cautions the advocate at every turn, for humor runs the risk of offending the audience and making the orator look foolish.

Narrative Focuses Attention

The story is told that when the novelist Harriet Beecher Stowe (1811–1896) was introduced to Abraham Lincoln, the president of the United States is reputed to have said, "So this is the little lady who started this great war." Lincoln was referring to Stowe's enormously popular novel, *Uncle Tom's Cabin*, which had helped hundreds of thousands of readers visualize the horrors of American slavery. Stowe, a social reformer, had cast much of her argument against slavery as a story of the experience of one slave, known as Uncle Tom. Her novel sold more than five hundred thousand copies in the United States alone between 1850 and 1855, and it was translated into more than twenty languages. Lincoln recognized the power of Stowe's story to galvanize American public opinion against the evils of slavery. In particular, Stowe had focused attention on the physical and emotional suffering inflicted upon slaves.

Chaim Perelman (1912–1985) was a Belgian lawyer and rhetorical theorist who did most of his writing in the second half of the twentieth century. One of his most influential ideas bears directly on the notion of persuasive narratives such as Harriet Beecher Stowe's *Uncle Tom's Cabin.* In his book *The New Rhetoric: A Treatise on Argumentation,* coauthored with L. Olbrechts-Tyteca, Perelman wrote that the immediate goal of argumentation was to make certain facts of a case visible to an audience. To focus an audience's attention on a particular fact or set of facts was to give those facts "presence." Perelman noted that presence was an essential but often neglected factor in contemporary theorics of argument, most of which focused on propositional argument to the exclusion of elements such as narrative (1969, 117). To experience the presence of a fact or an idea is more a sensory than a rational experience for an audience. "*Presence,*" Perelman writes, "acts directly on our sensibility" (116).

When employing narrative, a writer may bring his audience to the point of *seeing* a relevant fact, of *experiencing* an idea, and not simply of thinking about it. Thus, a writer might "make present, by verbal magic alone, what is actually absent" (117). Perelman himself told a story to make his point about presence as the "verbal magic" of making an audience "see" an important idea. He writes: "What we have in mind is illustrated by this lovely Chinese story: A king sees an ox on its way to sacrifice. He is moved to pity for it and orders that a sheep be used in its place. He confesses he did so because he could see the ox, but not the sheep" (116). In a persuasive essay, a story may allow the reader to visualize a point in a way that a traditional argument would likely fail to do, to experience the point as literally present.

Narratives Build Community

Ernest Bormann, a contemporary scholar in rhetoric and communication at the University of Minnesota, has explored the various ways stories can be used to build communities. Bormann began his work by noting that members of small problem-solving groups often share stories in their discussions together. Starting with the observation of Robert Bales that groups develop corporate "fantasies" or stories, Bormann noted that narratives are significant in creating agreements, shared meanings, and a sense of community. In an important essay titled "Fantasy and Rhetorical Vision," Bormann applied Bales' observations about group narratives to the sphere of public advocacy. Narratives become part of an organization's story about itself, thus serving to "sustain the members' sense of community" and "to impel them strongly to action" (1972, 398).

Bormann arrived at the conclusion that a community's identity arises out of the stories that have meaning for its various members. Bormann said that "symbolic convergence" occurs when members of a group begin to hold in common certain stories or "fantasy themes" that define the group and its values (1983, 108). Public advocates can play a similar role by helping a community shape its shared stories. A group's stories may include what Bormann termed inside jokes, which are encapsulated stories understood only by members of the group. The inside joke is not necessarily humorous; it is simply a story that is an abbreviated version of a longer narrative characterizing the group's life.

Bormann also discussed "fantasy types," which are basic plots repeated in a variety of group or organizational stories. For example, many corporations employ a fantasy type we might title "Our Founder Is Also a Decent Human Being." Various stories circulate within the organization about the founder's willingness to forgive an unintended insult by a new member of the group or about the founder's great generosity. Each of these stories is intended to reveal the founder as "a real human being." This particular fantasy type is part of the corporate story of many groups and organizations. When widely shared within a group, stories provide the basis for a shared vision that makes sense of the world, thus allowing the group to grow into a community. Over time, a shared vision will develop into what Bormann termed an "organizational saga." This is a longer story that presents the history of the group in the form of a legend (1983, 120).

Bormann's theory of the role of narratives in the life of a group, organization, or community is suggestive for writers and speakers. It reminds us just how important stories are as a group seeks to develop a shared identity. It also suggests that the telling of stories has great significance, for we forge personal and corporate identities out of the stories we tell about ourselves.

Conclusion

Stories can be an important part of the process of composing argumentative and other persuasive material. We have explored the narrative's power to bring ideas to life, to set ideas in contrast, and to allow marginalized voices to articulate their values and experiences. In addition, we have considered the humorous story's capacity to win the goodwill of an audience while at the same time demonstrating a writer's or speaker's intellectual capacities and character. Finally, narrative can also play a role in helping communities shape and articulate the values that unify them. For all of these reasons, narrative ought to be considered an important resource for the writer when functioning in the role of a public advocate.

Works Cited

Bakhtin, Mikhail. 1973. *Marxism and the Philosophy of Language.* Translated by L. Matejka and I. R. Titunik. New York: Seminar Press.

———. 1984. *Problems of Dostoevsky's Poetics.* Translated by Carol Emerson. Minneapolis: University of Minnesota.

Bormann, Ernest. 1972. "Fantasy and Rhetorical Vision: The Rhetorical Criticism of Social Reality." *Quarterly Journal of Speech* 59: 398.

————. 1983. "Symbolic Convergence: Organizational Communication and Culture." In *Communication and Organizations: An Interpretive Approach,* 99–122. Edited by L. L. Putnam and M. E. Pacanowsky. Newbury Park, CA: Sage.

Cicero, Marcus Tullius. 1976. *De Oratore*. Translated by E. W. Sutton and H. Rackham. Cambridge, MA: Harvard University Press.

Lewis, C. S. 1966. *Letters of C. S. Lewis.* Edited by W. H. Lewis. San Diego: Harcourt.

Perelman, Chaim, and L. Olbrechths-Tyteca. 1969. *The New Rhetoric: A Treatise on Rhetoric*. Translated by John Wilkinson and Purcell Weaver. Notre Dame, IN: University of Notre Dame Press.

Plato. 1952. *Gorgias*. Translated by W. C. Helmbold. Indianapolis, IN: Bobbs-Merrill.

Stories are almost universally enjoyed and draw people in to the argument or point a writer or speaker is trying to make. Why is its use not more employed more widely in academia?

3

Looking for Dr. Fuller: Story Strategies in Essays

Douglas Hesse

It's the next to next to last day of English 381: The Personal Essay. We're reading Annie Dillard's *Teaching a Stone to Talk,* and I call attention to the cover. A student asks about a blurb there from Dr. R. Buckminster Fuller. She doesn't know who Fuller is, and no one else does either, but the running speculation is that he's an evangelist. (He's not.) I suspect his name might be unfamiliar to you, too.

I fumble for an explanation of Fuller: architect, philosopher, voice of a lifestyle. I joke that I should bring in *The Whole Earth Catalog* so I can give them a short lesson on the mood of the seventies when I, like many of their parents, went off to college. I explain that, among other things, Fuller invented the geodesic dome. When some in the class aren't certain what that is, I scrawl a bad drawing on the board: a bunch of hexagonal panels fitted to make buildings shaped like huge basketballs with their bottom thirds cut off. Finally a student mentions the large entrance building at Disney World's Epcot Center. Yes! I remark that another dome is much closer to our classroom, standing ten miles down the road in the one-tavern town of Downs, Illinois. In my mind, I speculate that there could be an essay possibility exploring this odd connection between Disney World and Downs, Illinois. But that's not the story here.

* * *

Later at the library, I plug Fuller's name into the computer. Twenty books pop up, their call numbers ranging from C, to H, to P, to T, and I recognize one title: *Operating Manual for Spaceship Earth.* Out of curiosity, I also ask the computer to find *The Whole Earth Catalog,* call number AP2.W5. My book search will take me, then, to five of the library's six floors.

The Whole Earth Catalog is yellowing and brittle. Its publishers probably didn't expect back in 1969 that the book would spend thirty years on library shelves, so they didn't bother with acid-free paper. It's the shape of a *Rolling Stone* magazine but nearly two inches thick, with hundreds of pages of products, advice, and philosophy. The catalog's introduction promises tools to help "the individual . . . conduct his own education, find his own inspiration, shape his own environment, and share his adventure with whoever is interested." When I flip through the pages, I remember the day I bought a later edition in 1975 and, reading through it, came upon a recipe for baking bread. I was home on break. Bread making sounded like a fitting adventure for a freshman would-be intellectual, and so in my mother's kitchen I measured yeast and molasses and water and whole wheat and salt and oil and kneaded out six loaves. I took one to my girlfriend, figuring she'd think bread-baking boyfriends were intriguing, if not outright cool. She did. (You have to forgive me and remember that it *was* the mid-seventies). I bought the *Tassajara Bread* book and then *Tassajara Cooking*. The best thing in them is the tabouli recipe, though the honey cookies are good, too.

At this point we're in 1975 and wrist deep in tabouli. We're a long way from English 381, the year 2002, and this book. I could take you further down this road, perhaps to the time I shook George McGovern's hand one afternoon at the Moline airport fence, a few months before Richard Nixon blew him away 49 to 1 in the 1972 presidential election. Or earlier, to the summer I spent evenings in the park with Harry Gereau, singing Crosby, Stills, Nash, and Young songs. Way back there is my first cooking, after grade school when I'd trowel Miracle Whip onto Wonder Bread. But that's not the story line here, or at least I don't yet think so. *The Whole Earth Catalog*. R. Buckminster Fuller.

* * *

At this point you're rightly wondering where this story is heading or if it's even a story at all or just a self-indulgent collection of scattered memories. You've probably read enough to know that one of two things better happen if you and other readers are going to put up with this chapter, especially in a book promising to give advice about writing. One option is that a satisfying story will finally emerge. There will be some pivotal event, probably near the end, and maybe it will reveal a point, something that makes readers say, "So that's where all of this was heading." In O. Henry's famous short story "The Gift of the Magi," the narrator seems way too preoccupied with the wife's lovely hair and the husband's prized watch. Then, at the very end, each of them sacrifices the thing he or she loves best, and the meandering early stuff makes sense. In some pieces, then, the writer plays a sort of game with the reader, perhaps trying to see just how much chaos he can create before bringing everything together in an artful shape. The danger is that, like a diver attempting too high a degree of difficulty, he will flop.

The other option is that the writer has just begun with an anecdote, maybe to catch your attention or maybe to create some rapport with you. That opening story may even be beside the point. A couple of the most common conversational openings in our culture are "How are you?" and "How 'bout this weather?" Most of the time, the person asking doesn't really care about the answer; it just breaks the ice. Similarly, an opening story or anecdote can function like a welcoming handshake before the writer gets down to her real business. Some writers use this strategy when presenting ideas from a field unfamiliar to their readers. The late anthropologist Stephen Jay Gould, for example, very often spent the opening page of his essays recounting something that just happened to him before explaining to his lay readership some scientific principles or debates. It's as if Gould just wants to put us at ease, as if to say, "I know you're worried that some difficult ideas are on the way in this essay, but I want to reassure you that I'm a pretty normal guy who has your interests in mind." For example, in "The Perils of Hope" (1987), Gould starts by describing electronic gadgets he happened to see in a New York shop window. Then he discusses the theory that as engineers pack more and more computing power into less and less space, computers will become more human. From there he moves into the real heart of his essay, a critique of the belief that human intelligence is inexorably progressing. Gould's opening paragraph, then, apparently has nothing necessarily to do with his ultimate topic, but it does establish a human touch and allow him to ease us readers into a more complicated argument. If I were pursuing Gould's strategy in this essay, I would follow my opening anecdote by quickly moving into the concepts I really wanted to pursue and never turn back. But that's not entirely the approach I've taken.

These two options—having the parts of a story come together at the very end and using a story as a kind of disposable attention-getter—are traditional ways we think of stories working in essays. Beyond that we know that some essays consist entirely of a story, usually with the writer as the main character and first-person narrator. Some famous examples are George Orwell's "Hanging" (1993), E. B. White's "Death of a Pig" (1966), and Annie Dillard's "Death of the Moth" (1993). Orwell describes how, as a British soldier in Burma in the thirties, he watched a prisoner on the way to the gallows sidestep a puddle and, in that minor act, display his humanity. E. B. White tells how he ineffectively tries to care for a sick pig and how doing so transforms his sense of both himself and the animal. Annie Dillard watches a moth get trapped in a candle flame, its body becoming a second wick, a "holy flame" that Dillard wishes herself becoming. In each case, small incidents from real life, simply but powerfully narrated, are invested with greater meaning and significance.

Other essays are part story and part explanation, analysis, or argument. The conventional wisdom is that the writer has an argumentative or topical structure in mind, and telling a story or two helps illustrate points along the way or maybe keeps the reader interested. One traditional broad way to categorize essays in terms of form is to say that some are narrative and some are propositional. In fact, Jerome Bruner has described the narrative and the propositional as two fundamental ways of knowing.

Whether you have ever used this particular term, you are almost certainly familiar with propositional form. It's clearest in texts that are organized by thesis and support, often indicated by paragraphs that have topic sentences followed by evidence and explanations. The whole work is built as a logical progression of ideas.

Clearly these two ways of characterizing essays and their form are often helpful for both analyzing and writing. But many essays neither seem to consist entirely of stories nor seem to have a logical structure in which propositions all line up and point to a central thesis. Sometimes the essay is a succession of stories that don't seem clearly to add up to any simple point, a work like Joan Didion's "White Album" (1975). This forty-page essay consists of fifteen sections, mostly stories or scenes set in roughly the same time period in the late sixties. They include, for example, excerpts from Didion's psychological report, testimony from a murder trial, a Doors recording session, a car ride while listening to a radio, and interviews with the star witness against Charles Manson for the Sharon Tate murders. At one point, even Didion writes, "I believe this to be an authentically senseless chain of correspondences" (45), but the truth is that these sections are carefully organized to evoke the loss of meaning.

Sometimes the essay is a combination of story and ideas or information, but there doesn't seem to be a direct connection between these elements, as in a work like David Quammen's "Strawberries Under Ice" (1995). This essay juxtaposes two very different strands. One contains several pieces of very technical information about how ice forms and moves, through rivers and down mountains; this strand reads almost like an encyclopedia or textbook. The other consists of intensely personal stories about people he has known, including a dear friend who is killed. After that death, Quammen retreats to live for some time in a snow cave to come to terms with the death. Together, the two strands create a powerful metaphor of growth, change, and loss.

Still other essays may appear to have no narrative elements at all, but neither do their ideas or information seem to have a clearly logical pattern. It's as if the writer is moving purely by association, one thought triggering another. Critics like Paul Heilker and William Zeiger have described such essays as tracing the shape of thought. Scott Russell Sanders (1990) notes that they "violate the rules that many of us were taught in school" (35) and says,

> The writing of an essay is like finding one's way through a forest without being quite sure what game you are chasing, what landmark you are seeking. . . . Much of the pleasure in writing an essay—and, when the writing is any good, the pleasure in reading it—comes from this dodging and leaping, this movement of the mind. It must not be idle movement, however, if the essay is to hold up. (34)

As useful as this "movement of the mind" explanation is, I still don't think it accounts for what makes an essay "hold up," to use Sanders' term, for readers who can easily lose interest in works whose authors they may think are just taking them on a wild, incoherent ramble. Such readers might think that Didion is just being lazy not to write careful transitions between the sections of "The White Album" or that Quammen is making them do all the hard connecting work in "Strawberries Under Ice." Writers who don't use a clearly logical or propositional structure must, nonetheless, create a progression that has an emotional or intellectual payoff. When their essays are successful, even ones that have few or no characters or scenes, the readers' response at the end is "So that's why the writer told me those things and in that order."

* * *

I'm back in the library. The title page of the 1969 *Whole Earth Catalog* expresses the book's credo: "We *are* as gods and might as well get good at it." I worry that this sentence must sound pretentious to students who were born more than a decade after it was written. Then one day on my classroom bulletin board appears an announcement for a $5,000 essay contest. The challenge: "*Atlas Shrugged* depicts a society of diminishing economic freedom. What is the philosophical motivation behind these controls and what is the practical result? What is hero John Galt's answer, both practically and philosophically? Use the events in the novel to support your answer" ("4th Annual" 2002). A lot of my students are familiar with Ayn Rand's work, and I imagine the "whole Earth" phrase seeming familiar to them, even if Rand's philosophy is entirely different.

* * *

In the winter of 1975 I am standing in a kitchen in Vinton, Iowa, waiting for a girl to come home from playing basketball. I've never been in this kitchen before. It is my sophomore year of college, and I am meeting the mother for the first time. A doctor's wife, she asks as I walk in the door when I was born, not only date and year but time of day. As I stand in the kitchen, she hauls out various books and charts and begins casting my horoscope. It is snowing outside, and I still have my coat on, and Mary is still playing basketball, and I am wondering what stars might have led me to this place.

* * *

The very first entry in the 1969 *Whole Earth Catalog* is titled, simply, "Buckminster Fuller." He comes right under the heading "Understanding Whole Systems" and right before "The Population Bomb." Several quotations from Fuller's *World Design Science Decade* appear on page 3. For example,

"There is luck in everything. My luck is that I was born cross-eyed, was ejected so frequently from the establishment that I was finally forced either to perish or to employ some of those faculties with which we are all endowed." Fuller, already seventy years old, is trying to crunch a lifetime of design into a ten-year plan for the planet.

I decide I need to take a look at his books. At this point you need to know something of the scene, the sixth floor of Milner Library at Illinois State University, at a big table strewn with books, overlooking the ranch houses of eastern Normal. (Yes, that's the town's real name.) In *World Design Science Decade* is a plan for a pyramid-shaped floating city for a million people. Each family would have two thousand square feet of living space, with access to the outside. The artist pictures the city floating in San Francisco Bay, where its design is earthquake-proof. Fuller notes that this million-person city can be extended symmetrically.

Also on my library table someone has left various art books and gallery catalogs. As I often do, I browse one out of curiosity. It presents the work of Jennifer Bartlett, an artist apparently famous enough to merit a book. There is a plate on pages 142–143 of a work titled *East 19th Street* (Goldwater, Smith, and Tompkins 1985). It consists of a succession of pyramidal forms. The book lies side by side with Fuller's tetrahedral city. Pure chance?

The associational chain stops here. Almost. What brought me to the library, to this artist, to George McGovern, to long-ago girlfriends? What brought me to writing these words? Does it add up somehow? What's the narrative or line? For I have traveled a journey in time and space as well as words and I can't yet see what the map might be.

* * *

Essayists frequently use walking or meandering as a way to structure their works. Describing a journey, no matter how mundane the trip may be, provides a framework on which one can hang almost any idea. In "Looking for a Lost Dog," Gretel Ehrlich (1986) uses the frame of a winter day spent searching a Wyoming ranch for a lost dog to meditate on everything from music to Henry David Thoreau. Of course, the essay is a story about looking for the animal, which Ehrlich worries may have fallen into a hollow created by deep snow. But it is about other things, too, about Ehrlich's search at that time for other things in her life, even about the act of writing essays. In "Cloud Crossing," Scott Russell Sanders (1987) uses the story of climbing a mountain to carry ideas about parenting and responsibility. Sanders and Ehrlich's strategy is by no means a new one. An essay written in 1711 by Joseph Addison begins, "When I am in a serious Humour I very often walk by my self in Westminster Abbey" (1973, 170). Addison goes on to describe spending an afternoon in the famous church, and as he moves from place to place, different sights conjure different thoughts.

What many essayists in the centuries since the genre's origin in the late sixteenth century have realized is that reporting a journey, even one as mundane as an afternoon walk, can give shape to ideas and information that otherwise might be so fleeting or out-of-the-blue as to be nearly impossible to put into some structure. A random thought—or even a profound idea—can be presented as occurring at a certain moment in time. That's true of George Orwell in "Shooting an Elephant" (1970). At the moment Orwell recognizes that if he doesn't kill an elephant the local people might think him weak, Orwell says that he learns a deeper truth: imperialists enslave themselves as well as the people they are ruling.[1] There is a structure in something as simple as "I left my house, I walked around, and I came back home," and presenting even random ideas as coming to the writer during that sequence makes them part of the story and gives them structure. But of course, all of us have heard dull stories that consist of endless "and thens," with nothing very interesting happening or seemingly no point to the whole thing. There are subtle issues of craft in using the journey strategy. The reader has to find the trip worthwhile.

More often the stories that essayists use are less obvious. Annie Dillard's "Expedition to the Pole" (1982) is a complicated piece that juxtaposes two kinds of materials. In one thread, Dillard narrates attending a Roman Catholic mass where all the music is provided by a group of folk musicians that she finds increasingly annoying. Dillard's other material is historical information about several polar expeditions in the nineteenth and early twentieth centuries, all of them ending in tragedy because the explorers were so ill-prepared for arctic rigors. What can these things possibly have to do with each other? The story of the mass gives some narrative structure to the piece, but the interruptions of the historical material don't make sense—that is, until we begin to realize near the end that Dillard is making a point about religion and worship: people who approach worship in ways as shallow as she believes the organizers of the mass have done are putting themselves at as much risk as the foolish organizers of those polar expeditions. By the end of the essay she brings the two strands together in an imaginative scene, with both the folk musicians and the explorers together on an iceberg.

Richard Rodriguez's "Late Victorians" (1991) tells of moving to San Francisco and meeting people there. He also describes the city's architecture and how ironic it is that buildings inspired by the nineteenth-century Victorian era of sexual repression would be so embraced by the gay culture. He recounts, finally, the spread of AIDS in the eighties. While Rodriguez sits meekly at a funeral, the several elements coalesce, and the essay comes to a powerful end.

---

1. I talk more about "Shooting the Elephant" and this strategy in "Stories in Essays, Essays as Stories" (1989).

In all of these essays—and in myriad ones like them—the narrative elements signal how we might read them. Instead of searching for main points that build a logical structure of assertion and evidence, or instead of accepting them as formless, albeit often intriguing, meanderings (Samuel Johnson thought the essay an "irregular and undigested bit of composition"), we should recognize that essays often have the shape of stories. The events in those essays are often scenes and stories themselves, but they may just as often be information and ideas. Just as works of fiction contain both narrative and exposition (or action and explanation), so do many essays. Writers expand their range of strategies by understanding the strategies that are available for including stories in essays. They can deploy a single story at the beginning of an essay and then move into discussion of the issues it raises, or they may save that story for the middle or the end. Writers can break a story into pieces, interrupting those pieces with all manner of reflection, analysis, or even other stories, as they depend on the overarching narrative to make everything hang together.

Using stories or story forms to hold together even your disconnected ideas and experiences is a useful and powerful tool. In a frequently quoted observation, Joan Didion asserts that "we live entirely, especially if we are writers, by the imposition of a narrative line upon disparate images, by the 'ideas' with which we have learned to freeze the shifting phantasmagoria which is our actual experience" (1979, 11). Our experience never stops generating the kinds of disparate events and ideas that almost dare us to give them a place in the plot of our lives.

* * *

Not long after finishing the first draft of this essay, I'm at a writing convention in Chicago where, out of the blue, I come across a book by Ayn Rand titled *The Art of Nonfiction*. I think immediately of the contest poster in my classroom and of *The Whole Earth Catalog*. What should I make of this phenomenon? And the day I'm writing my final revision of this very paragraph, a student sends me an e-mail that describes a festival at Black Mountain College and mentions, among other people, Dr. Buckminster Fuller (Benton 2002). It's almost as if, once you start paying writerly attention to something, it's hard to stop the chain of associations.

I can't know who your personal Dr. Fullers might be. They are people or ideas peripherally meaningful to you, perhaps mysterious to others. They reenter your consciousness perhaps by chance and become more important through the memories they stir and the connections they cause. As you explain it all to someone else—choosing certain of your experiences and ideas and arranging them to tell a story—you may find yourself back in your mother's kitchen, learning how to bake bread or cook an egg. And if you've done it well, that surprising journey will make sense.

Works Cited

Addison, Joseph. 1973. "The Spectator, No. 26 [Westminster Abbey]." In *Selected Essays from the Tatler, the Spectator,* and *the Guardian,* 170–173. Edited by Daniel McDonald. Indianapolis, IN: Bobbs-Merrill.

Benton, Michael. 2002. "Black Mountain College 50 Year Celebration." E-mail. 20 August.

Bruner, Jerome. 1986. *Actual Minds, Possible Worlds.* Cambridge: Harvard University Press.

Butrym, Alexander, ed. 1990. *Essays on the Essay.* Athens: University of Georgia Press.

Didion, Joan. 1979. "The White Album." In *The White Album,* 11–50 by Joan Didion. New York: Simon and Schuster.

Dillard, Annie. 1993. "Death of a Moth." In *In Depth Essayists for Our Time,* 183–185. 2nd ed. Edited by Carl Klaus, Chris Anderson, Rebecca Faery. Fort Worth, TX: Harcourt.

———. 1982. "Expedition to the Pole." In *Teaching a Stone to Talk,* 119–134. New York: Harper and Rowe.

Ehrlich, Gretel. 1986. "Looking for a Lost Dog." In *Graywolf Anthology Three,* 89–92. Edited by Scott Walker. St. Paul, MN: Graywolf.

"4th Annual Essay Contest on Ayn Rand's Novel *Atlas Shrugged.*" 2002. www.aynrand.org/contests/atlas.html. 8 February.

Goldwater, Marge, Roberta Smith, and Calvin Tompkins. 1985. *Jennifer Bartlett.* New York: Abbeville Press.

Gould, Stephen Jay. 1987. "The Perils of Hope." In *An Urchin in the Storm,* 208–215. By Stephen Jay Gould. New York: W. W. Norton.

Heilker, Paul. 1996. *The Essay: Theory and Pedagogy for an Active Form.* Urbana, IL: NCTE.

Hesse, Douglas. 1989 "Stories in Essays, Essays as Stories." In *Literary Nonfiction,* 176–196. Edited by Chris Anderson. Carbondale: Southern Illinois University Press.

Kauffmann, R. Lane. 1990. "The Skewed Path: Essaying as Unmethodical Method." In *Essays on the Essay,* 221–240. Edited by Alexander Butrym. Athens: University of Georgia Press.

Orwell, George. 1993. "Hanging." In *In Depth: Essayists for Our Time,* 518–521. 2nd ed. Edited by Carl Klaus, Chris Anderson, Rebecca Faery. Fort Worth, TX: Harcourt.

———. 1970. "Shooting an Elephant." In *A Collection of Essays,* 148–155. By George Orwell. New York: Harcourt Brace.

Quammen, David. 1995. "Strawberries Under Ice." In *Literary Journalism,* 195–208. Edited by Norman Sims and Mark Kramer. New York: Ballantine.

Rodriquez, Richard. 1991. "Late Victorians. In *The Best American Essays,* 119–134. Edited by Joyce Carol Oates. New York: Ticknor and Fields.

Sanders, Scott Russell. 1987. "Cloud Crossing." In *The Paradise of Bombs,* 49–57. By Scott Russell Sanders. Athens: University of Georgia Press.

———. 1990. "The Singular First Person." In *Essays on the Essay,* 23–25. Edited by Alexander Butrym. Athens: University of Georgia Press.

White, E. B. 1966. "Death of a Pig." In *An E. B. White Reader,* 157–166. Edited by William W. Watt and Robert W. Bradford. New York: Harper and Row.

The Whole Earth Catalog. 1969 ed. Menlo Park, CA: Portola Institute.

Zeiger, William. 1985. "The Exploratory Essay: Enfranchising the Spirit of Inquiry in College Composition." *College English* 47: 454–466.

Sharing Ideas

1. Have you had professors like Hans Ostrom who arrive early? What's your sense of these professors' purposes in doing so? (Or, if you have professors who are chronically late, what does that sort of arrival say to you?) Keep some notes in your courses: What stories are being told? What can be learned before or as a class opens? Do you agree that these stories begin or help to define you? Your class? Your generation?

2. From different perspectives, Hans Ostrom, James Herrick, and Douglas Hesse contrast narrative, or storytelling, with other modes of expression. (For example, Hesse contrasts narrative writing with propositional writing.) In addition to narrative, what other kinds of writing and speaking do you find yourself doing in college? How would you describe these kinds or modes of writing? How would you label them? What are their characteristics? Which ones are most and least difficult for you at this point?

3. All three contributors to this section discuss how stories often help build groups and communities, and James Herrick in particular discusses the work of Ernest Bormann in this regard. Herrick discusses Bormann's notion of inside jokes—special information or specific stories of which only members of a particular group are aware. Using this figurative, not literal, use of the inside joke, how would you characterize the special information or specific stories that help hold together a group to which you belong? Are there stories only you and a few of your friends know? To what extent does retelling or referring to the stories help maintain a group identity—a sense of an inside or of a closed circle? To what extent are the stories used to exclude people from the group, placing them on the outside? How do inside jokes (special stories) function in other groups to which you belong?

> Examples: sports teams; musical groups; a group of workers; a group of volunteers; a group based on a special activity (for lack of a better word), such as skateboarding, surfing, participating in a particular faith or religion, playing electronic games, computer hacking, rock climbing, customizing cars, body piercing.

4. Reading Douglas Hesse's essay, one might conclude that, for many members of his generation, *The Whole Earth Catalog* is a kind of inside joke—a text that evokes particular memories and emotions and one that helps cement a group identity. To what extent does your generation have a similar text or cultural object? Looking ahead twenty, thirty, or forty years, think about cultural items that might possibly evoke particular memories and emotions for your generation or subgroups within your generation when they reflect back.

5. Toward the beginning of his essay, James Herrick discusses how C. S. Lewis used fiction, primarily novels, to advance arguments—arguments in the sense of points of view about particular subjects, such as theology. How might one of your favorite novels be seen not just as fiction but as fiction that is making an argument? For instance, perhaps you have read a science-fiction novel that implicitly suggests how humans should or should not live their lives. Or maybe you've read a contemporary novel that makes an argument about what's wrong with American society. Why does the argument the book makes appeal to you? How effective is this novel as an argument? What are the advantages and disadvantages of using fiction for rhetorical purposes? Feel free to apply similar analysis to films, plays, songs, or television shows.

6. Think—and write—about a story that one of your parents or another older relative tends to retell. Perhaps the story concerns the person herself, perhaps not. The crucial element here is that the story is one the person retells from time to time. Why, in your view, does this parent or other relative retell the story? Are there explicit and implicit points the storyteller hopes to make? How do you and others respond to the story? How much has the story changed over the months and years, if at all? Do you ever tell that same story to others? Why or why not? In what sense is the story an accurate representation of this parent or other relative? Now scrutinize yourself: what story or stories do you tend to retell and why?

7. Consider a short story, a novel, an autobiography, a biography, or a film that recounts a journey that you found especially appealing. Think—and write—about why this particular journey appeals to you. How much did the style of storytelling contribute to the appeal, and to what extent are you able to separate the telling from the tale—the style of moviemaking (for example) from the journey the movie presents? Why do you identify with this particular journey, and what does it mean to identify with a journey?

8. James Herrick's essay refers to Plato's use of dialogues—plays, really—to discuss philosophical questions. Read all or part of one dialogue by Plato. Then write your own dialogue that explores a philosophical, religious, political, or social issue. What two or three characters, such as Socrates, will you create to serve as spokespersons for different positions, beliefs, points of view?

Part II
Story, Discovery, and Recovery

I've known rivers.

—Langston Hughes

4

Storytelling, Writing, and Finding Yourself

John Boe

I grew up listening to and telling stories. I learned storytelling from my mother's stories, the stories of her day, her life, other people's lives. Then in imitation I learned to tell my own stories. The voice I want now when telling a story (aloud or in writing) is that remembered kitchen table voice: relaxed, confident, having fun.

It's never too late to learn to value kitchen table stories, the celebration of the seemingly trivial, of laughter and gossip. Think of King Lear (who'd ever but slenderly known himself), past eighty and imprisoned with his daughter Cordelia. Lear shows he's finally wised up when he says to his daughter:

> Come, let's away to prison:
> We two alone will sing like birds i' the cage:
> When thou dost ask me blessing, I'll kneel down,
> And ask of thee forgiveness: so we'll live,
> And pray, and sing, and tell old tales, and laugh
> At gilded butterflies, and hear poor rogues
> Talk of court news; and we'll talk with them too,
> Who loses and who wins; who's in, who's out;
> And take upon's the mystery of things,
> As if we were God's spies. (Shakespeare 1963, V.iii.8–17)

Strung together with eight *ands,* this eighty-one-word sentence could be corrected by a writing teacher. But I love its flowing list of life's valuable things. In these trivialities of daily life—the stuff of kitchen table conversations with my mother and sisters—we take upon ourselves the mystery of things, become spies for (or on) God. Lear, after a lifetime of puffing himself up with power, has learned the secret of life, has learned how to relate to his daughter in the feminine, feeling world: praying and singing and telling old tales and laughing and gossiping. Most of us don't have anything earth-shattering to say, but we can learn, like Lear (like my mother), to celebrate the little stories that make up our own precious lives.

My other best homeschooling came from the shows my sisters and I and various visiting children would put on for adults at parties. These were the post World War II, pre-VCR and going-out-to-eat days, when adults (especially my parents) had all kinds of parties: canasta and poker parties, drinking parties, singing parties, charades parties, treasure hunt parties. While the adults were carrying on, the kids would be in another room making up a play, writing out parts and rehearsing.

In entertaining the adults (sort of like Bottom and his unsophisticated cohorts performing for nobles at the end of *A Midsummer Night's Dream*), I first experienced the rewards of writing linked with performing. These shows for the adults had a parallel in my regular play, where my sisters and I would write, draw, and act out elaborate fantasies (a childhood activity perfected by the Brontë children). Not enough kids get to do such performances these days, at least at home. There aren't so many siblings, parties, or video-free environments. (TV and videos do satisfy our addiction to stories but unfortunately eliminate our role as the storymakers.)

The connection between writing and performance has roots in classical rhetoric, and it was a norm in education even in Shakespeare's day. As a recent biographer of Shakespeare's points out, in the Elizabethan era "we can see connections between a golden age of drama and an educational program constructed on the basis of dialogue, colloquy, and imagined speeches, and which so prized eloquence and verbal inventiveness" (Kay 1992, 45). Shakespeare's probably Stratford schoolmasters were educated according to the pedagogy of Richard Mulcaster: "To cultivate eloquence in English composition, and to inculcate what he called 'audacity' as well as 'good pronunciation' among his charges, he advocated teaching through drama, more specifically through acting" (45).

Why shouldn't education today be more like the education of the greatest genius of our language, Shakespeare, and stress "eloquence, performance, and 'audacity'"? (46). So much contemporary education, especially the mass education of the research university, seems aimed at diminishing rather than increasing audacity (that wonderful combo of daring, originality, and fearlessness). One way to learn audacity is to tell stories. For in speaking publicly in your own voice, you bravely confront one of the great fears: stage fright.

Finding Your Story, Finding Your Personality

Like ideal method actors, people telling stories from their own lives in their own voices are playing (thus finding) themselves. When you make an audience experience a story from your life, you experience that same story with a clearer consciousness. The stories I tell and how I tell them define me for myself as well as for my audience.

And so I can tell stories that show that I am a man who met and had sex with his wife in high school, whose father was a gambler, whose mother was a piano player. Or, on a less personal level, I could tell you about Shakespeare, jazz, basketball, and mathematics.

The psychologist Carl Jung thought that the central goal of life was finding your self, your personality. He thought that "the optimum development of the whole individual human being" (1961, 171), what he called "personality," should be the main business of education. While we all have some sense of what "personality" means, Jung defined it in different interesting ways, one time saying it is "a well-rounded psychic whole that is capable of resistance and abounding energy" (169), and another time simply saying "personality is Tao" (186).

Tao, the goal of the followers of the ancient religion Taoism, means "the way, the path." The Chinese diagram symbolic of the Tao is the yin/yang circle, suggesting that the way involves a balance of opposites: light/dark, male/female, active/passive, and so on. If you find your own personality, you have found *your* way of living in the world, *your* way of balancing the oppositions that make up all of life. To be in Tao, then, is to be your self, to have a genuine personality, to have your own path. When you are in Tao, you are acting out of your own personality. (And if you are in Tao, your personality can have a psychological magic, charming others.)

I was once teaching a storytelling class to college freshmen and had asked them to write an interesting story from their life experience, then to rewrite the story (shaping it, improving it), and then finally to tell the story to the whole class. (While in writing classes I sometimes use storytelling as the rough draft, in storytelling classes I more often use writing as the rough draft.) One young woman, Antonia, came to my office and sadly said that she had no story to tell because nothing interesting had ever happened to her. I told her that if this were true, she should drop out of college and get a life. I explained that the Constitution of the United States guaranteed her the right to an interesting life, for it promised her the right to life, liberty, and the pursuit of happiness. While the right to happiness itself is not guaranteed, the pursuit of happiness is, and this pursuit, I insisted, inevitably leads to an interesting life—and thus to stories.

But Antonia turned out to have no interest in dropping out of school. She wanted only to complete my assignment. So I asked her just to tell me a story of her life, anything, no matter how trivial or stupid. After a long period of silence, she told me how as a child, living in Richmond, California, she had found an injured robin on the street and had picked it up and brought it to her mother. Her busy mother was not pleased, but Antonia insisted the bird needed help, so finally her mother, fuming, drove the girl and the wounded bird from Richmond to Berkeley, where there was an emergency avian care facility. The bird was left there with a good prognosis for recovery, but the ride home went in stony silence, with Antonia having to suppress her exuberant joy over having rescued the bird. Then, a week later, Antonia, amazingly, found another wounded robin in the street, and over her mother's horrified protests, the scene was repeated. This little story ended up as a lovely piece of writing and performance piece. That I still remember this story is a tribute to its power. And I remain convinced that this story tells me a lot about Antonia's admirable personality.

To realize you have a self is to realize you have unique stories, your own way (Tao). To crystallize this self, you need to capture your memories, to make your stories conscious by telling or writing them. One of the best reasons for writing (and for taking writing classes) is because in writing you find (and remember) your stories, become conscious of your own life history. When you become conscious of the power of your own unique stories, as Antonia did, you are reminded that despite living in an overpopulated world, you are a unique personality, that you are not just another interchangeable worker. You find your personality by finding your stories, and thus your stories become your fate. As psychologist James Hillman wrote, "The way we imagine our lives is the way we are going to go on living our lives" (1983, 23).

Finding Your Storytelling Voice(s)

Mine is an old-fashioned argument for self-knowledge, or perhaps I should say selves-knowledge. You don't just find your storytelling or writing voice; over time, you find voices. A writer finds a voice and then in different contexts or genres, different voices. We human actors play many parts, and storytelling helps us get in touch with these various parts. By embodying our complexity in a wide variety of stories, we get a sense of our full personalities.

The challenges in writing or in telling a story are the same: finding material and finding the right voice for expressing that material. So one way to improve as a writer is to improve as a storyteller. You can start this work by performing your rough drafts, telling them (without notes) to friends or even performing your drafts for your entire class. Once you start performing your drafts, you naturally take a crucial first step toward being a better writer: you try to avoid being boring. It is easy to write in a pompous, academic, trying-to-be-smart way on a paper, but with your friend you tend to just try to be yourself, which is often the best strategy for a writer anyway.

If you are afraid of such performing, you shouldn't be. Most people in any audience want to like the speaker. Most of the time, humans enjoy looking at and listening to other humans. My best advice for people with performance anxiety is from a scene in one of my favorite movies, *Meatballs,* where Bill Murray, as the camp counselor, motivates the camp kids before a big sports meet with the rival and more talented camp by having them chant over and over, "It just doesn't matter! It just doesn't matter!" If you can really believe that such performances don't really matter, as of course they don't, then it is easy to relax. You don't have to be clever, you only need be your self.

Since storytelling is a natural activity, there are no rules to learn. You need only to keep it natural. So you should *not* use notes when you tell a story; you must know your stories well enough to tell them by heart, just as you tell a story by heart to a friend when you are sitting together at a table or in a car.

The physical experience of having a real audience makes unnecessary the imaginary audience often invoked by writing teachers. "Whom are you writing for?" teachers ask students, but if there is a real audience, you know whom you are speaking to. And your audience will let you know the funny parts by laughing, the boring parts by looking bored. You can tell how your audience is reacting because, having no notes to look at, you look at them.

Thus you can test the worth of a story by trying it out loud on an audience. Such performance has obvious benefits for a would-be writer: (1) you may find it easier subsequently to write the story in a more natural voice; (2) you can modify your story based on the response of your audience; and (3) you may discover the stories that are important to you and that others agree are important (while these stories may be personal, they need not always be so).

Responding to Stories

One response to a story (written or told) is just to honestly tell how the story affected you. Another response is to comment on the surface of the story: Did it have a strong beginning and resolving ending? Were there any really good phrases? Was there something missing? Would more dialogue or description help?

These two ways of responding to a story (focusing on your responses or on the surface) are not mutually exclusive, although the literary critical versions of them (Reader-Response and New Criticism) are often thought to be. When I was a college student in the '60s, New Criticism was the dominant critical paradigm: you talked about what happened on the page. The New Critics rejected the "affective fallacy" as valuing how a poem affects a reader rather than what a poem is. Amazingly, talking about how a poem affected you was actually labeled a fallacy!

Then in the late '60s, Reader-Response Criticism arose as an academic countercultural reaction against the New Criticism, with the goal being to talk more about readers than about words on the page, to talk about what a poem does more than what it is. The psychologically oriented hypothesis was that literature took place not on the page but in a reader's mind. Unfortunately, in recent decades, the growing prominence of abstract postmodern literary theory has erased much of the influence of Reader-Response Criticism. As Peter Elbow has commented,

> It's interesting what's happened with reader-response criticism. It was fashionable for a while, then it was dropped like a hot potato. My hypothesis is that English departments dropped it because it looked as though there were

some danger of actually having to talk honestly. And English professors didn't want to do that, especially the theorists. (Boe and Schroeder, 1992, 29–30)

But when responding to a story, everyone, even an English professor, should start with honesty.

I try to respond to stories as if I were a human being, just saying what I liked. This process is easy, for what I liked is usually the same as what I remember. My memory naturally tells me what it thinks is worth remembering, what it was struck with. (Memory plays the same selective role in reflecting on my own life as well.)

In responding to a told story, of course it can be useful to talk about the surface, about voice, eye contact, speech patterns—just as in talking about writing, it can be useful to talk about mechanics. But it is usually more useful to offer reader or listener response criticism, talking honestly about your responses. The opening questions are obvious: What did you especially like? What were you bored by? What more would you want in the story? What stories were you reminded of?

Like life, most stories from life are not simple. But if you don't reduce your story to a single meaning, you can still find interesting ways to talk about it. You start by saying why this story is important to you, why it is one of the stories you remember from your life. (The bad thing about most people's lives is how much they forget; the good news is that what they remember is, by virtue of being remembered, important.)

As a teller, you learn from the responses of your audience, and those responses transform subsequent retelling or (re)writing. A guru in an old joke I heard when I was a teenager epitomizes for me a teller's ideal openness to audience response:

A man reached a spiritual crisis and decided to give up everything and search for the meaning of life. He studied the philosophers, but they didn't satisfy. He tried psychology—Freud, Jung, Reich, EST. He tried religion—Christianity, Judaism, Islam, Hinduism, then Transcendental Mediation, Zen, and then Tantric Buddhism—but still he didn't find the meaning of life. Finally his Tantric master told him that his own guru might indeed know the meaning of life. So the seeker sold everything he had to pay for a trip to India. After long searching he found his guru's guru and asked him the meaning of life.

"I'm sorry," the guru replied. "I don't know, but perhaps you should ask my guru, who lives deep in the jungle." So the seeker, now totally broke, wandered into the jungle with only the rags he was wearing and his begging bowl. After some months, he came to the cave of his guru's guru's guru, where he again asked what was the meaning of life.

"So sorry," his guru's guru's guru replied, "but to be honest, I don't really know, but my guru, who lives in a cave on a high mountain in the Himalayas, is the one person who may know."

The seeker, frustrated but still hopeful, hiked off, and after a year of searching, he found himself struggling up a steep mountain path, with a vision of a sunlit cave hovering above him on the peak. Finally, with his last ounce of strength, he pulled himself up onto the floor of the cave and saw a beatific figure bathed in white light.

"Please, master," he begged, "before I die of exhaustion, tell me the meaning of life."

The wise old man drew a deep, slow breath and replied softly, "My son, life is like a fountain." And then he smiled in silence.

The seeker looked at his guru's guru's guru's guru in disappointment, then grew angry and started screaming: "How dare you, after I have searched for years, sacrificing my time, my money, and my health, studying with philosophers, psychologists, and spiritual teachers, coming to India in search of one guru after another, then hiking into the wild jungle, finally clawing my way to the top of this desolate mountain—how dare you have the nerve to tell me that life is like a goddamn fountain!"

At this the guru raised his eyebrows and replied with genuine curiosity, "You mean life isn't like a fountain?"

When, in trying to reflect on or interpret a story, someone offers a stupid Forrest Gump moral ("Life is like a fountain"), I want to scream like the seeker in the joke: "Goddamnit, this is my life here! Don't bore me! Don't give me clichés!" In such situations, if the teller were as wise as the guru in the story, a correct response would be to really listen. I love how the guru, who at first thinks he is giving words of wisdom, so quickly responds to his angry audience. On the basis of the response, he is willing to revise his point of view, to start a dialogue by asking, "You mean life isn't like a fountain?" In this moment, ironically, the guru shows that he is indeed a guru!

The guru does especially well considering that he is in an impossible position, for the question "What is the meaning of life?" is unanswerable, and from a logical perspective, meaningless. (Douglas Adams' answer in *A Hitchhiker's Guide to the Universe*—"42"—is as good as any.) Everyone ought to know that a real story from life (like life itself) can't be reduced to one simple meaning, but students are often too much like the seeker in the joke. They think they are supposed to find *the* meaning of a given story, especially of an important story from their own lives. There is an understandable naïveté about this position: If only life were as simple and clear as a word or a sentence whose meaning we easily understand! If only our lives were like parables or fables. Sometimes, I wish they were, too. But they're not.

Often it is good to clearly separate the telling of a story from any interpretation of it. Story, as Aristotle pointed out, has a beginning, a middle, and an end, so in working on how you tell a story, it makes sense to concentrate on these three phases. But reflective writing (almost all academic writing) brings in an additional element: interpretation. The essay, for example, is basically a form built around a story or stories interspersed with or followed by commentary.

Even the lab report follows the story-plus-commentary structure. The first part tells the story and can be divided in various ways, all of which follow the beginning, middle, and end structure: intro, materials and methods or procedure, culminating in the results section (the end of the story). But then there is the fourth element: the discussion section, which is often seen as the most important section of all. The procedure is often the same in science and in storytelling and writing: First you find your story (the real experiences you are recounting) and tell it as well as you can. Then you spend some time thinking about your story (the fourth part) and try to talk about it in an interesting way, without oversimplifying it.

Anyone writing an essay for school can easily imagine a need to make explicit what has been learned, for learning is, after all, the purpose of school. And indeed this explicit statement of what you have learned is required in most academic writing, for example, in writing the discussion section of a lab report. But life learning usually can't be translated into a simple phrase or rule (as if life were like mathematics, with algorithms we can all learn and agree on). While I do believe in learning, I have become increasingly skeptical about anyone's explicit claims as to what she has learned, about how she now clearly understands this or that part of her soul, life, or mind. The older I get, the less I myself seem to have learned. So while the stories people tell about their lives are more and more interesting, the lessons seem more and more obscure.

So don't tell me a story and then quickly say your story shows that life is like a fountain. Just tell me a story that makes me feel the fountain of life, that carries me along like a river. Then maybe we can work out a way to say something interesting about the story.

Comparing Stories

One of the best ways to talk about a story is to compare it with other stories. If you have a story about having almost died by drowning (as I do), you compare it with other such stories you read or hear. You look at parallel stories in order to move closer to the meanings of your own story.

When I hear someone else's story, I will often tell a related story of my own and solicit others to tell their related stories: "Have any of you ever been arrested?" "Have any of you ever snuck out of your house without your parents knowing?" "Have any of you almost died?" This process is a good model for the writer's life as I have sometimes known it writing nonfiction for newspapers and magazines. Once, for example, when I got an assignment from a magazine to do an article on palm reading, I got my palm read by five different readers, and I read parts of a number of books, but I also asked all my friends and almost anyone else I talked to if they had any experience with palm reading. And much of my published material came from the stories people told me. Libraries and the Internet are great sources for research, but you shouldn't forget that people have stories to share. You need only ask.

From life you get stories. You get the rough material for your stories from living, but you really get the stories themselves only from the telling. You can mine your life for stories by gathering, writing, and telling them: your parents' stories, the stories of your childhood, the stories of your day; to have a story to tell is to have something of value. At the end of the day, as at the end of your life, you are left with your stories.

What I want from other people are stories. So even when someone starts to tell a joke, I don't let on if I have heard it before; there is a pleasure in hearing a story more than once and thus learning it. The great Tulalip storyteller Johnny Moses, when he performs at a storytelling festival, often will repeat stories throughout the course of the weekend. He explains that in his northwestern Native American culture, once you have heard a story three times, you are then obliged to tell it. What a great rule! (Children often feel the same way about repeating stories; if it was good, do it again.)

It is easy for people, especially young people, not to realize that they are owners of wonderful, memorable stories. I still remember stories I read twenty years ago in composition classes (like the one by a young woman who had become pregnant but despite her parents' urging refused to have an abortion; she wrote about eating alone upstairs, listening to the sounds of a raucous Christmas dinner downstairs, because her parents wanted to hide her condition from their extended family). If you are able to find your stories, you will inevitably write a successful paper, and your teacher may remember your story for years, or at least till dinner table conversation and the natural talking about the interesting events of the day.

Everyone has stories, and if you don't know what yours are, start looking for them. And if someone you know has a really good story, you should look forward to hearing it again and again and again (until you can tell it yourself and it thus becomes your story, too). As I grow older I more and more value people who will tell stories. People are the storytelling animals.

Using Story as Therapy

Telling stories is a kind of therapy, for, as I have been arguing, in telling stories you find out who you are. Traditional psychoanalysis is a storytelling therapy, where the patients tell the analyst their life and dream stories. As Carl Jung expressed it in his autobiography,

> In many cases in psychiatry the patient who comes to us has a story that is not told, and which as a rule no one knows of. To my mind, therapy only really begins after the investigation of the wholly personal story. It is the patient's secret, the rock against which he is shattered. If I know his secret story I have a key to treatment. (1961, 117)

As Jung points out, our own stories can even be secret from ourselves. This is where an analyst or a teacher can help. Individual stories can take various forms—confessional, scientific, historical, comical, whatever. But if you work on telling them well and often enough—for me, it helps to go back and forth between writing and telling—your stories become your own myth, and you create a feeling of meaning in your life. Your stories are finally *yours* and so express a felt truth about your self.

There is perhaps a danger as you get older and live your life and find your stories—the danger exemplified by the boring old person who tells the same stories over and over again. As a professional storyteller, I know how easy it is to know your stories so well you tell them on automatic pilot. The Hodja, the wise fool of Middle Eastern folklore, was once asked how to attain wisdom. He replied, "Always listen attentively to what those who know tell you. And if someone is listening to you, listen carefully to what you are saying" (Downing, 1961, 32). So when I am telling a story, I need to let myself be affected by it, to look closely at it, to see what I can think or say about it, to make conscious that I find meaning in this particular story. If someone is actually listening to me, I need also to listen afresh to what I am saying, to understand my own stories with my heart and my head.

In listening to my own stories, I have to pay attention to more than the surface (just as in writing, I have to care not only about commas and spelling). I can't be so concerned with how I tell a story that I lose its emotional impact on me. There are very successful professional storytellers who turn me off because they seem so focused on the style of their telling that I end up paying more attention to them than to their stories. They seem more like actors than like people. The compliment should not go to the teller but to the tale.

I know it sounds like California wisdom, but it's true and, hell, Shakespeare said it (in the third to last line of *King Lear*) before there even was a California: "Speak what you feel not what you're meant to say." But before I can speak what I feel, I have to know what I feel. Life is the first teacher here, but I also find out what I feel by telling my stories in a voice that expresses my feelings as opposed to telling them in an official academic style (what I'm meant to say, how I'm meant to say it).

If people are listening to me tell a story, or even just listening to me talk (such attention is a delight in itself), obviously I should listen to myself as well. Not only will I improve my technique as a storyteller, but I'll also improve my understanding of who I am. And I'll demonstrate the delight of having a story to tell, a story that allows for the wonderful moment when someone else who is also paying attention suddenly can say, "That reminds *me* of a story."

Works Cited

Boe, John, and Eric Schroeder. 1992. "Looking Two Ways at Once: An Interview with Peter Elbow." *Writing on the Edge* 4.l: 9–30.

Hillman, James. 1983. *Healing Fiction.* Woodstock, CT: Spring Press.

Jung, C. G. 1954. *The Development of Personality*. By C. G. Jung. Translated by R. F. D. Hull. New York: Pantheon Books.

————. 1961. *Memories, Dreams, Reflections*. New York: Pantheon Books.

Kay, Dennis. 1992. *Shakespeare: His Life, Work, and Era*. New York: William Morrow and Company.

Shakespeare, William. 1963. *King Lear*. Edited by Kenneth Muir. London: Arden Shakespeare/Methuen and Co. Ltd.

Tales of the Hodja. 1964. Retold by Charles Downing. London: Oxford University Press.

5

Remembering Great Ancestors: Story as Recovery, Story as Quest

Stuart H. D. Ching

At the funeral of my grandfather, or *gung gung,* Hong Sing Ching, there was a great metal drum in the funeral hall, and in this drum were thousands of dollars of burning money. Through my child's perspective, both container and fire seemed enormous, and my cousins and I, none of us above the age of ten, took pleasure in lavish spending, casting play money in tens of thousands into the metal drum and watching the riches ignite into flames. Though I did not know at the time, according to cultural practice, this money was the great purse that would sustain my grandfather in his journey through the afterlife. Then, amid the immediate laughter of children surrounding me, I heard a loud wailing from the opposite end of the hall. And I remember, now, sometimes in my most quiet moments, the image of my grandmother, or *popo,* Ethel Yuk Hin Ching, approaching us and weeping uncontrollably, braced on both sides by the arms of two men whose faces I can no longer see. I cannot recall if my older cousins comprehended the family's loss. I was only four years old, engrossed in the activity. Even as Popo wept and passed me, I giggled and tossed handfuls of play money into the burning metal drum.

After the funeral and during much of my childhood, there was a period of forgetting. The image of Popo weeping must have been buried beneath the daily preoccupations of childhood play, school, baseball games, karate practice, surfing, and Pop-Warner football. But in my adolescence and up to the present day, I have continued to recover and realize the symbolic meaning of Gung Gung's funeral:

> *I'm four years old and peering into Gung Gung's open casket. I'm more curious than sad, not understanding that his spirit has entered the infinity of*

afterlife—that my only interaction with and connection to him in this finite material world from this day on will be through remembering.

I'm watching Popo collapse under the weight of grief. I hear her wailing voice rising into the high ceiling and rafters of the funeral hall. As she passes me, I'm throwing play money into the burning drum and not comprehending what I will only know years later—that all of Popo's strength is gone, that she is sustained, held upright, only by her community and memory. I do not understand that she would take great comfort if one of her grandchildren, perhaps I, would reach with my child's hand to caress her face, would kiss her cheek—taste the salt of her tears.

I'm at Diamond Head Cemetery, walking with my family back to the car. The cemetery is peaceful; the silence through which the moment passes seems immense. Glancing back, I study Gung Gung's burial site: the green canopy and, beneath it, the fresh mound of earth blanketed with flowers and wreaths marking Gung Gung's final resting place. Without realizing why, I prolong my gaze. Many years later, I still remember.

I open with these recollections to emphasize two purposes that cultural narratives serve when we translate them from oral into literary discourses: First, telling the story enables recovery. That is, in many cases, the descendant dreams of repaying his ancestors (I use the male-gender pronoun with direct reference to myself). But because the descendant understands that his ancestors have made great sacrifices—endured extreme hardship (sometimes even death) so that their progeny might reap a better future—repayment often seems impossible. Thus, the descendant's only recompense is to remember. And as he writes, he hopes that through inscribing his ancestors' lives within his own story, he may more clearly comprehend his ancestors' experiences, express gratitude for their dreams of a better life, and bear their struggle.

Second, remembering ancestry through story involves questing. Through memory, the descendant claims his ancestral connection. In addition, he simultaneously separates himself from his ancestry, defining a new identity that differs from that of his forebears yet still emerges from their memory and legacy. And as he remembers, the descendant realizes that his memories only approximate his ancestors' experiences, that he is both familiar and strange to his forebears. His writing, then, becomes all of the following: affirmation, homage, apology, revision, and quest.[1]

In this chapter, the functions of story that I will illustrate—story as recovery, story as quest—should neither predetermine your artistic choices nor precede the experiences that inspire you to write. More productively, I hope that

---

1. My perspectives on memory comprise both personal reflection and ideas that I have learned from researchers and writers: Ruth Behar (on memory as salvation and duty); M. A. Syverson, Michael Fischer, Gloria Anzaldúa, and James Clifford (on memory as cultural reinvention and travel).

my inquiry into the subject—story—supports your own artistic and intellectual inquiries in the following ways: I hope that a dialogue among my stories, yours, and those of other writers in your class will complicate and enrich your understanding of story's cultural functions. In addition, I hope that the invitations at the end of this chapter will encourage you to generate, complicate, and develop the stories that simultaneously recover your cultural and historical pasts and support your quest for cultural identity in the present.

In Search of the Past

Thirty-four years old, I return home to Hawaii in summer 1999 to research my family's genealogy. I interview relatives, do extensive research in the University of Hawaii's Asia/Pacific collection, and sift through microfiche for news articles on the Chinese in Hawaii. Looking for a book on the early Chinese in rural Punaluu, the fertile coastal region on Oahu's north shore, I visit the Hawaii Chinese History Center in Honolulu's Chinatown. Walking through Chinatown, I pass familiar landmarks: a modernized Fort Street Mall; the red-brick-and-iron-gate facade of the Chinese Chamber of Commerce; and the long-established open-air Oahu Market. I don't enter the market, but I know from memory, from weekly childhood visits, how the aisles are arranged: crates and baskets holding vegetables; chicken, duck, and pork, some raw and some roasted or reddened with *char siu* sauce, hanging from meat hooks in glass display cases; and beds of chipped ice bearing assorted fish. Across the street from Oahu Market, a weathered, T-shaped neon sign marks the Ting Yin Chop Suey restaurant. Next to Ting Yin is the C. Q. Yee Hop Co. building, where the Hawaii Chinese History Center, a cramped two-room office, is located on an upper floor. There an elderly man named Wah Chan Ching, who speaks with the authority of a scholar and historian and who has roots in the early Punaluu community, sells me a copy of James Chun's *Early Chinese in Punaluu.* To my surprise, he also shares stories about my great-grandfather, Ching Wai Yum, when I identify myself as the grandson of Hong Sing Ching (Ching Wai Yum's son).

I visit other sites of memory. My father drives me to the area in Punaluu where Gung Gung, Hong Sing Ching, first resided in Hawaii. According to my father, the area remains largely unchanged, a small green house amid a wide and fertile wetland. A few hours later, in Honolulu, we visit Manoa Valley, the site of Popo's childhood house, where Gung Gung and Popo initially lived after marriage. As my father drives into Manoa Valley, he tells me that these routes were once unpaved, narrow dirt roads with deep wheel ruts. As a little boy riding in the backseat of the family car, he would poke his hand through the window and pluck leaves from the shrubs and trees crowding the road and scraping the sides of the automobile. He also shows me where the house opened on a farm of wet taro on the east side of the valley. Behind the house, a Japanese family named the Mitsunagas owned and managed a dairy farm.

Nearby, dairy cows grazed in a pasture, and through the pasture cut a mountain stream in which my father would play. Beyond the taro field and cow pasture was Manoa housing, shanties made with flimsy pressboard walls that quickly bore holes from exposure to weather. Today, house, pasture, stream, and housing area are gone. The University of Hawaii Press, the Manoa Public Library, the Manoa Shopping Center, and an elementary school have taken their places.

My father drives deeper into the valley to the Manoa Chinese Cemetery, where, amid myriad gravestones, he locates the markers of my two great-grandparents, Ethel Yuk Hin Ching's parents. Their two upright markers, located at opposite sides of the cemetery, are severely weathered. I read the markers carefully, discerning the names: Chun Tai (family patriarch) and Chung Chun Ngit Shee (family matriarch).

Several weeks later, I revisit the Manoa Chinese Cemetery by myself. Concerned that memory might one day fail me, I sketch the grounds on a notepad. I base my map on two of the cemetery's prominent landmarks, the cemetery's ornate gateway, framed by two decorative dragons and, at the back of the cemetery where the terrain ascends upward, an enormous banyan tree up high on a hill. From these landmarks and with notepad in hand, I draw my map, walking to each grave, gauging my distance, carefully numbering the steps that I take to reach my ancestors.

To reach my ancestors, I travel through stories that I recall from experience and stories that elders tell me. In this way, my family and I selectively recover and construct our history. In reality, memory is nonlinear, fragmented and full of gaps, disconnected, jumbled, disorganized, and contradictory. It comes to us in glimpses and brief moments of insight. Jose Garcia Villa's fictional work "Untitled Story" (1993), a mosaic of fragments numbered one through seventy-four, reminds me that we purposely compose culture through story when we number memory to give it meaning, order, artifice, linearity, and power.

Through orchestrating memory this way, we assign power to the family heirloom, the family photo, the family tradition—the family story. I have received heirlooms, photos, and stories, and I have participated in many family traditions. Collectively, they compose the memory that my elders wish to give me. My mother tells me that Popo's mother, my great-grandmother, or *taipo*—Chung Chun Ngit, whom I never knew—had bound feet. Taipo told her daughter (my grandmother, Ethel Yuk Hin Ching), who then told her daughter-in-law (my mother), who then told me, that had she known her parents were sending her from Hawaii back to China to have her feet bound, she would have run away. But she did not know, and so she returned to Hawaii with her feet crushed, bound tightly in cloth. As my father describes them, her feet resembled small hooves. In China, bound feet signified membership in the upper class because those with bound feet obviously needed attendants. And so in Hawaii, six or seven servants should have tended to and transported Taipo. But in Hawaii, Taipo tended to herself, and in her adult years, she removed the bindings and walked on extremely reduced feet.

Popo told a version of this story to my mother. And my mother told a variation to me. I realize that every time a family member retells the story, she adapts it to her social and historical context. But in this transformation, she still recovers some valuable part of the past, maintains a sense of continuity, and gives a piece of memory to the next generation. Because of this story, I have imagined my great-grandmother many times. Most often, I see her walking. Her deliberate steps signify the strength of the women in my family. In the space of imagination, each of Taipo's small steps teaches me a lesson of great distance.

I have two photographs taken in summer 1999 at the Manoa Chinese Cemetery at the graves of Popo's parents: the first, my father and I sitting on both sides of my great-grandfather's (Chun Tai's) grave marker, the other, my father and I standing on both sides of my great-grandmother's (Chung Chun Ngit's) marker. In each photo, my father and I—sitting in one photo and standing in the other—are flanking the grave marker and resting one hand on the upright weathered stone.

We posed for those photos during my third visit that summer to the Manoa Chinese Cemetery. Several weeks before, my father had taken me to visit the grave site. Then I had gone a second time by myself to sketch a map. When Jann, my spouse, arrived from Nebraska a few weeks later, I asked her if she wanted to see the cemetery, too. She did. That day at the Manoa Chinese Cemetery, Jann suggested that she take pictures of my father and me. Agreeing, we all climbed out of my father's Buick, and Jann photographed my father and me at the grave site of Chun Tai, my great-grandfather. Then my father drove the Buick up the narrow, ascending cemetery road to the grave of Chung Chun Ngit, my great-grandmother. During the brief ride, Jann asked my father if he remembered Chun Tai. My father vaguely recollected his grandfather, but he remembered Chung Chun Ngit, his grandmother, very well. "My *popo* and I were buddies," he said. Then addressing me, he said, "She really took good care of me, just like your *popo* took care of you." When we reached the far end of the cemetery, up high on the hill where the road loops beneath an enormous banyan tree, we parked the car and stepped out. We walked some forty yards down the weathered concrete stairs with green grass growing between the uneven bricks. I walked in front, and having previously visited the grave twice, once with my father and once by myself, I located Chung Chun Ngit's marker easily. Just before taking the photo, Jann, as she had spontaneously suggested shortly before at my great-grandfather's grave, directed my father and me to place our hands on the marker. Dad and I moved closer to the marker and each rested a hand just above my great-grandmother's name: Chung Chun Ngit Shee.

At the time, I did not realize the gesture's significance, but now looking at the photo, I see the story that the gesture evokes. Placing our hands above

Chung Chun Ngit's name, my father and I touch two different memories: his, the recollection of childhood, mine, a story unfolding before my memory begins. Somehow the gesture of touching joins our sites of memory, evokes a narrative across time and space, and affirms that Chung Chun Ngit's material presence bears us both.

The Potential of Story: An Invitation

The recollections in this chapter largely refer to the deaths of ancestors. But I think that death alone does not account for each story's cultural significance. More importantly, these stories achieve cultural importance because their endings imply that other stories follow and that endings also mark beginnings. That is, the stories achieve their emotive and cathartic potential because they define the connecting point between the passing of one culture and the creation of another, the passing of one generation, whose gift is life for the next.

In the January 8, 1989, Sunday edition of the *Honolulu Star Bulletin and Advertiser*, two photos documenting the Hawaii Bicentennial Celebration importantly link four generations of Hawaii's Chinese community through this master narrative of rebirth.[2] In one photo, a 620-foot-7-inch dragon extends two city blocks and dances amid a throng crowding North King Street in Honolulu's Chinatown. Amid beating drums and clanging symbols, the dancing dragon represents two hundred years of Chinese residence in Hawaii: the first Chinese who arrived as craftsmen and rice farmers; the coolies who followed and labored on the sugar plantations; and the laborers who left the plantations, migrated to Honolulu, and became merchants. The dragon dance also signifies the generation that endured Chinese exclusion legislation, survived the outbreak of bubonic plague, and overcame the devastating fire of 1900, which burned Chinatown to an ashen wasteland. Finally, the dragon dance recalls the subsequent generation of Chinese women and men who rose from the ash and rubble and gained prominence in island commerce after the mid-1900s.

The second photo portrays Jackson Lee, one of four men designated to carry the dragon's head. In the photo, Lee's forearms, folded across his chest, are enormous. His shoulders and biceps are thick and muscled; they bulge beneath his T-shirt. Though he looks directly into the camera and not at the bejeweled dragon's head beside him, his awareness of the high honor he bears in carrying the dragon's head is obvious. Lee's expression is stoic yet concentrated. His facial features, like my ancestors', are distinctly Chinese, but because his expression seems more Eastern than my Westernized face, I sense

---

2. These photos appear in Vicki Viotti's article "A Dragon to End All Dragons Kicks Off Festival."

a great distance both separating and joining the images of Jackson Lee's face and my own. Lee's Eastern features, imposed on two hundred years of memory, make my ancestors' mythical journey across the Pacific Ocean immediate. My ancestors and I have all passed through Honolulu's Chinatown, but we have imagined it differently. Because of our different historical circumstances, we have occupied diverse cultural and linguistic sites. We are separate identities. Still, we are joined by a story.

In asserting that cultures exist in a state of "medias res" (1997, 3), James Clifford reminds us that cultures die even as they are reborn. Clifford's statement suggests that just as cultures exist within the continuum of evolution, we, as cultural beings and as *writers composing culturally,* also occupy a fluid space between the passing of one generation and the birth of another. It is at this connecting point where we can thrive. We can compose our lives, resurrecting our ancestors—and ourselves—in the stories that we are compelled to tell.

Invitations for Writing

As I have told my stories, I now invite you to tell yours.

* * *

In this chapter, I have suggested that places bear memory of events—pivotal singular events or events retold so many times that they resist an exact time and place. These are events of sadness, sacrifice, struggle, achievement, kindness, happiness, fortune, and hope. In your lived past or even in the past that you know only through family stories, identify a place, perhaps a house, a kitchen, a landscape, a neighborhood, a burial site, or another site from which memory, traditions, ceremonies, rituals, and family gatherings originate. Describe this place and tell the stories that give this place its symbolic power.

* * *

I have also suggested that objects similarly bear memory. They serve as memorials—over time and across generations, these objects become metaphors of homage, duty, obligation, apology, and celebration. I can readily name several objects that have inspired me to write, among these, the jade bracelet that Popo passed down to Jann on our wedding day, a photo of Popo and Gung Gung's gravestones adorned with flowers from their children's gardens, a photo of the orchid plant (now in full bloom) that I gave to Popo shortly before her passing. Find a family photo or heirloom, and research its genealogy. Narrate the events, lives, and stories that assign emotion and symbolic meaning to this object.

* * *

Homage, duty, obligation, apology, and celebration—these are all motives for writing, and each motive originates within a complex weave of relationships, historical events, and sociopolitical circumstances. Rather than start with an object or place, I often begin with a motive, a context or event within my past or present life that provokes me to write. Similarly, a political or social circumstance—for example, an injustice, a promise kept or broken, a dream realized or postponed, a misperception, a stereotype, a historical account or recent event that demands contest or celebration, an intergenerational tension within your community, or a tension among several communities—may move you to compose. Rather than begin with a place or object, start with a motive, and then let your storytelling emerge from and clarify this motive in its full complexity (see also additional invitations in Hint Sheet A).

* * *

My writing largely involves inquiring into my family stories' deeper meanings—the lessons and memory behind subtle expression and gesture. These meanings bind my extended family even before utterance and evoke a symbolic past that I cannot always articulate fully at the initial stages of composing. I often start a project with fragments—for example, the sound of my grandmother's voice, the shape and texture of her hands, her face, her posture when she would sit at a nine-course Chinese dinner and preside over three generations of her family. These images compel me to write. As I develop these images, I attempt to forge connections among them, and I try to articulate the larger meanings, or the master narratives of great distance that my elders and I, as cultural beings, tell, revise, and recover. Similarly, you do not need a whole, coherent idea before you begin writing. Perhaps several pieces of memory readily compel you to write. Begin with these pieces of memory; describe them vividly. Then generate and define their connections. What narratives enable you to connect these pieces of memory into several stories of power and distance? What stories differentiate or link the identities and values of subsequent generations in your community? As you write your stories or as you revisit, focus, extend, and reshape the material you've produced in response to the preceding invitations, I encourage you to move beyond surface events and to recover and generate the deeper meanings—the master narratives—that illuminate and sustain your cultural existence.

Great Ancestor: Ritual

When Popo is still alive, I am visiting her on Chinese New Year so that I can pour her tea. "Kung Hee Fat Choy! Happy new year!" my mother, brother, and I call as we walk up the wooden steps leading from the garage to the second-floor kitchen entrance of the Kapahulu house.

"Kung Hee Fat Choy!" Popo calls back to us.

As we enter the kitchen, Popo appears from her bedroom at the entrance of the adjoining hallway. A child in elementary school, I know from Chinese New Years past that she has retrieved and now holds in her pants pocket two *li see*, red paper encasing money, for my brother, Stanton, and me. As reward for our remembering her and our demonstration of filial respect and loyalty, she has prepared for us *li see*, her gift of happiness, which we must spend on a personal treat. Popo takes her seat at the kitchen table, and my mother busily opens the box of dried, candied fruit and vegetables that we've brought from a Chinatown bakery. Inside are candied pieces of carrot, papaya, squash, lily root, pineapple, and coconut. While my mother arranges the candied fruits and vegetables attractively in the box, I take a few pieces of coconut and nibble on the dried, sugared strips—they have long been my favorite.

That the ritual takes place in Popo's kitchen is appropriate, since her kitchen is our family's gathering place. As a child, I cannot articulate this but can sense it readily. In the morning, we come to pour tea for her in this kitchen. Throughout the day, in this kitchen, she and my aunt Priscilla will cook the extended family's supper: among the dishes, ham-turkey jook (rice soup), oyster rolls, ginger chicken, and jai (a vegetarian meal of bean curd, ginkgo nuts, dried mushrooms, chestnuts, algae, and other nonmeat ingredients). The kitchen is simple, consisting of linoleum tile flooring, a white stove and oven, a sink without a disposer, nondecorative but well-painted kitchen cabinets, and a dining table. Visible outside the kitchen window is the aluminum patio roof and, beyond, the narrow lane bordering one side of the property and the top of the ponderous mango tree shading the backyard and encroaching on the lane.

Popo's tea is kept warm in a tan thermos with a red cap. According to the Chinese tradition of following the order of oldest to youngest, my brother, Stanton, who is two years my elder, pours tea first. With my mother's coaching, he places several pieces of sweet fruit into Popo's cup and then carefully pours the tea. Then, as my mother has taught him, he lifts the cup with two hands and presents it respectfully to Popo. Popo receives the cup with two hands, lifts it carefully to her lips, sips the tea, then places the cup on the table. Now my brother must perform the important second pouring, the refill, or tim cha. And so he warms her cup with just a "spot" extra. Popo sips the tea again.

Now it is my turn.

I'm only a child. I do not know yet as I prepare tea in a fresh cup that one day, in retrospect, I will write about Popo—about this moment—that one day and for many days after, I will remember her, even after she has long passed, with such clarity. I do not know yet that one day, many years later in the fresh wake of her passing, I will want to touch her one last time, and my mother, standing beside me and understanding without being told, will say to me, a grown man, "You can, Stuart. It's okay." Weeping, I will place my hand inside

Popo's coffin and hold her arm. When it is time to close the coffin, the aunts and uncles (Popo's children), the in-laws, the grandchildren, the great-grandchildren who are old enough to understand, will all intuitively turn our backs to the coffin because we know without being reminded that our people say the final good-bye this way. And now as a child bringing in the new year of the Chinese calendar by pouring tea for my grandmother, I do not know yet that one day I will write about her so that I can always be like her, and during the writing I will realize that in my words are her stories and the stories of many others before and after her. I do not know yet that I will write about her so that I can, in one sense, return home. And while writing myself home, I will realize that I am also trying to set myself free. I'm still a child, but already, as I carefully fill a fresh tea cup and then pass the cup with two hands to Popo's, the texture of her hands as she receives mine, her smile, her quiet nod of approval—all these have already played before me many times in memory. I do not know yet that years later, I will realize that such images, like the delicious scent of food wafting through a busy Chinese kitchen, exist fragmented in the mind, broken, fluid, their traces and material images drifting in and out of consciousness—always recuperative.

I am only a child performing the tea-pouring ritual for my grandmother, and as Popo takes the cup, I study her face. She is smiling, happy. Good grandson, my youngest. She can say this to me without speaking. I smile back, already remembering the traces of her countenance.

Works Cited

Anzaldúa, Gloria. 1987. *Borderlands/La Frontera: The New Mestiza.* San Francisco: Aunt Lute Books.

Behar, Ruth. 1996. *The Vulnerable Observer: Anthropology That Breaks Your Heart.* Boston: Beacon Press.

Clifford, James. 1997. *Routes: Travel and Translation in the Late Twentieth Century.* Cambridge: Harvard University Press.

Fischer, Michael M. J. 1986. "Ethnicity and the Post-Modern Arts of Memory." In *Writing Culture,* 194–266. Edited by James Clifford and George Marcus. Berkeley: University of California Press.

Syverson, M. A. 1992. "The *Community* of Memory: A Reznikoff Family Chronicle." *Sagetrieb* 11 (1–2): 127–170.

Villa, Jose Garcia. 1993. "Untitled Story." In *Charlie Chan Is Dead: An Anthology of Contemporary Asian American Fiction,* 462–475. Edited by Jessica Hegedorn. New York: Penguin Books.

Viotti, Vicki. 1989. "A Dragon to End All Dragons Kicks Off Festival." *Honolulu Star Bulletin and Advertiser* 8 January, Sunday ed.: A-3.

6

The Stories We Are

Old Meshikee and the Winter of 1929

Michael Spooner

Among many First Nation cultures, the time for telling stories is winter—at least after the first frost. Of course, some stories are sacred and can be told only during certain ceremonies, but the stories that Grandmother or Grandfather might tell the children—about animals, ancestors, events in history, how things came to be—these are traditionally told on a winter's evening.

My Ojibwe relatives tell me that the old people often built their winter lodges (or wigwams) in a circle, and the snow was piled high between and behind them so that the center of the circle was kept clear for work during the day. In the evening, members of the family would gather inside to play or to work around the fire at small tasks like repairing clothing or tools. If you've ever camped outside in the winter—or even simply enjoyed time on a winter evening with your family inside one small room without a television—then you know how cozy such a moment can be.

After a while, Grandfather might call you over to him.

"Little one," he'd say. "Come here." And reaching into a pouch, he might draw out a long pinch of *kinnick-kinnick,* and he'd close your child-sized hand around it tight as a nut. And he'd say, "Go now; you can tell them this time." So this was how the word would go around: you would stop at each lodge in the family circle, and you'd give the grown-ups a pinch of tobacco, and you'd tell them to come, bring the children: Grandfather is telling the stories tonight.

Old Meshikee is living on an island, maybe not too far from here, in the middle of a beautiful lake. Old Meshikee is a happy fellow. He loves his life on the island and he loves to swim in the lake. And in the evening after a warm summer day, he loves to play his drum and sing.

Now, Old Meshikee is a big old turtle, so he has a big old drum; and when he plays it, it makes a big sound.

51

DRUMDRUM DRUMDRUM DRUMDRUM
You can hear him for miles around.

On the shore of his lake live the little *shagizenz* (sand crabs). They're such busy people, the *shagizenz,* always working in the sand, always digging, always building something. But not always too smart. And on a summer evening, after working hard all day, the *shagizenz* like nothing better than to pull out their drums and have a good dance and sing.

Now, the *shagizenz* are little people, you know, so they have little drums, that sound like this:

drumdrum drumdrum! drumdrum drumdrum!

Not too loud, but it's fine for them.

Trouble is, every time the *shagizenz* get out their little drums (drumdrum drumdrummmm), Old Meshikee starts up his evening racket (DRRRUMDRUM DRUMDRUMMM), and the *shagizenz* can hardly hear their little drums at all.

When the old ladies in my family told me about it, they called 1929 in northern Wisconsin "the winter of all that sickness and all that snow." By February, the snow was to your thighs in the forests, to your waist in the fields. The cows stayed close to the barns; the horses struggled to pull a wagon or a sleigh or a car down the lane. It was impossible to keep the few roads clear for long. As soon as the plow went through, the breeze would throw a drift across the road. It snowed until the train from Minneapolis couldn't get through. It snowed until only people like Uncle Paul Babcock, who delivered the mail on his '23 Ski-Doo, or those with snowshoes, like my Ojibwe relatives, could get around much at all. And still the snow came down. And sickness? All that sickness—influenza, pneumonia, croup, measles, polio. More than one family lost a baby or an elder. It was the winter of 1929, and the darkness and snow descended with a steady leveling.

Late in February, in the upstairs bedroom of the farmhouse (such a cold room, the old ladies told me), a woman in her thirties labored with a difficult birth. Her name was Estelle. She was tall, with black hair modestly pulled back and large light brown eyes. And she was a sweet woman, kind and practical, devout and patient and serene. More than seventy years later, they still speak of her gentleness and her joy. They speak of how she could sing and how beautifully she played the piano. But her struggle in the upstairs bedroom was not beautiful. Maybe it was a breech birth—no one can remember now—but it was a very difficult one. Someone went for the doctor, but it was a long way to town, and the drifts were deep, and the snow still falling. So Estelle gave birth without the doctor, in a cold upstairs bedroom, while the winter of all that sickness and all that snow descended outside her window.

One of the women who told me this story was Aunt Signe, the wife of Estelle's brother Paul, who carried the mail on his '23 Ski-Doo. The other was Lolita, Estelle's niece by marriage. Lolita made it, probably on snowshoes or by horse and wagon, from her home on Connor's Lake to Estelle's home on Devil's Lake. Things did not look good. The child was fine—a healthy boy named Robert, who was getting all the attention that newborns deserve. But Estelle was not fine. An infection had set in, and apparently for a while she was the only one aware of it.

"Leave the child," she whispered to Lolita. "Someone should tend to me." But this was 1929, winter in Wisconsin, and there was nothing the family could do for her. The doctor arrived, but too late. Estelle died of what the old ladies called "childbed fever," in the winter of all that sickness and all that snow.

Estelle was my grandmother. The child she would never know was my father.

Lolita was a young woman, unmarried, and she moved in with my baby father's family to help raise him and his two older brothers. Their cousin, but the little boys thought of her as an aunt: Aunt Lite, they called her. Years later, she would tell me Robert was a quiet child. He spent a lot of time outdoors, never seemed to mind the snow. Aunt Lite was Ojibwe on her mother's side, and on winter evenings in the Great Depression, she would gather those three boys around the stove, and she would tell them stories she had learned from her Ojibwe grandfather.

"DRUMDRUM," she'd say, and "drumdrum drumdrum," they'd answer.

One day the *shagizenz* decide that something must be done about Old Meshikee and his big old drum, so they call a meeting in the big wigwam. When they come out of the meeting, the *shagizenz* are clapping their hands and singing:

"That's what we'll do! That's what we'll do!" and some of them are dragging a long rope they have made from the inside bark of an elm tree. Very quietly, they push off in their big canoe and paddle across to Old Meshikee's island. The day is warm, and the *shagizenz* are not surprised to find Old Meshikee dozing in the sun. Quickly, quickly, they tie him up and throw him into the big canoe.

Back on their own shore again, the *shagizenz* tumble Old Meshikee onto the yellow sand, where all their children play. But what will they do with Old Meshikee now that they have him? They gather in the big wigwam for another meeting.

Old Meshikee doesn't mind the children teasing him. But what are the *shagizenz* saying in their meeting? Old Meshikee smiles. He can just imagine.

Now the *shagizenz* are coming out of the big wigwam, very pleased. "That's what we'll do! That's what we'll do!" they sing, and they spread out immediately to gather wood for a fire. Some pluck tiny dry twigs from the lowest branches of a pine tree; some gather middle-sized sticks from the forest; and the largest of the *shagizenz* are going down the beach to drag an old gray drift log to the fire. Old Meshikee makes his voice sound worried. "What you gonna do?" he asks. "What you gonna do?"

"Oh," says one of the *shagizenz*, "we're gonna fix you good, Old Meshikee. We're gonna make this big old fire, and then we're gonna throw you in! Then you won't be playing your big old drum anymore!"

Old Meshikee shrugs at this, as if he doesn't care.

"*Mah-jon, mah-jon,*" he says in a loud voice. "Throw me in your silly fire. But don't you know I'll kick, and I'll thrash, and all these burning sticks will scatter on your children?" Well, that makes the *shagizenz* stop and think.

"Hmmm," they say, looking at all the children digging in the yellow sand near Old Meshikee. "Can't do that. Can't do that."

"Anyway," shrugs Old Meshikee, "I don't care about fire; it's only water that worries me." So, off go the *shagizenz* to have another meeting. But they don't take too long. They come out of the council meeting just as pleased as before, but this time the largest of them are dragging an old copper kettle, and they're singing:

"That's what we'll do! That's what we'll do!" Some of the *shagizenz* settle the kettle on top of the firewood. Other *shagizenz* are going down to the lake with baskets made of birch bark, which they dip full and carry back to the kettle.

"What you gonna do, little *shagizenz?*" Old Meshikee cries. "What you gonna do?"

One of the *shagizenz* stops a moment to boast. "Old Meshikee," he says, "we're gonna fix you good this time. You see this kettle full of water? We are gonna heat this water till it's boiling hot, and then we're gonna push you in! Then you won't be playing your noisy old drum anymore."

Old Meshikee shrugs. "*Mah-jon, mah-jon,*" he says. "Drop me in your silly kettle if you want. But don't blame me when I kick and I splash and when boiling water goes splattering all over these fine children of yours!" Once again the *shagizenz* have to stop and think.

"Hmmm," they say, scratching their chins and counting the children who are still playing in the sand around Old Meshikee, around the kettle— in fact, all up and down the shore of the lake. How can there be so many children? "Can't do that," they mutter, "can't do that." Then, of course, they go off to have another meeting.

Would you please tell me what it is about children that they are so infatuated with stories? When my son Isaac was small, he couldn't even get through breakfast without making up some kind of narrative. "I have to go to the bathroom. I'll be back as soon as I can and do my homework." He was three when he said that; don't ask me where he heard about homework. Then there's the one about when he grows up, his parents will be babies: "When I get ten, from nine, then Dad will be little and I'll have to carry him." I've met lots of kids who believe that one for a year or two. (And in one sense, of course, they're right. Parent-child roles do seem to reverse as we get older.) Isaac's version of the Jonah story from the Old Testament was a keeper, too.

> Well, Jonah didn't like the city, so he ran away to a big ship. And he fell down, down, down into the water, and he saw a big fish. And the fish ate up him. And inside the fish were hearts, broken hearts. And then the fish spit him out on the shore. And Jonah let go of his fishing pole, because he didn't want to be eaten up again. The end.

Creating those kinds of stories is important, because they show a child's imagination at work and because they develop flexible minds. But, obviously, children like to hear stories as well as make them up. They like the stories in books, in movies, and in television (many of which I would just as soon they *didn't* enjoy), but even more fundamentally, they like stories about their own world, their own family, themselves.

When I was a child, the time I heard the best stories about my parents was after supper while my sister and I did dishes with my mother. We loved her stories about when she was little. How she lived in the city (unlike us). How she cut her ankle on the sprinkler. How she broke her nose. How she used to escape into books. And then her stories about other family members, like her grandfather, who worked for the railroad briefly in South Dakota and was shot by some bullies who wanted his paycheck. (He lived.) And we always loved the one about her sister Elayne, whose boyfriend was stationed in the Pacific during World War II. The navy would censor any reference to the location of their troops, but the boyfriend managed to let Elayne know where he was by using a different middle initial in her name on the address each time he wrote to her. She could put several envelopes together and spell out the name of the island where he was stationed.

And you have stories from your family, too. Do you have favorite ones about family members? It's through stories like these that, as children, we gradually build our understanding of who we are, who our family is, where we come from.

We know what English teachers often mean by *story*. There are some formal ideas, like "a story must have a beginning, middle, and end," and "a story proceeds through the stages of conflict, climax, denouement," and "it has five equal parts: introduction, complication, crisis, resignation, and resolution."

These are useful formulations for when we're telling or writing a story, but they're too formal and formulaic for just thinking about story. In the way I'm using it, *story* isn't formal terminology. If I tell you the story of Old Meshikee and the *shagizenz*, it will have a plot and characters and a point of view and other elements we recognize. If I tell you the story of my father's birth and how he first heard "Old Meshikee," that narrative, too, will have plot and characters and point of view and so on. But those things probably tell us the least important meanings in the story. Instead, we need to listen to personal narratives like that one—and like those from your own family and your own experience—for what they tell us about pain and passion, humor and courage, disappointment and desire . . . in short, about life.

Ultimately, some researchers say, we understand life itself as a story. And maybe we think of life this way because we're so used to hearing and telling (formal and informal) stories, or maybe when we tell stories, we're just creating small versions of life, the world, and time. Either way, storymaking and storytelling is powerful and important work. The writer Ursula LeGuin reminds us that "there have been great societies that did not use the wheel, but there have been *no* societies that did not tell stories."

This is no surprise, of course. We're used to thinking of societies telling stories—especially societies from the past, or cultures that we might call ethnic or traditional or tribal. And we know a little about the function of storytelling in culture: how it conveys values and history and tradition and lore from one generation to the next, how it passes on wisdom about the world, about nature, about interpersonal relations. Just as stories work with children to tell them who they are, stories also work to help a society or a culture build and convey a sense of who it is: a cultural self-image that becomes the transcending story of who we are to ourselves. Not only that, but our cultural stories can become the voice by which we are known to other cultures and other times. Are there traditional stories you learned in childhood that came from your cultural heritage? What do they tell you in subtle ways about yourself?

At a sidewalk cafe, a disheveled man pulled out a chair at the table next to me. "Can I sit here if we're very quiet?" he asked. I made room, and he sat down. Very soon, he was whispering, then muttering, then speaking aloud. We all talk to ourselves, but this man had several selves that were talking to one another. In a whisper, he would insist that you can't trust them. In a "normal" voice, he would answer that they were only trying to help. A sarcastic voice would interrupt, and then the moderating normal voice would reply. The issue seemed to be whether it was wise or not to go back to Saigon, though I never understood why Saigon, what it meant to him, whether he'd ever really been there, or whether anything about him could be taken at face value. But one of his voices saw Saigon as the only answer; another voice advised against it; another kept cracking jokes. In all, I counted four different personalities in the argument.

We can take story a step further. We can think of mental or spiritual health as the state of being well connected to our own story. There are psychiatric researchers who describe it just this way. Often, where something has gotten out of balance, it has to do with a disruption in the continuity of our personal narrative. A part of a person's own story—a story within the story—cannot be remembered or is yet undiscovered. In other cases, a fantasy becomes the substitute for a life story that has become disconnected from reality. And these disconnections affect us at our most fundamental level: our sense of our own identity. The suppression of story can cause a serious psychological wound. We can see this in broader ways, too. We know that historically, as one nation would conquer another, it often systematically destroyed and outlawed the cultural symbols that were important to the identity of the conquered people. For example, when the American army set out to destroy the buffalo, they were trying to break down the cultural identity of the Plains Nations. When sixteenth-century Christian priests and soldiers burned the books of the Islamic citizens of Spain, that was an attempt to erase a cultural identity. Of course, these are not the stories that Americans or Christians usually tell. But we know why that is: because these stories threaten their sense of who they are.

Is it possible that there's a part of your own story that you've come unglued from? Where's the empty place, and what do you think the story is that goes there? Who can tell it to you?

My father never told me the story of Old Meshikee. The death of his mother in the winter of 1929 was only one in a string of family tragedies: his father's father had died before her, and soon his father's brother died, too. Then the Depression struck, and the family lost their house and land and pretty much all their worldly goods. As sometimes happens, I think his family had no way to cope with these trials but simply never to speak of them. They did not allow themselves to grieve the loss of their loved ones, nor to seek help from well-to-do relatives for their financial problems, nor in a hundred small ways to acknowledge the heavy emotional toll this period of time was exacting from them. Instead, they pushed these things down inside and never spoke of them again. Consequently, my father never learned much about his own mother, and he never asked, as far as I know. His brothers (men in their sixties and seventies when I knew them) would leave the room if conversation turned to these subjects. Their generation, and their parents' generation, deliberately lost

these crucial stories. I don't think they knew that they would lose
their voice, too.

So I was twenty-six or twenty-seven years old when I heard
"Old Meshikee" for the first time, and I heard it from Lite, the
same woman who cared for my father when he was a child, who
told the story to him and his brothers. Born in 1908, Lite was
an adult witness to the generation of trouble in the family; she
remembers the main characters vividly and fondly. But as a
niece and cousin, she was far enough on the outside to maintain
a perspective, to see what the family was losing. On the other
side of her family, Lite is a member of the Eagle Clan, Fond du
Lac Band in far northern Wisconsin—the land of Gitchi Goomi,
Nokomis, and Hiawatha—and she treasures those family connections as well. She is old enough to have experienced the last
years of the traditional life, to know the old people, to have lived
for extended periods in wigwams made of birchbark. She married a man who would become a tribal chairman, and their son
would later become chairman, too. As a child, Lite learned the old
ways and the old stories from her grandfather, and she learned
the importance of passing them on to the next generation. She
pursued an education and became a teacher and a local historian. As sometimes happens when a person lives a long life in a
rural area, there are now people from four generations who
claim her as their mentor, their favorite teacher. And not least of
all, in time she took on the mantle of oral historian to the family. Though my father moved away as soon as he was old enough
to hitchhike, eventually settling in Alaska, Aunt Lite still lives in
the same county where she was born.

She was one of the few people my father spoke of from his
childhood, so when I went to visit her in 1980, it was like making a pilgrimage. I went to her seeking to reconstruct the stories
of my family, and I think she enjoyed telling them to me, because
finally here was someone from the Spooner side who was willing
to hear and learn and pass on the stories of the family. It was
from her that I learned about the death of Estelle, my grandmother, and about a dozen other important characters from the
family's past.

And she taught me about the Ojibwe side of the family, too.
She told me the children's stories that she learned at her grandfather's knee—the same ones she had told my father fifty years
before. She told me about Winabozho and the gopher skin, about
the Spirit of the Corn, about the gift of vision, which Great Spirit
gave to the first people to see them through the trials of this

Are59

life. And she told me the story of Old Meshikee and the
shagizenz.

Soon come the older *shagizenz,* marching out of the big wigwam.
"That's what we'll do! That's what we'll do!" they are singing. Straight-
away, they push Old Meshikee onto his back and start to drag him away.
"What you gonna do, little *shagizenz?*" Old Meshikee cries out, "What
you gonna do?"
Someone holding down his head laughs and boasts.
"Oh, Old Meshikee, we're gonna fix you for the last time. You see that
hill up there—the highest sand bank on the lake? Well, that's where you're
going, Old Meshikee, 'cause we're gonna pitch you off the very top. And
when you hit that water, you're gonna drop straight to the cold and deep!
Drowned Turtle, hee hee hee!"
"Oh no!" cries Old Meshikee.
"Then you'll never play that big old noisy old drum again!"
Old Meshikee kicks and waves his arms, but it seems that the more
he struggles, the more determined the *shagizenz* become. They drag him
way up to the lip of the hill, where he can see nothing below but the beautiful lake itself. And when the *shagizenz* give one mighty push, over he
goes, tumbling, tumbling down the great sandy hill, down toward the water,
down toward the bottom of the lake.
SPLASH!

My wife and I were hunting with my father in the Talkeetna
Mountains. The peaks of red and gray thrust up at sharp angles,
with aspen and blueberry and dwarf birch coloring the slopes and
icy mountain streams crashing over boulders. Not far away, the
Matanuska Glacier, a field of ice hundreds of feet thick, spilled
among the canyons, valleys, and hollows for hundreds of square
miles. We were hunting mountain sheep, but this area was also a
gathering place for caribou herds in the fall. We saw them graz-
ing along the ridges, their antlers outlined against the sky, and
once in a while a roving band would high-step through the brush
just a few yards beyond our camp.

In the evenings, we sat around the fire, talking quietly as we
ate or repaired tools and dried our wet clothing. One night, the
conversation turned to family things. I had been to see the old
folks in Wisconsin more recently than he had (no surprise there),
so I brought him up to date on their doings and their greetings.
He asked about Aunt Lite, of course, who had turned eighty years
old that summer. Finally, I had to ask him.
"How come you never told me the story of Old Meshikee?"
"Which story?"

"Don't you remember Lite telling stories when you were little? Especially a story about an old turtle and his drum?"
"I don't think so," he said. "How does it go?"

* * *

There are moments when you are given the chance to bring some-one a chapter from his life story that he has lost entirely, or per-haps has not discovered. You'd think you could see such a moment coming, yet so often it's unexpected—you're into it and done before you know it. But if you've been on the receiving side of this exchange, it is such a gift. Not always life-changing, but something deep and full, like a small stone from another country passing from someone's hand into your own.

As the dark came down around our circle, I told my father the story of Old Meshikee and the silly *shagizenz*. "DRUMDRUM," I said, and "drumdrum." "What you gonna do?" I said, and "Can't do that, can't do that." I told this folktale to my taciturn father, and I felt absolutely foolish: imagine reciting a children's story to frowsy grown-ups against a mise-en-scène of mountains, rough brush and antlers, guns and gloves and wet wool socks—not a child within a hundred miles. But I felt the power of the moment, too; what a sacred nibble of time it was.

Of course, I couldn't read my father's thoughts one bit. When I was finished, he raised his eyebrows slightly, looking away into the dark. Then he smiled to himself. Yes, he said, maybe parts of that did sound familiar, and he stirred the fire gently with a stick.

* * *

The theoretical way to get at what I'm saying is that every one of us has a need to understand our self, whether we frame that understanding in terms of the traditional, unitary, authentic self or the postmodern, disintegral, shifting sub-ject. We need to know who we are. And one important way we learn who we are is by telling ourselves about ourselves. We construct an autobiographical narrative. Some psychological researchers think it's an imperative natural process: we just do it—continually, unconsciously, we are working on this nar-rative. It's our life story. It's our drum. We play it because it's what we have.

If we turn this slightly and think about life as a story that we construct as we live it, then we begin to think of ourselves and other people as artists—maybe inadvertent novelists with a work in progress. Where our lives intersect with others, we become more aware of our own roles as characters in *their* sto-ries and *their* lives. Usually, we'll be a minor character, but we want to be the sort of character who makes a difference. We can have an extraordinary range in this respect. We want to offer them something they need, some small thing, perhaps as small as a children's folktale, that will help them connect to themselves and enrich the telling of their own life story. We want them to hear Old Meshikee's drum, which is the irrepressible power of the story that they are.

* * *

All the way back down the hill, the *shagizenz* are laughing and clapping their hands and telling each other the story of how they finally got rid of Old Meshikee and his big old drum. They're so happy.

And when they get back to their village, the first thing that the *shagizenz* want to do is to bring out their drums and have a dance. Some of them build a fire, and some of them put on their best moccasins and vests.

drumdrum drumdrum. The *shagizenz* are playing their drums.

Hey hey, hey hey! the *shagizenz* are singing their favorite songs.

Drumdrum. Hey hey! But wait . . . what's that sound?

DM DM

Is it coming from the island?

DRUM DRUM

Oh no, it can't be.

DRUMDRUM DRUMDRUM

But it is!

Safe on his island, Old Meshikee is playing his big drum and laughing very loudly.

7

The Poems Came Late: Literacy as Cultural Dialogue

David Wallace

For me, becoming fully literate meant speaking and writing in a voice that did not edit the words to please my father, my god, my dissertation directors, my journal editors, my department chair, or my dean before the words were uttered. It meant saying words that I'd been scared to say for a very long time, words that might estrange me from my family and friends, words that would mark me as "other" in society, words that might put me physically at risk. It meant claiming words like *queer, fag,* and *homo*, which small-minded people had spat at me in derision all my life. Fortunately, becoming literate also meant discovering that I could be gay and accepted.

In this chapter, I invite you to consider that literacy may be something other than what we have imagined it to be—that it is cultural dialogue. In *The Order of Discourse,* French literary theorist Michel Foucault argues that we do not so much speak as we are spoken by the discourses in which we participate. By *discourse* I mean spoken and written language in the contexts in which it is used. Although Foucault admits in his essay that individuals can take agency in speaking and writing, he sees the critical aspect of language and literacy as examining how individuals are situated in the discourses in which they partic- ipate. For example, as children we learn to speak with a slow Georgian drawl or a nasal Jersey twang because we imitate the talk that we hear around us. Thus, in a sense, the discourse we hear teaches us how to speak. Foucault's point is particularly telling when we consider that the discourses we first hear have effects on us that extend far beyond accent. Children who hear their mothers and other adult women referred to as girls or chicks or babes are also learning something about how society views women—lessons they may need to unlearn later in life. In addition, Foucault's position suggests that speaking and writing—participating in discourse—may be more difficult for those of us whom the dominant culture defines in stereotypic ways or renders invisible (e.g., lesbians, gay men, physically disabled people).

Seeing literacy as cultural dialogue stands in direct contrast to how most people in American society understand the term: as the basic ability to read and write. I want to argue here that literacy is more than a fundamental set of skills that children must master to succeed in school, a foundation of grammar and usage knowledge that students should have before entering college, or a set of genres one must master to join a profession. Although literacy can be seen as "basic" in these senses, for me, becoming fully literate meant much more than learning my ABCs, enriching my vocabulary, diagramming sentences, and learning new genres and discourse practices. In a sense, then, becoming literate means finding a voice that allows you to represent yourself in various kinds of dialogue. For me, taking such a literate stance meant rewriting my life against cultural narratives that had led me for too long to see my sexual identity as sinful and unspeakable and then later as tolerated but invisible.

The notion of literacy as cultural dialogue is critical for many people. For example, my colleague and friend, Brenda Daly, writes that as a victim of childhood sexual abuse she had to actively author her life. She says, "The poisonous lesson of my childhood was that I could speak, I even could cry out, but no one would hear me, no one would listen" (1998, 5). For Daly, authoring involved more than simply finding words to speak; she also needed an audience to "bear witness" (15). She explains that early in her life, her abuse story was not a welcome one; indeed, the lesson she learned from the discourses of her childhood in family, church, and home was that her problem didn't exist, that she had imagined it, or, worse, that she had caused it. It wasn't until other victims of incest and sexual abuse began to speak of their experiences publicly that Daly found a discourse that she could join. Still, she felt that telling her story meant she had to be a bad girl, at least from the standpoint of her cultural heritage. She says, "To free myself from this debilitating childhood lesson, I would have to transgress conventions of 'good taste'" (20). Like Daly, I have come to see that becoming fully literate required that I rewrite my life, that I deconstruct the discourses that had led me to a place of relative privilege and safety (although at the cost of years of denial). It meant transgressing the version of morality that had shaped my life. It meant writing poems that explored the trials of flirtation, courtship, and intimacy that most people explore as teenagers. These poems came late.

In the pages that follow, I use stories and poems from my life to illustrate the process by which I became literate—that is, able to speak and write myself as a gay man. I invite you to consider how your experiences are similar to and different from mine and also to consider how schooling has affected the kind of voice that you have been invited to take.

**Scene 1: Miss Balfour's Academic-Track Senior English Class,
Homer-Center High School, Fall 1977**

"Exemplary. Who can use exemplary in a sentence?"

Hands shoot up around the room.

"Kim Jones."

"Marie Antoinette led an exemplary life."

*"What! Marie Antoinette certainly did not lead an exemplary life! She
was beheaded because of her cavalier attitude; when she heard that the peas-
ants complained that they had no bread, she said, 'Then let them eat cake!'"*

*Kim slides down in her seat; classmates exchange furtive but sympa-
thetic glances.*

"Now who can use exemplary correctly in a sentence?"

A few nervous hands go up.

**Scene 2: Holistic Scoring Session,
Indiana University of Pennsylvania; Summer 1987**

*Six people sit around tables in the English department library. Each pours
over a stack of hastily scrawled drafts written on every other line by nearly
first-year college students reflecting on the strengths and weaknesses of their
high school education for administrators who will never read their papers.
The stacks get smaller and pages of numbers next to the students' social security numbers fill up. The sticky afternoon wears on in silent reading, broken
only by sighs or the occasional chuckle followed by "listen to this one."*

"When Sister Mary Frances died, the whole school was totally lugubrious."

The raters smile, snicker a bit, and then return to their reading.

Shallow Literacy

In the ten years that passed between scene 1 and scene 2, I went from being
one of those students nervously trying to help Kim Jones recover from what
our twelfth-grade English teacher saw as a deplorable lack of cultural knowledge to being one of those six people charged with deciding which students
were ready for college writing courses at the local university. The vocabulary
issues here are, of course, just indications of wider issues. Like most of the
seniors at my rural Pennsylvania high school, I didn't have the cultural knowledge to know that Marie Antoinette was not an exemplary figure, but ten years
later I'd developed the kind of sensitivity to linguistic register to know that
lugubrious was completely out of context in that student's placement essay.
Indeed, my twelfth-grade English teacher's attempts at vocabulary enrichment
are likely the same kind of stopgap educational attempts that led the student
writing about Sister Mary Frances to throw in an impressive-sounding word.

According to the usual definitions of *literacy,* I became literate, even hyperliterate in those ten years. I learned to write essays, news stories, and term papers; I learned to distinguish between *affect* and *effect* and to identify sentence fragments and run-on sentences. I survived the "weeding-out process" in higher education that "sifts the relatively few 'worthy' members for the rewards that come with social promotion" (Ryan and Sackrey 1998, 114). Yet this new literacy was shallow because I was never invited to consider how I was being acculturated in those years—to consider the implications of leaving my working-class roots and becoming someone who knows both how and when to use such words as *psycholinguistics, deconstruction,* and *eco-feminism.*

I bought into what Cheryl Geisler calls the great appeal of higher education: "to make expertise universally accessible" (1994, 79). The problem with such an assumption is that it led me to believe that the ways in which I was taught to speak and write as well as the topics I was encouraged to write and speak about were natural, normal, the way things ought to be. No one invited me to consider why certain topics were never mentioned. And this brand of academic and professional literacy did not occur by accident or descend as holy writ from some language god. Rather, as Geisler notes, it was a part of a larger repackaging of "Anglo-Protestant elitist culture as neutral expertise" by the men who set the initial standards for professional status and the terms by which higher education would bestow that status (75). And for many years, I bought into this presumption, probably because, on the surface, the match between my rural Pennsylvanian, fundamentalist Christian values and the values of higher education was fairly good. I was a smart, white, Protestant male who was trying to appear both straight and middle class. And school itself served as a kind of sanctuary for me—a place where it was okay for a skinny, awkward, deeply closeted gay boy to be smart. Indeed, graduate education eventually provided me the perspective and tools to step back from my evangelical heritage and its attendant condemnation of homosexuality. However, the culture of higher education—at least as I've experienced it— did not immediately encourage me to integrate my sexual identity into my professional life. Thus, school has played a complicated role in the development of my literacy.

Athletes

1971
Last picked, the outfield moves in, easy out.
Swing and a miss; a foul tip has the line of batters reaching.
Across the playground the girls double dutch and hopscotch.
"Just hit this one."
Eyes squeezed shut at contact; the dull thud tells me to release the bat
    and run.
Always a step slower than the throw, but just the second out.

I shuffle back to the end of the line, eyes focused on the gravel beneath
    my feet.
The top of the order grips the bat in his coarse hands.
Arms swing; hips rotate forward; the ball falls over the heads of fielders
    who forgot to adjust.
He rounds second and beats the relay home.
Pop fly, the third out. I trot out to hide in deep right, an inning closer to
    the safety of math problems and phonics lessons.

1977

Head down, eyes focused on a chip of gray paint separating from the
    steel, I pull up my shorts.
The door next to me bangs closed, metal meeting metal, followed by the
    soft click of the locking mechanism falling into place.
My neighbor spins the dial to hide the last number.
"Better hurry."
A white t-shirt hangs loose on my narrow frame, I pull out my shoes,
    sitting to tie them.
From the back of the stall, I see the broad shoulders that stretch tight
    knit shirts across his smooth chest.
His stance is wide and balanced, supporting loud boasts.
I follow the long torso as it narrows to a jock strap, then turn my eyes to
    examine the rust spot obscuring the number plate riveted to the
    door.
I push my locker shut, step over the wooden bench, and weave through
    bodies I cannot touch, careful not to see the ample globes freed
    from their usual home in his Levis.
In class, this jock admires my quick answers; here, I'm on my own.

1981

A knurled bar and two full plates, I press the weight.
Third rep, the bar stalls, arms quiver between achievement and collapse.
Quick steps bring a hand to guide the bar up.
"Maybe you shouldn't try so much next time."
Bi's and tri's, quads and lats, delts; the room slowly empties.
One more set; I brush away the sweat dammed in my eye brows.
He bounces in, smiles, and flips on the sauna.
His jeans drop to the floor; he steps out of them bending slightly at the
    waist.
Today, tight blue cotton caresses his full cheeks.
Will I join him? He's brought an extra towel.
The heat would lessen tomorrow's ache.
Fine beads of sweat form on his tanned skin, but his thick black hair
    resists the damp.
He sits on the cedar slats, shoulders slumped slightly forward—hands
    lightly holding the edge of the bench.
He laughs, showing straight white teeth, briefly holding eye contact but
    then looking down between his feet.
This pretty boy sees more than a brain, but I fumble his pass.

1998
A knurled bar, four full plates and two quarters; I want four reps.
I stretch one shoulder against the side of the bench, and then the other,
    catching a glimpse of Tony at the fountain.
I stand, check the weights, and wait for him to pass.
"Excuse me, could you give me a spot?"
I lie looking up past the bar at his tight chest and arms. I close my eyes.
We lift on three, and then the weight is mine.
The first is down and up, easy. I feel the second. The third is steady but
    slow.
A couple short breaths and I release my locked elbows, letting the bar
    sink to within a whisker of my chest.
I explode back up, pressing; the weight stalls.
His hands hover, not quite touching the bar.
I press again; a red vein stands out on my forehead. I lock my arms.
His hands close around the bar, guiding it back to the supports.
"Nice lift." The cute ones always make me work a little harder.

                                            March 1999
                                            Ames, Iowa

Heterosexist Literacy

No one was openly gay in my high school, in my church, in my Bible college.
Sure, my tenth-grade typing teacher talked in a high nasal voice and was called
Suzie behind his back. But he wasn't to be taken seriously. Sure, there were the
two spinster ladies in our church: the butch one who always had a new car and
brought a whistle when she baby-sat us and the sweet feminine one who never
raised her voice. But they were just best friends for forty years. Sure, there was
a string of friends in Bible college who had been gay and given it up for Jesus
or who discovered they were gay after graduation. But we never kissed during
our lonely talks or dared to even think of holding each other's hands during the
long walks by the lake. Unfortunately, the message that homosexuality didn't
or shouldn't exist was not limited to my rural western Pennsylvania high
school, my evangelical Christian church, or my fundamentalist Bible college.
It also appeared in my secular graduate training in English: we collectively
winked at Truman Capote's "flamboyant" lifestyle and focused on the sub-
stance of what Socrates said to Phaedrus rather than on their flirtation.

Scene 3: Rhetorical History Course, Summer 1986

*The air-conditioning system couldn't quite pull enough of the humidity out
of the air, so the eight or ten of us gathered in the English department's
library to discuss ancient Greek rhetoric sat slightly sticky on a warm summer evening. A new master's student, I mostly sat in silence as the teacher
and the Ph.D. students discussed the text we'd read. I scribbled some notes,*

but I wasn't sure exactly what I was supposed to do with them, as there would be no tests. As we were collecting our books to leave, the teacher gave us a last-minute warning about the Phaedrus, *which we were reading for the next class session: "Ah, you will encounter passages that seem homoerotic; don't pay much attention to them because, ah, the sexual tension between Socrates and Phaedrus is largely a literary device."*

I'm not sure why my instructor made that statement. Apparently, he did not see it as important to discuss the obvious sexual tension when Socrates says, "Where is that boy I was talking to? He must listen to me once more, not rush off to yield to his non-lover before he hears what I have to say." And Phaedrus responds, "Here he is, quite close to you, whenever you want him" (Hackforth 1952, 53). I'm fairly sure that the instructor was aware of the tradition of homoeroticism in ancient Greek education, but I don't know if his statement to us was a vestige of homophobia or whether he simply believed that, as a scholarly matter, the answer to the question of whether Socrates and Phaedrus were lovers was so obviously negative that it didn't bear discussion. Whatever his intent, the message that I took as a fledging rhetorician (who was still deeply closeted) was that homosexuality was not fit subject matter for discussion in our classroom.

Scene 4: The Blazing Saddle, Des Moines, Iowa, September 1998

"You go in first," said Brad as he pulled open the door.

"No, you go first," I replied, pushing him forward, "I've never been to a gay bar before; I don't know what to expect."

The bar was packed with men in Levis and T-shirts; most had stomachs that lopped over their belts. Heavy eyes fell on us as we pushed through the crowd to get to the bar.

"Where are the cute guys?" I asked when Brad returned from the bar.

He laughed. "They've probably moved on to the Garden to dance by now."

We sipped our drinks, and I scanned the room, trying to find at least one man whom I found attractive.

"I'm going to leave you now, because no one will hit on you if I stand here with you."

"No," I grabbed Brad's arm and held it in a vice-tight grip.

He shook himself free. "I have to go to the bathroom."

I scowled at him, suspicious.

"As soon as I leave, someone will hit on you because you're fresh meat."

"No, really? I don't see anyone whom I want to hit on me, and what would I say?"

"You'll think of something," and he melted into the crowd, moving toward the back of the bar.

"I haven't seen you in here before."

I turned to face the voice; Brad hadn't been gone thirty seconds yet.

"It's my first time."
"My name is Justin, and this is Chad."
I shook hands. "I'm David."
"You have very nice arms; you must work out a lot," Chad was lightly
squeezing my bicep between his thumb and forefinger and smiling.
"Um, ah, thanks, I don't really work out that much." Chad was kind of
cute.
"Well, whatever you do, it's working."
*I stumbled through three more minutes of conversation before I bolted,
"I've got to go the restroom," and I pressed into the crowd in the direction
Brad had gone.*

Pride Parade

We are
leather and lace, spikes and boas, lamé and denim,
flannel and sequins, pinstripes and pumps, pancake and eyeliner

We are
fags, dykes, homos, bitches, queens, twinks, mothers,
fathers, sisters, brothers, daughters, sons

We are
confused teenagers silenced by locker room taunts

We are
lascivious and lonely, handsome and homely
svelte and skank, built and butch

We are
smart, dumb, fat, thin, tall, short, bald, hairy, drunk, sober, bold, timid,
positive, negative, happy, sad

We are
servers, technicians, doctors, cooks, lawyers, decorators, mortgage
adjusters, reporters, office managers, college profs, secretaries, senators

We are here; we are proud; we are not alone.

June 1999
Des Moines, Iowa

Scene 5: Room 213, Pearson Hall, Iowa State University, April 2001

*"I'm not sure I should read you this one." I held the transparency of
"Lifestyles" in my hand, five minutes before class ended. I'd just read "Pride
Parade" to my first-year composition students. They got the point—poems
don't have to have a regular rhythm and rhyme like those singsong poems
from* Chicken Soup for the Teen-age Soul *that the group in charge of class
had given them to read. The group's plan had been good: to try to use the*

*poems to get the class to think about what it was like to be in someone else's
shoes, someone who had been identified as "other" by the dominant school
group and treated badly. I was pushing for a second point with my poems: I
wanted the class to be challenged by texts written by someone who was the
"other," in this case me, a homosexual.*

"*Well, now you have to show it to us,*" *they teased.*

"*Okay, class is officially over; you don't have stay for this one,*" *but who
would leave before the drama was over? I took a deep breath, wondering if
I should let my students glimpse even this much of my sex life.* "*Here goes.*"

Lifestyle

Thighs and hips
Tongues and lips
Boys in g-strings dance for tips

Rum and coke
X and smoke
Meat so thick it makes me choke

Whispers and groan
Dicks come bone
Friends in bed, now not alone

Bottom and top
Press, don't stop
A different kind of sock hop

Anal and oral
Sex in plural
Not what the Boy Scouts call moral.

November 2000
Athens and Atlanta, Georgia

By anal *the class is laughing nervously; Chris gets up and leaves the
room in a pretend huff, only to return a few seconds later, smiling. Students
chat in knots of two or three.*

"*We'll talk more about this one next time.*"

*I begin the next class session reviewing the piece about making pickles
that I shared with the class during our first session together. I remind the class
that I've been sharing my writing with them all semester. They understand the
point; I've been trying to show them that they should write about things that
matter to them by reading them pieces in which I take emotional risks. Then I
put "Lifestyles" back up on the overhead projector. In a few minutes I will
pass out the course evaluation forms.* "'*Meat so thick it makes me choke. Anal
and oral, sex in plural.' Why do you think I chose to begin and end the course
with these two pieces? Why did I share this poem with you last time?*"

"*Well, you wanted to show us an example of a good poem.*"

"Yeah, but I could have quit with 'Pride Parade' if that were just my goal." My usually talkative class is silent. No one makes eye contact with me.

"Has it occurred to any of you that none of the poems we read for the last class were written from the point of view of the person who was labeled as 'other'?" Apparently it hadn't. *"Has it occurred to any of you that I am labeled as 'other' in many situations?"* A few brows wrinkle, but no one breaks the silence. *"I showed you this poem to show you that this stuff is a part of who I am. I wanted you to see that to accept me as a person who makes pickles and strawberry jam to grieve for his mother and grandmother is also to accept me as a person who has sex with other men. It's all part of the same package."*

I hand out the course evaluation sheets and—following university rules—I go out in the hall until the students are finished.

A New Literacy

At age thirty-seven, I began learning how to interact as a gay man. Despite the awkwardness of my first exposure to a gay bar, I took to flirting and the pickup games that go on in gay bars fairly easily. I became literate quickly. I learned that in some kinds of bars, men I don't know will feel free to grab my ass and that with the right kind of look I could stop them short. I learned that it was okay to let my eyes linger on an attractive man, but that if we made eye contact, I had to decide in a millisecond whether to hold it and indicate interest or break it immediately. I learned to distinguish between accidental touches on the dance floor and subtle overtures.

Learning to be a gay man in my classrooms was harder. In fact, it was three years after my first experience in a gay bar that I explicitly outed myself to a writing class. I saw the need to be out with this particular class when I received two papers early on in which students defined homosexuals as outside of their circles of humanity. One student wrote:

> The first people I exclude from my circle [of humanity] are homosexuals. They have no right to be able to do those sick and unpure actions. Not even the dumbest animal on earth performs these disgusting acts. It is against the whole plan of Human Nature.

For the first time in my teaching career, I was not content to sit back and pretend that such statements did not affect me, to hide in a safe, supposedly straight, middle-class, educated, white, male, above-it-all teacher role. I stood in for the millions of lesbian, gay, bisexual, transgendered, and transexual people whom these students were writing off and let them know in my responses to their work that their arguments affected me as a gay man. Later in the course, I outed myself to the class as a whole when, as an example of how to develop a focused argument, I used a letter to the editor I'd written responding to a state senator who was upset about Iowa State University's recent decision to grant domestic partner benefits. Yet this was not enough. I was still safe in my teacher's role; I'd won most of the class over early in the semester by reading them some pieces about my mother's death. I'd been patient with them, met with them outside of class, but in Helene Cixous' (2002) terms, I hadn't written my body for them. I hadn't made them see that the sensitive son grieving for his mother, the caring patient teacher, and the man who flirted with men in bars were all me.

The occasion in which I chose to push past some students' comfort level with my homosexuality arose as a response to several poems a group of students had chosen for their class discussion. As I read the poems about an hour before class, I was annoyed that in one of the predictable, singsong poems, the hero was a pretty, popular girl who got assigned to work with a group with a boy who could barely speak English and two girls who were fashion-challenged. And so, at age forty, in 213 Pearson Hall on a bright April afternoon, I found a new academic voice. I found a small way to speak back to the discourses both throughout my life and in that very classroom that had tried to make me see myself as abnormal, sinful, and needing to be silent. My choice to make my sexual identity explicit by reading "Lifestyles" to my class was far from safe. In the course evaluations, the students' responses were mixed. Several cited "Lifestyles" as offensive, as over the line; others saw it as a more natural part of the series of revelations that I'd made throughout the semester and were grateful for the chance to have substantive interaction with an openly gay man for the first time in their lives.

Although I have not read "Lifestyles" to any other of my writing classes, I continue to share my poems and stories with my classes, and I always share something that involves an emotional risk for me. The main reason I make myself vulnerable to my students in this way is to invite them to tell stories that society has encouraged them to keep to themselves. This semester a beautiful young woman wrote a paper in which she admitted for the first time that she was bulimic; a self-described computer nerd wrote about a recent romantic rejection and shame at never having had a girlfriend; and a budding feminist wrote about her secret desire for larger breasts, the kind that turn men's heads. To be completely honest, though, I also take these risks—particularly those related to my gay identity—because I need to, because I'm still recovering from a personal and educational history that discouraged me from accepting myself.

Authoring Your Life

Although I wrote thousands of words in elementary, junior high, and high school and tens of thousands as an undergraduate and graduate student, the poems came late, came last. School provided me with many important intellectual tools: I learned to read others' texts and summarize them fairly and efficiently; I learned to question authors' assumptions and examine the support that they provided for their claims; I learned to construct my own arguments, to make a clear point and support it well. Rarely, however, did school invite me to consider who I was or what assumptions other authors were making about me. I learned to explore my own life in relationship to others only as I taught myself to write stories and poems.

Along with the other authors in this book, I want to invite you to consider the power of story to enliven your writing (see also Hint Sheet B). The writing teachers in this book as well as those in your classrooms have much to teach you about new techniques and exploring unfamiliar genres. However, they may or may not encourage you to author your own life, and so I conclude by extending that invitation: write yourself; write what matters to you. Twist and turn teachers' assignments until you find an angle that lets you say something that you simply must say. Take a risk; write the things that you've been hiding under covers of silence or forced eloquence. I can't guarantee that your teachers, your family, or your friends will like what you write, but at least you won't wait as long as I did to write your poems and stories, your essays and letters to the editor, your paintings and portraits. Write yourself.

Works Cited

Cixous, Helene. 2001. *The Laugh of the Medusa.* In *The Rhetorical Tradition: Readings for Classical Times to the Present,* 2nd ed., 1524–1537. Edited by Patricia Bizzell and Bruce Herzberg. Boston: St. Martin's Press.

Daly, Brenda. 1998. *Authoring a Life: A Woman's Survival in and through Literary Studies.* Albany: State University of New York Press.

Foucault, Michel. 2001. *The Order of Discourse.* In *The Rhetorical Tradition: Readings for Classical Times to the Present,* 2nd ed., 1460–1470. Edited by Patricia Bizzell and Bruce Herzberg. Boston: St. Martin's Press.

Geisler, Cheryl. 1994. *Academic Literacy and the Nature of Expertise: Reading, Writing and Knowing in Academic Philosophy.* Hillsdale, NJ: Erlbaum.

Hackforth, R. 1952. *Plato's Phaedrus: Translated with an Introduction and Commentary.* London: Cambridge University Press.

Ryan, Jake, and Charles Sackrey. 1985. *Strangers in Paradise: Academics from the Working Class.* Boston: South End Press.

Sharing Ideas

1. John Boe stresses how much can be learned from stories told by families and friends. Think and write about what you believe you have learned from stories that your friends and members of your family have told. Start, perhaps, by making lists of stories, of people in your life who tell or have told stories, and of memorable storytelling moments in your life. Move from the lists to other kinds of writing: journal entries, essays, stories, a series of vignettes, poems.

2. Audacity should be one aim of education, suggests John Boe. To what extent do you agree with him? To what extent are you viewed by others as *audacious*? Why or why not? If you were to imagine yourself becoming more audacious in a way that you would like, what specific form would that audacity take? Think and write about one or more of these questions surrounding the topic of audacity.

3. Part of what makes us individuals is that we have unique stories to tell; this is another point that John Boe's essay makes. Assume for a moment that you agree with this point. Make a list of the stories you have inside you that are not just distinctive but unique—one-of-a-kind. Then write one of these stories or tell it to someone.

4. Stuart Ching's essay begins by recounting a child's perspective on a ritual. Think and write about a ritual that you witnessed as a child. Examples of rituals include a wedding, a funeral, a baptism, a bar mitzvah, a festival, a traditional parade, a holiday (holy day) meal.

5. Michael Spooner tells us that, in his experience, winter was the time of telling stories. In your experience, what is the time of telling stories? When you think of family members telling stories, do you think of a certain season, occasion, or time of day? What place(s) do you associate with storytelling: a porch, a place of work, a backyard, a park, a kitchen table, an automobile? When do you tend to tell stories? Where are you most comfortable telling stories? Think and write about one or more of these questions.

6. David Wallace writes about storytelling as a mode of dialogue through which people have an opportunity to bridge gaps of misunderstanding, fear, and prejudice. He also gives an example of story told in a class that had the potential of causing discomfort and triggering fear and prejudice. Try to think of a moment in your life when you listened to or read a story that caused you discomfort or otherwise touched a nerve but that, perhaps, led eventually to greater understanding. If you had been in Wallace's class, how might you have reacted to the stories told and why?

7. Much of David Wallace's education, whatever its strengths, did not address certain issues, experiences, and matters of identity that were crucial to him. To what extent has your education addressed or not addressed such issues, experiences, and matters in your life? To what extent has your education been unsatisfying and why? Think and write about these questions.

8. To some degree, all of the writers in this section discuss the extent to which storytelling and education ought to involve some level of risk. One example of such risk is sharing a story with someone, a story that might cause you discomfort or embarrassment or that might cause an unforeseen response in your listeners or readers. To what extent do you agree that this

kind of risk, or that risk in general, is appropriate and desired in educational settings? Write an essay in which you take a position on the issue of *risk*. Think and write about a time in your education when you took a risk or were asked to take a risk of some kind. To what extent was this experience positive and productive? Why or why not?

———————————

Part III
Story in Context: Responsibility, Community, Heritage

All codes become codes by doing some things regularly
and not others, and it is not so much the ultimate logic
of these regularities that makes them obligatory but rather
the fact that, logical or no, they have become habitual to
those who communicate within that code.

—Mina Shaughnessey

8

Personal Experience Narratives: What Are Our Responsibilities as Storytellers?

Robert Brooke, Rochelle Harris, Jeannine Nyangira

Here's how we imagine you: Like us, you're a writer in an English class, and you have a personal story to tell. It might be the story of a trip you took, say to a culture not your own where you met someone who changed you. Or the story of a loss, perhaps of a relative or a close friend. Or the story of a relationship, of how you clarified a belief or an aspect of your personality because something once went wrong in the way you loved someone. We all have stories; they change us; teachers ask for them in various ways. Perhaps you're in a literature class, and your teacher has requested a journal relating personal experience to the novel you just read. Perhaps your composition teacher has asked you to describe how your childhood family taught you to read and write. Or perhaps, as in the class the three of us shared, your teacher has asked you to develop your own writing project, as long as you can connect it to a "written conversation" going on in the literary nonfiction you're reading.

So you have a story to tell, and an English class that seems, in its own way, to be asking for that story. Like us, you are considering how to write about this story, and a host of questions are sparking somewhere in the back of your mind: *What would my family think if they knew I was writing about them? How do I feel about revealing this story? Is this the right place to write this story? What will the teacher and the other students think about it? What do I want them to think?* If you're like us, these background questions are present in your mind, interfering (to a degree) with the work of just writing the story. To us, they are questions about our responsibilities and about the people who can be affected by the way we write our stories—the people represented in the stories, the people with whom we share our drafts, the people we want the stories to change.

In this chapter, we want to think with you about our responsibilities and our stories. We'll gather our thoughts around three particular responsibilities: ownership, process, and purpose. We have stories to share about each of these responsibilities, stories with a moral (or if not a moral, at least a question). We think our stories and responsibilities are important, and part of the work of being a writer is negotiating among them, in English classes and beyond.

A Story About Ownership:
Jeannine Asks, "Who owns my stories?"

I'm still not sure what I would have done. What if she had said no?

Here I was, finally enrolled in a university creative nonfiction course, staring at my first blank page and my fingers itching to write. "Write what you know," the experts said. Okay, I thought, but what I knew was this snarled ball of yarn—no, make that barbed wire—in my head called "Jeannine's family history." In some regards, my past was smooth and secure. But at regular intervals certain snags punctuated its narrative, making it tangled, unwieldy. It had to do with the strange tale of Mama and Nick, my parents. If someone tried to market their story for some after-school special, the spiel would read: *White girl from Nebraska meets boy from Kenya in 1960s New York. Fall in love, get married. Girl's family has minor meltdown. Boy keeps secrets—drinking and women and another family on the side. They move back to Kenya, but by the time his secrets come out, daughter is born. White girl tries to save marriage. Mother and daughter escape from Kenya, move back to Nebraska. Daughter grows up safe but confused.*

This tale had been told to me in pieces through Mama's bedtime stories, tales full of hard fact yet free from any hostility. At night I'd learn about a country and a family and a father that I couldn't remember, and I inhaled these stories until they seemed to become part of my own memory. Still, there was so much in it to untangle—barbed threads of racism, alcoholism, infidelity, and those questions of belonging that often come with being biracial. So although Mama had (amazingly) chosen to recount these stories with grace, I still spent my days rummaging through them, scrambling for tools to bring order to their disarray. Sometime the tool I used was denial, then bitterness, then rage, and finally forgiveness, thanks to some serious spiritual intervention. And now in this writing class, I finally had a chance to pull these scenes out of my head and onto paper in order to map where I was and where I wanted to go.

But here I faced a dilemma: whose story, exactly, was this—mine or my parents'? For I realized that in order to explore my own issues, I would inevitably have to write about Mama's and Nick's as well. Our stories were so commingled that the essence of one narrative became the essence of another, and I couldn't tell my secrets without also telling someone else's. In my Nebraskan German-descended family, there are several understood tenets of behavior: *be clean, always work at least two jobs, and don't tell your business to anyone. If necessary, go only to a family member.* So the question remained: if story is property, to whom did this family history belong?

For the record, let me state: I love Mama. I'm indebted to Mama. And after an eight-year stint in Chicago, I again live with Mama. As her only child, I've become so fiercely protective of her that sometimes she literally has to pat me on the arm, tell me to calm down. Yet while learning from her how to forgive, I've also picked up from her to be careful of whom I trust. Somewhere along the line, though, I also learned the sweet release in the type of written self-disclosure to which Gertrude Stein pointed when she said, "I write for myself and for strangers." In writing, I discovered, I could pull that barbed wire out of my head and weave it into narrative through a certain voice that seemed to materialize only in print. Writing for my own catharsis or for that faceless audience out there didn't faze me. It was just those people in between—those that I knew—that made things so sticky.

Had I written any personal essays earlier in life, they would've been full of crackling ache and fury: at a father who refused to choose the things that matter, at a loving white mother who naively thought she could raise her mixed daughter as colorless, and at an extended family that kept Mama and me on its periphery. But now I wanted to understand the multidimensionality of these characters. I needed to understand causality—what had made them into themselves? Had they also been hurt? For me, writing could function as a site of wrestling and epiphany and forgiveness and tribute, a place to do things like honor Mama's graciousness through her own abandonment. Yet would she view my documentation of her betrayal as a form of betrayal in itself? There was no way to truly know without asking. One evening I sat upstairs, staring at my blank computer screen and feeling the stories impatiently moving up out of me, yet knowing what I still had to do: go downstairs and ask Mama how much I could tell. I dreaded this asking, having little idea how she would answer and absolutely no idea what I would do if she said no. What would I choose: allegiance with Mama or allegiance with writing?

Such moments of tension have long been debated by authors who choose to abide by the wishes of others and those who choose to ultimately follow their writing craft, despite any fallout from family. Creative nonfiction is fraught with the negotiation of these choices. Take the dedication of Maxine Hong Kingston's *Woman Warrior:* "To Mother and Father." Now take its opening line: "'You must not tell anyone,' my mother said, 'what I am about to tell you'" (1976, 1). Family secrets then spill out like water.

One can cite pragmatic reasons for allowing family input in shaping a narrative. Besides my own larger concern that my writing could exacerbate Mama's difficult past, I also just don't want to be uncomfortable at the breakfast table when I go downstairs in the morning. Annie Dillard, author of *An American Childhood,* explains her own reasons:

> My parents are quite young. My sisters are watching this book carefully.
> Everybody I'm writing about is alive and well, in full possession of his facul-

ties, and possibly willing to sue. . . . I've promised my family that each may pass on the book. I've promised to take out anything that anyone objects to—anything at all. . . . I don't believe in a writer's kicking around people who don't have access to a printing press. They can't defend themselves. (1987, 69–70)

But there are obviously other ways to look at this. Kim Barnes, author of memoirs *In the Wilderness* and *Hungry for the World,* chooses to fundamentally embrace her craft but does so through a certain understanding of the role of memory:

See, before they were handed the manuscript, I had talked with my family . . . about things from memory that they disagreed on to illustrate how hard it is to say that there is one memory of any given situation. . . . I think memoir writers and personal essay writers would be further ahead if, instead of talking to their families about the details of the story, they would talk about the idea of writing such a thing—why we write what we do, how our goals are to come to a greater understanding of what we're made of and what our memory is made of." (2000, 177–178)

There's so much to be said about memory and ownership of stories, I know. Yet I'm still upstairs, trying to foresee Mama's response to my writing. If she refuses to let me write this story, perhaps I could lie low for a while and later return with my own spin on memory theory. "True, Mama," I would say, "I don't remember your parents or Nick or Kenya like you do—actually, I don't remember them at all—but this is how it feels to *me*. This is who they've become to *me*." Or I could push: "Look" (despite my love for her, I can be strong-willed), "when you birthed me, your story automatically *became* my story." Technically I have a right to do this. I have a right to memory—and even to explore my lack of memory. Yet it's a right I haven't always granted. How many times have I stopped Mama from talking to others about Nick? I've policed her hard, kicking her under the table or abruptly changing the subject while inwardly fuming, *you can't tell that part of me*. Sometimes she'd acquiesce and quiet down, and sometimes she'd pin me down with this exasperated look that clearly asked, *just who do you think lived through all this?* The truth is that this story is *our* story, mutual property of which, admittedly, I could take "my half" and run. But an apparition still resurfaces: my future deathbed, laden with my published texts and a literary prize or two, but no Mama. No family at all. And, wheezing, I ask my lonely, dying self, "Was it worth it?"

So I take a deep breath, sigh, and make my way downstairs to where Mama's sitting on the couch watching PBS. On the arm of the easy chair I sit and wait, realizing that my question—and her answer—could well determine my writing future. "Um, Mama? I have a question. How much about you and Nick am I allowed to . . ."

And she doesn't even let me finish. She glances away from *The Lehrer News Hour* or *Antiques Roadshow* and swiftly answers, "All of it. I don't care. It's over."

This I wasn't ready for. A fight, yes. Quiet disappointment or persistent cajoling, sure. But given carte blanche? Find an analogy for this: I am a soldier, sword unsheathed, only to discover that there is no duel. Or a beggar who discovers that the goods are free. This time I get it all, the writing *and* the Mama. Yet there'll still be times when I'll hesitate to show her my writing, like the piece interrogating the racism of her mother, my white grandmother. And I'll also wonder, now that I've asked for permission to tell the Mama-and-Nick story, will she assume that I'll always get clearance before I write or publish anything? I can't answer this. I do know, however, that when it came to the most important story and the most important person, I had to get permission.

But of course I'll still wonder: what if she had said no?

A Story of Process:
Robert Asks, "How and when do
I write my story, and with whose help?"

Jeannine's section raises the question of ownership. In crafting a personal story, she asks, How much is ours to tell? How much belongs to others? Her response to this dilemma—seeking permission for the story—is one I value.

But I'd like to raise another, related question, more about the reasons we might want to write certain stories rather than about ownership. My question is about process: when should I choose to write a given personal story, and why then? My response to this question, finally, will be to seek discernment, as a writer, for the dangers and possibilities of writing in a given context.

A personal story, emphasizing danger: In the late 1980s, my eldest brother died, in an accident involving alcohol. All of us scattered siblings came home for the memorial service, to join in mourning with Dad and Mom and our youngest sisters still at home. All ten of us came, with spouses and children, for a gathering of near thirty. We cleaned his apartment, divided what we could, and went back to our lives, often in separate states. We each enacted our mourning as fit our personalities and abilities.

Since I am a writer and writing teacher, I wrote about my brother and my family off and on for the next two years. I wrote in my weekly writing group, in classes with students, in summer institutes for schoolteachers. Finally, when I thought I'd finished the writing, I shared a partial draft with my parents. I soon learned that they felt hurt by the writing: they asked me not to publish it. I have respected their wishes and have kept that piece in a filing cabinet drawer.

This version of the story of my writing, thus, emphasizes ownership and danger—my family also owns the information about my brother and I faced danger in sharing it with them.

But another version of this story, emphasizing possibility: For most of the time I wrote about my brother, I didn't think about ownership or danger. I was thinking, instead, about the meaning of his death, or what meaning I could take from it. Most of my writing was, as Paul Heilker describes, an essay in the oldest sense of the word: an essaying forth, an exploration, a seeking for understanding. Heilker defines the essay as

> [a] textual attempt to come to some understanding of a problem, however partial, provisional, and ephemeral; a weighing of alternatives; an experiment in thinking whose outcome is unknown at the outset; a Montaignean exploration of a self and world in flux that leaves the known behind . . . its form being not the form of a thing, but rather the form of an activity. (1996, 161–169)

In the activity of writing, I was trying to understand how my brother's life could have taken the path it did, what shaped it, whether and how it might have been possible to intervene so his story would have ended differently.

So the writing, for me, was a learning activity, a process of discernment. Certainly some of what I wrote was fairly straightforward story writing, telling what happened and painting with words the particulars of specific scenes. But this story also led me to reading, to talking with others, to getting more informed. I spent some time, for instance, talking with members of our local Al-Anon group and reading their literature. I read some studies of family dynamics, birth order and its effects on personality, especially for the oldest children of large families. I read a lot about the negotiation of religion and sexual identity for young people in their teens and twenties. This reading was, for me, surrounded also by real conversation. The other writers in my weekly writing group responded to my drafts by sharing their own confrontations with similar issues. Schoolteachers would tell me stories from their classrooms. Students in my writing classes would write their own stories or would talk to me in office hours about their negotiations of family and faith and identity. The discernment process was, for me, centrally located in the social contexts of these conversations.

The writing process of this personal story, in short, engaged me in three activities, all of which were full of possibility:

- I needed to articulate on paper what I understood from this story, and I needed to be able to revise this articulation regularly in response to new information and new perspectives;
- I needed to immerse myself in learning that broadened my sense of the scope and meaning and relevance of my personal story; and
- I needed regular discussion with people of many ages, experiences, and backgrounds, through which I could test out my articulation and understanding.

When I look at this personal story from this perspective, I see that the process of writing was certainly, for me, more important than the potential published product. I needed to write this story at this time, and I needed to do so in the semipublic space of writing groups in and out of classes. In order to work out what my brother's story meant for me, I needed to explore what his story might mean to others and how his story might reflect patterns in other people's lives.

Kim Stafford writes of the sharing of stories: "Stories work to make us more than citizens. . . . Saved stories make us flexible" (1986, 126). Through all this writing, reading, and conversation, I believe I came to a more flexible understanding of some of the tensions of young adulthood, not just for my brother and myself, but for those I worked with. And I think during those years my personal writing in classes modeled writing as a process of understanding and discernment that may have served some students well.

All of which leads to a worry about audience: I started this section asking, "When should I choose to write a given personal story?" I think I've given two contradictory answers to that: For the story as product, maybe I shouldn't write a story when it has the potential to hurt those involved with it. For the story as process, maybe I need to write a story when I am in search of understanding. But I don't want to make too much of that product/process distinction when the real issue may well be audience.

I think our writing process has an audience every bit as much as our finished writings. During the two years I wrote about my brother, I was lucky to be in a position to choose (mostly) the people with whom I read and discussed my work. I knew the people in my weekly writing group were all good writers and caring teachers, and I could be safe just exploring in their company. As a writing teacher, I could set the tone for writing in my classes and open those courses to writing for understanding. Since I had those two audiences, I could wait to share my writing with my family or with editors until I had done most of the working-through the story required. For me, having these specific readers for my writing process made all the difference.

Which leads me to conclude: Perhaps my question about process—"when should I write this story?"—is also a question about the audience that surrounds our writing process. I needed the kind of readers who would support the essaying I was doing, and that need suggests a moment of discernment as we writers approach the dangerous possibilities of our stories. We writers might want to discern whether this class, this writing group, this teacher or colleague can be the sort of reader our process needs. If such readers aren't immediately available, then we are left with the task of finding readers to support the writing, of discerning when they are available.

A Story of Purpose:
Rochelle Asks, "Why am I writing, and what responsibility do I have to that?"

Jeannine and Robert have been reflecting on the responsibilities of ownership and process. My reflections have to do with the responsibility of the writer to herself when she tells stories. I often wrestle with trusting the meaning I make of my stories as well as letting them out into the world for others to read. Here is a writing story about this responsibility.

Visiting Jack

I printed off an extra copy before I left, stuffing it in a folder with all the other things I wanted Jack to read. I was off for my annual summer visit, driving myself and my cat a thousand-plus miles to see family, then to visit Jack and his wife, Elizabeth. I had had a productive writing summer and was eager to share a certain essay.

Eventually the moment came. Everyone who smoked had a cigarette; everyone who drank had an adult beverage. We were outside under the carport, watching the sunset fade and the stars come out. I slipped inside through the squeaky screen door and grabbed my folder. Jack grinned and took the essay. I think it must have been a relaxed evening after two days of good conversation. Maybe it was that I was really proud of this essay—several others had read and liked it. Maybe it was that I had been trying to write a good essay about the mountains for three years. Maybe I just didn't realize how much of myself I had invested in this piece.

Jack's forehead wrinkled like he was puzzled. I began to get tense, palms sweaty. It was a short piece, so he finished quickly, scanned through it again and said, "It's interesting how you write about the mountains." What did *that* mean, I thought. "I don't think people from the mountains would describe them the way you do." I was tuning out, surprised by any negative or even neutral critique. I mean, the hook for the essay, which I called "Shouting the Mountains," was the unusual way I tried to think about the mountains—as a kind of sound, a full, earthy, sharp sound. Did he not like the hook? Was he bored by the mother-daughter story, another important aspect of the essay? Couldn't he see how much I loved the mountains from my descriptions? Jack did eventually tell me what he liked about this piece, pointing to a couple of lines about moss and rhododendron he thought were good. I just nodded. Then as soon as I could, I stuffed the paper back in the folder.

What Happened?

It's not a big moment. It's not even that dramatic a moment—two friends hanging out, reading their work, saying what they think. I didn't burn my essay afterward. But while this was happening, I was mad, worried, and scared. Quite a reaction. I wanted to figure it out, to see what I had at stake in this essay, to find out why I responded the way I did.

My reaction has layers, I believe. In one way, here were my deepest writing fears coming true. His doubt about the narrator's story of her and her mother was an echo of my doubt in trusting myself as a storyteller. His inability to see this essay as one about identity and relationships *and* mountains mirrored my fear of an inability to craft an essay around those ideas.

I bet many writers have had a similar experience. I wonder if it has even happened in class when a peer is responding, and all the student can hear is that her writing isn't good or doesn't work. My experience with this essay brought into relief two writing issues I've started working on: the capacity to trust what I write and to name the purposes for the pieces I write. I want to believe that my writing process and the texts I produce can be successful and authentic, appealing to readers and well-crafted. I want to have that "intangible authority" as a narrator about which the essayist Edward Hoagland writes (1999, xv).

There is something so powerful about putting a memory down on paper. Yet this is also an inherently vulnerable act. Anne Lamott, a novelist, believes writing is about exposing the unexposed, that "writing can be a pretty desperate endeavor, because it is about some of our deepest needs: our need to be visible, to be heard, our need to make sense of our lives" (1994, 19). When I read Natalie Goldberg, also a novelist, I found out she lived with these tensions, too: "You are exposing your life, not how your ego would like to see you represented, but how you are as a human being" (1986, 36). How relieving it is to know that I'm not alone, that other writers feel anxious and fearful but keep writing, to know that sometimes there is much at stake when a person puts words on paper. Jeannine and Robert have talked powerfully about the different responsibilities we have as writers and storytellers to our families and audiences, but I learned through Jack that my primary responsibility is to myself.

Another way to state that idea is with two questions about the purpose of an essay: what is it I want my essay to do as an essay, a specifically and deliberately composed piece of writing that reflects on the meaning of an experience in my life, and what do I want this essay to do for me, as a writer trying to trust her writing and her writing process? When I answer these questions for the essay that Jack read, I see that I wanted my text to be a thoughtful piece about the mountains, which are very important to me, and to be proof that I *am* a good writer.

Then there is the layer of audience. It might seem after a reader like Jack that getting response is too much trouble. I am firmly convinced, though, in having readers—like a writing group in a composition class or a few close friends—give me feedback. I write because I believe the act of composing teaches me something about life and living; I need readers to let me know what it is they're learning from my texts. Crafting a story into an essay is a combination of inspiration, that elusive almost mystical moment of creating, and of making choices, where I shape and mold the ideas into a text. Readers help me make those choices.

Underneath this layer is, I believe, the strongest reason my response to Jack's reading was so sharp: responsibility to myself. Now that doesn't mean I refuse to revise or listen to people's comments or that I'm only selfishly concerned with myself. Quite the contrary. I seek out opinions and ideas; I revise repeatedly. "Shouting the Mountains" went through about five revisions before

Jack read it. It just means that I believe telling my stories is a way of making meaning of the world around me. The essayist Joseph Epstein says the "self of the writer is in good part what the essay is about" (1993, xv). Joyce Carol Oates, a nonfiction writer, simply calls essays "truth-telling" (1991, xvi) and Philip Lopate, a personal essayist, describes them as "a mode of inquiry, another way of getting at the truth" (1995, xiv). When I wrote "Shouting the Mountains," I finally felt like I made sense of how the mountains are all tangled up with thoughts of home, my mother, and growing up. Because of that, my essay was a success. Yet on another level, I am trying to convince readers that my experience is valid and legitimate, that I have learned something.

Why This Is Important

Anne Lamott suggests "a writer always tries, I think, to be a part of the solution, to understand a little about life and to pass this on" (1994, 107). I wrote this quote on an index card and taped it to my computer. Ultimately, I think, this is what I try to do when I write an essay and give it to a friend. Sometimes that means putting scary things down on paper, like how my mother's choice to move to the mountains changed both our lives. Sometimes it means being uncomfortable while a friend reads my essay. Sometimes it just means living with the meaning I make in my writing. It is all a process, this learning to trust my decisions and tell my stories.

A Final Responsibility: Writing the Story

Here's where we want to leave you: write the story you've brought to your English class. It might be a story you're itching to write if you can only get permission for it—a story like Jeannine's. It might be a story you need to write, though you may need to attend to process—a story like Robert's. Or it might be a story with effects you especially want to address—a story like Rochelle's. Write the story. And, in writing it, be responsible—to the content, to the process, to your own practice as a writer.

Part of story writing, we believe, is managing the responsibilities of that writing. Those responsibilities won't go away. They are there anytime we represent other people in our work. They are there anytime the force of our words might affect ourselves or others. Story writing is a social act, deeply embedded in our social world of family and friends, classmates and acquaintances. We aren't behaving responsibly if we believe otherwise, if we choose to ignore the power of our words to affect others.

But such responsibilities aren't, finally, reasons *not* to write. They are, instead, considerations for *how* to write. Part of that *how*, certainly, involves considering what your words will mean to those who read them in and out of class. And part involves considering how to manage the process of developing your writing, whom you share drafts with, and how you ask for response, advice, and permission. This is all part of the work of having a story to tell, a story that teaches you and your readers a little bit more about the world in which we live.

Works Cited

Barnes, Kim. 2000. "Interview with Kim Barnes." By Robert Root Jr. *Fourth Genre* 2.1 (spring): 170–190.

Dillard, Annie. 1987. "To Fashion a Text." In *Inventing the Truth,* 54–76. Edited by William Zinsser. Boston: Houghton-Mifflin.

Elbow, Peter. 1981. *Writing with Power: Techniques for Mastering the Writing Process.* New York: Oxford University Press.

Epstein, Joseph. 1993. Introduction to *The Best American Essays 1993,* xiii–xviii. Edited by Robert Atwan. New York: Ticknor and Fields.

Goldberg, Natalie. 1986. *Writing Down the Bones: Freeing the Writer Within.* Boston: Shambhala.

Heilker, Paul. 1996. *The Essay: Theory and Pedagogy for an Active Form.* Urbana, IL: NCTE.

Hoagland, Edward. 1999. Introduction to *The Best American Essays 1999,* xiii–xix. Edited by Robert Atwan. Boston: Houghton-Mifflin.

Kingston, Maxine Hong. 1976. *The Woman Warrior: Memoirs of a Girlhood Among Ghosts.* New York: Knopf.

Lamott, Anne. 1994. *Bird by Bird: Some Instructions on Writing and Life.* New York: Anchor Books.

L'Engle, Madeleine. 1980. *Walking on Water: Reflections on Faith and Art.* Wheaton, IL: Harold Shaw Publishers.

Lopate, Phillip. 1995. *The Art of the Personal Essay.* New York: Anchor Books.

Oates, Joyce Carol. 1991. Introduction to *The Best American Essays 1991,* xiii–xxiii. Edited by Robert Atwan. New York: Ticknor and Fields.

Stafford, Kim. 1986. *Having Everything Right: Essays of Place.* Seattle, WA: Sasquatch.

9

Sympathy for the Devil? Risk Taking in Writing About Fear

Carolyn Alessio

The high school freshmen were whispering during class, exclaiming over an open note in one girl's lap. Finally she folded it up and attempted to pass it to another classmate, but in transit the note fell to the floor. When the instructor opened it, she saw photos from the Internet of the smoldering World Trade Center. Embedded in the plumes of rising smoke were the outlines of two forboding faces. The handwritten note below said, "Melissa: The Faces of Satan?!"

The faces were a photo hoax, one of many circulated through the Internet, and the students were not the only ones who believed them. The doctored photos offered a sort of comfort for terror-stricken viewers—by putting a known face on evil, part of the tragic story was already solved.

Many emotions can fuel stories. Eudora Welty once wrote, "all writers speak from, and to, emotions eternally the same in all of us: Love, pity, fear do not show favorites or leave any of us out" (1984, 230). But not every feeling is equally easy to harness for the novice. As fiction writers, especially beginning ones, we tend to think more about love, a subject that at first seems the most accessible. Unfortunately, it is also the most susceptible to clichés, a point that Rainer Maria Rilke makes eloquently in *Letters to a Young Poet:* "avoid at first those forms that are too facile and commonplace: they are the most difficult, for it takes a great, fully matured power to give something of your own where good and even excellent traditions come to mind in quantity" (1934, 19).

Pity, the second emotion pinpointed by Welty, may appear in the stories of novices, but too often it takes the form of heavy moral symbols, such as a homeless person with a heart of gold who triggers a spiritual awakening in a passer-by. When I think of stories that poignantly demonstrate pity—or self-pity—I turn to the end of James Joyce's "Araby," in which the adolescent narrator relates, "Gazing up into the darkness I saw myself as a creature driven and derided by vanity; and my eyes burned with anguish and anger" (1995, 696).

Fear, then, remains the most viable for a new writer to attempt. Fear is always immediate. Nobody is impervious to it, and everyone, to take off from Franklin Delano Roosevelt's famous pronouncement, dreads the very topic of fear.

Even the denial of fear can be a powerful prompt for a story. Last September, I asked a class of high school freshmen if they were scared about entering a new school. Nobody raised his or her hand. I stared out at the classroom and saw twenty-six impassive faces. Though I was aware of the teen code not to reveal anything in one's face to an adult, I knew that these students had plenty to worry about: a neighborhood riddled with gangs, relatives with immigration problems, poverty, the task of mastering English as a second language after their native Spanish. Coming to the high school, which is selective, also presented plenty of challenges—to finance their private tuition, the students each had to work one day a week at a job downtown. Had I been faced with any one of these situations as a fourteen-year-old, I knew that I would have struggled immensely. So looking out at the blank faces, I repeated my question, "Did *anyone* have any fears?" Again, nobody responded.

Toward the end of that class, I asked the students to write me letters about themselves. Looking over the letters that night, I found a litany of anxieties and fears: of forgetting locker combinations, losing scholarships because of bad grades, not making new friends, having a boss who did not like him or her. More than one student wrote that he or she feared the school would not offer driver's ed.

Fears are not always colossal, but everyone has them. For many of us, fears come in such diverse forms as not having enough money to pay rent or tuition, going gray before thirty, being rejected from a sorority or fraternity, and finding army ants coming in through the basement. Though these scenarios may pale in comparison to, say, ethnic deportation or the threat of anthrax in the mail, they share an important root: all threaten to upset balance.

The upset of balance and routine can be the foundation of a story. This shifting of the ordinary allows writers a chance to show their characters as vulnerable, as reacting in unexpected and sometimes even primal ways. The writer (and the reader) is called upon to reconcile the characters' past with the present.

Too often, we think of fears and phobias as nuisances that need to be conquered. Sigmund Freud wrote about humans' attempts to ward off their fear of death with routines. But that desire for control is what makes fear such an effective tool in fiction, capable of driving a narrative when unleashed.

New writers sometimes are encouraged to begin a story with a fait accompli, or an act of God that has already occurred, such as the death of a character's beloved, a tornado, or a maiming accident. In these stories the triggers are already clear; emotion and character motivation stem from that source. This method can work quite well, as in Gabriel Garcia Marquez's "Handsomest Drowned Man in the World" (1984), a story in which a village becomes enamored of the body of a stranger who washes up on their beach, and Bharati Mukherjee's "Management of Grief" (1995), in which a Canadian woman loses her entire family to a terrorist bomb on a plane bound for India. In the Garcia Marquez story, the villagers learn about themselves through their treatment of the beguiling corpse, and in the Mukherjee story, disorientation provides the protagonist with the incentive to consider life options she had never fully realized. Mukherjee starts the story with the exposition askew and the sense that even the narrator's home is no longer her own: "A woman I don't know is boiling tea the Indian way in my kitchen. There are a lot of women I don't know in my kitchen, whispering and moving tactfully" (975).

This initial aura of confusion in both the Marquez and the Mukherjee stories is powerful, and a ready-made, exposition-making emergency. Both stories are searing and sophisticated, but in a way, the stories' work, or part of it, already has been done. For a novice (and often even an advanced writer), the weight of these acts of God can be overpowering. To begin a story with a death, especially a violent one, can prompt clichéd scenes, such as characters weeping and having flashbacks to tender, sentimental times. Instead of offering us a window into the characters' psyches, tragedies can force a story into obvious patterns.

One way to avoid some of these pitfalls is to begin by making a list of things you fear. Don't rule out anything: a flat tire in the middle of a busy intersection; the news of a family member's terminal illness, burglary, baldness. *An invitation:* Pick one of these situations and write a brief story about it happening to someone you despise. Next, write about the same situation happening to someone you dearly love. Finally, write about the situation happening to you.

With a writing partner or by yourself, examine the stories. For each, begin by picking out the emotions each character feels. Do not be afraid to use huge, vague labels that normally are taboo in writing classes. Go ahead—tell and don't show, at least for now. After you have written down large, basic feelings such as outrage, sadness, and shock, look for the ways in which you and your writing partner translated these reactions to specific details, acts, and words. Here are some questions to keep in mind:

1. Which of the three scenarios is the most compelling? Why?
2. In coping (or failing to cope), does the character surprise herself and others? Why or why not?
3. Which character most successfully shows the reader his past as well as his (fractured) present? How?
4. Which story shows the most about a character even *outside* of the incident? How?

One goal in this exercise (and all writing about fears) is to shift the focus of the story away from the devastating event and to the heart of the character. If you are having trouble summoning up authentic reactions for your characters, try to think of a specific situation in which you already have felt one of these emotions. Do not worry if the situation had little to do with the one you are currently exploring. Pretend you are a method actor. As the British actor Simon Callow recently said in an interview, "The job of an actor is to think the thoughts of another human being." Through summoning up an emotion from another vivid experience, transfer it to the situation you are exploring in your fiction. The episode from your past may have nothing to do with the one you are writing about, but mine that emotion. Think about Eudora Welty's comment about the universality of emotions.

Even writing about frightening circumstances takes courage. Many times, students teach me about the importance of risk taking. As part of this process, they also show me what it means to create and care for a true villain. In exploring and making our villains more whole, we come closer to a frightening but evocative cauldron of possibilities that might exist in all of us.

Last summer, I learned about the essence of writing about villains at a summer writing workshop. I was teaching a class for incoming college students, and we were talking about finding ideas or prompts for stories in actual news events, a la *Law and Order*'s "ripped from the headlines" technique. We looked at prompts or triggers ranging from the quirky (police reports about amateur burglars—one even broke into a house to go to the bathroom) to the more serious (a mother who had killed herself and her three children by driving into a highway divider). In all, we looked first for characters' motivations. In what moment did this character make the decision to act? Did it have its origin over a long period of time, or was it instantaneous?

Sometimes this asking of why? can devolve quickly into a B-movie scene in which adults read over a teenager's suicide note and look helplessly skyward. In this class, however, we examined the newspaper articles and first imagined the emotions in the character's minds, then translated them into actions and backstories. A *backstory,* a term often used in filmwriting, is a secondary tale or situation that has happened outside of the primary plot but which has bearing on it. The reader (or viewer) may learn about this secondary story in hints or flashbacks. Sometimes backstories are cut completely from a story or film, but the process of creating them is valuable for the creator. In a well-written story, even though the reader does not see a deleted section, he or she will sense its presence. Ernest Hemingway had a famous philosophy about what a writer leaves out: "If a writer of prose knows enough about what he is writing about he may omit things that he knows and the reader, if the writer is writing truly enough, will have a feeling of those things as strongly as though the writer had stated them" (Phillips 1999, 77).

When we work on stories inspired by actual events, students sometimes argue that it is impossible to tell what is in a character's mind, especially when a villain is based on an actual person. As an example, we turn to Eudora Welty's 1963 story "Where Is This Story Coming From?" The brief story was written on the night Medgar Evers, the civil rights leader, was assassinated in Welty's hometown of Jackson, Mississippi. Welty wrote the story quickly and sent it to the *New Yorker,* where it was accepted immediately for the next issue. When her editor, William Maxwell, called to edit the piece with Welty, the authorities already held a suspect in the case. Though Welty had had no personal knowledge of the suspect, the facts of her story's "outward details" too closely resembled those of the suspect being held, so Welty had to make some changes.

Was she psychic? ask students, like those in my summer class. To answer this question, we went to Welty's own words about the matter, in the preface to her *Collected Stories* (1984). On the night of the assassination, Welty said that she thought, "Whoever the murderer is, I know him: not his identity, but his coming about, in this time and place. That is, I ought to have learned by now, from here, what such a man, intent on such a deed, had going on in his mind. I wrote his story—my fiction—in the first person: about that character's point of view, I felt, through my shock and revolt, I could make no mistake."

Even more incredible than Welty's intuition, though, was her skill in presenting the assassin as a plausible, round character. A *round* character is believable because she has more than one side to her personality. When I asked the students in the summer class how Welty made her assassin round, how she put aside her own "shock and revolt" to create an engaging character, at first they pointed to details in the story. These included the sign at the local bank that showed the temperature in lights, "all night long even," the truck borrowed from a brother-in-law, the brief anecdote about how as a child, the narrator ran away from home and his parents placed a plea in the newspaper that read "SON: You are not being hunted for anything but to find you."

These humanizing details, the students pointed out, made it easier to keep following the story of a narrator capable of planning such an odious act. At one point the narrator even explains, "I done what I done for my own pure-D satisfaction."

I was impressed by the students' abilities to pinpoint specific details that helped to humanize the character, but I also wanted to move deeper and discuss the guiding emotions or source for the story. I found myself nearly moving into bad-teacher mode and explaining what I thought the students were missing. Fortunately, I was rescued by an incoming college freshman named Ramah David. Welty made her assassin compelling, he said, because she "showed the part of him that we all have: fear."

The summer class inspired me in many ways, but most of all it made me think of what I fear most, and that is the alienation of people who are different.

I took my own prompt from the news and formed a story around it. The process taught me more about writing about evil and wrongdoing; I learned that the witnesses to malice are as important as the perpetrators. Any story about fear and evil, I discovered, is incomplete until every character has engaged the sympathies of the reader (if only for a moment).

The news clip that inspired me concerned a suburb of Chicago, where the house of an African American family was vandalized with racist graffiti. Afterward, the homeowners refused to paint over the graffiti, even when the predominantly white community pleaded with them.

When I heard the story on the radio, I responded in two ways: first, with terror that somebody would commit such an intimidating (and clichéd) act, and second, with delight that the homeowners had the guts to make the community face the offensive graffiti. Such a homeowner, I thought, was resilient and ironic.

In drafting a story around this event, I purposefully stayed away from too many specific details about the actual homeowners. I wanted to use the situation without mimicking everything about the characters. For a narrator, I chose the point of view of an African American widow whose only child was soon to go away to college. I also made the mother and daughter former city dwellers who had moved to the suburbs in the past few years. (The deceased father had opposed moving to a mostly white suburb.) I recently had covered Lorraine Hansberry's play *A Raisin in the Sun* with my high school students, so I was already thinking about the theme of racially hostile neighborhoods.

To show the suburb, I found myself going back to my own suburban childhood and my deep ambivalence about my first home. The suburb had some wonderful qualities, such as the lovely, old elm trees that curved over many of the streets and the excellent schools, but it also had a stereotypical homogeneity. Most of my neighbors and peers also were white and middle-class. In few places did I see reflected the wide range of people I encountered in my reading. The difference between my everyday world and the one in my imagination was vast.

While writing my story, at first I relied too much on my own memories of suburbia; the first draft featured neighbors who were bland and largely unsympathetic. They were not overtly racist—it would have been too obvious—but they were obtuse when it came to the nuances of racism. Basically, they stood around and gawked like pale cardboard cutouts.

The neighbors, while probably not the perpetrators of the offensive graffiti, turned out to be increasingly important in the development of the story. As I worked through subsequent drafts, I realized that the neighbors were as critical as the narrator and the person who had written the graffiti, because the neighbors were crucial witnesses. They responded to the evil act, and the adults set examples for the children of the neighborhood.

In later drafts I created a specific neighbor, a (white) mother of triplets who was outraged by the graffiti and who wanted to paint over it immediately. She urged the narrator to think of all the children who would see the heinous message.

The neighbor was still suburban in some clichéd ways—she and her husband had had triplets as a result of fertility treatments—but she also surprised me as I developed her character. Some of the changes I made seemed small and involved a word or two. For example, in the first draft, at the beginning of the story, the narrator watched the neighbor and her husband walk past with their triplets in an "absurdly" long stroller. Reading over this line, I saw that this adverb carried too much judgment—the reader had hardly even met the neighbors and already the narrator was mocking them. I changed "absurdly" to "awkward" because I wanted a more objective or even sympathetic adjective. It is a small alteration, but this way, the reader and the narrator did not reach any early conclusions.

Other changes involved whole scenes. In one, when the neighbor was imploring the narrator to paint over the graffiti, she clicked a bracelet on the kitchen table. The narrator noticed with surprise that it was a medical alert bracelet. The moment is brief, but through it the narrator (and I) realized that even the neighbor, with her ardent but naive liberalism, was vulnerable. In that same scene, I also showed the neighbor interacting with the narrator's daughter in an unexpected way. Suddenly, all the women in the kitchen were connected by their fears. Nobody had a definitive answer about the proper way to proceed.

Writing this story taught me about the importance of making all of one's characters human. Starting out, I had assumed the narrator would be an obvious heroine and the neighbors predictable suburbanites. I also had expected to show more about the villains, the writers of the graffiti. As I worked on the story, though, I discovered that even the message spray painted on the garage door was less important than the interaction between the narrator and the neighbors. While the authors of the pernicious graffiti skulked off into the night, the narrator, her daughter, and the neighbors were left to gaze at the message in daylight. Their responses to the graffiti and the narrator's decision to guard over it were the kernel of the story.

Developing my own story and talking to students about the Welty story showed me something surprising about my fears. Initially I thought that the story was merely about the perpetrators of racism. Soon, though, I saw that my fear was more about the people who witness racism and do not respond or respond in an unproductive way. My characters showed me that the subtleties of witness can be difficult to decipher. I used to believe that people reacted to wrong in obvious, immediate ways. But after many drafts, I saw that my story was more about the social cues involved in reacting to violence.

Writing about fear is not only cathartic but instructive. As we examine evil and misfortune, we appeal to every character's sense of anger, injustice, and vulnerability. One of the most important things to remember in writing about fear is that you, the writer, should surprise yourself in the process. By writing about fear, you take a risk. This risk should be at least as great as the one the reader takes in trusting you as a guide.

Works Cited

Garcia Marquez, Gabriel. 1984. "Handsomest Drowned Man in the World." In *Collected Stories*, 230–236. By Gabriel Garcia Marquez. New York: Harper and Row.

Joyce, James. 1995. "Araby." In *The Story and Its Writer,* 692–696. Edited by Ann Charters. Boston: Bedford Books.

Mukherjee, Bharati. 1995. "The Management of Grief." In *The Story and Its Writer,* 975–986. Edited by Ann Charters. Boston: Bedford Books.

Phillips, Larry W. ed. 1999. *Ernest Hemingway on Writing.* New York: Touchstone/Simon and Schuster.

Rilke, Rainer Maria. 1934. *Letters to a Young Poet.* New York: W. W. Norton.

Welty, Eudora. 1980. "Where Is This Story Coming From?" In *The Collected Stories of Eudora Welty,* 603–607. New York: Harcourt.

———. 1983. *One Writer's Beginning.* New York: Warner Books.

———. 1984. *The Collected Stories of Eudora Welty.* New York: Harcourt Brace Jovanovich.

10

Necessary Confessions: Personal Stories, Personal Writing, and Writerly Communities

Joseph Eng

Introduction

First, let me tell you a story titled "Now I Get It":

In the fall of 1992, I took up my first full-time teaching job as an English instructor at a community college of four thousand in the suburb of St. Paul, Minnesota. Still shocked by the heavy teaching load and some less-than-motivated students at midquarter, I decided to tell my composition class a classic Chinese story on the relationship between knowledge and perspective. "Long, long time ago, there were two teenage monks engaging in a debate in front of a flag post. While speculating on the movement of the flag flying in the wind, one of them says, 'The flag is moving.' The other monk responds, 'No, the wind, not the flag, is actually moving.' They continue for a while until the Grand Master appears. Hearing what they have said, he quickly gives the monks knocks on their heads and says, 'Nothing is really moving except your busy minds!'" My class responded with a minute of silence and then slowly expressed their surprises about the philosophical overtone of the story. I chipped in a thought about the importance of developing perspectives in the world as we know it. Later, two interesting incidents followed that telling.

At a one-on-one conference after class, Katie, a fair-complexioned young woman in her usual sweatshirt and khaki jeans, seemed to sidetrack from talking about a draft copy of her paper. Instead, she expressed her concern about my telling the story.

"You know, Mr. Eng, some of us were not very comfortable hearing the story. . . ." She hesitated to continue.

"Why?" I asked.

She explained, without looking directly at me, "You know, people don't use the word *monk* because it is a bad word."

"Oh, really?" I was genuinely surprised.

"You know, the word *monks* means *stupid* people?" she added, "You can get into trouble just by saying that. . . ."

"Well, I never thought about it that way—I thought I meant the priests in the Buddhist context." I professed nothing but ignorance.

At another conference, Jennifer, in her typically dark makeup and L. A. Raiders attire, seemed confused about why I questioned some parts of her mapping exercise, in which she had gathered ideas for her essay topic, "interracial dating." In one of her circles of ideas, she had "dealing with kids" and "planning on having more kids" as two relevant issues. Reading it again, I was not sure if both ideas really belonged in the paper; I asked her instead, "Are you expanding on the topic now, Jennifer? Is it interracial *dating* or interracial *marriages*?"

"No," she sounded quite certain about it, "I don't want to talk about marriages."

"But," I continued, "people who date don't plan on having kids unless they *are* getting married, right?"

"No, some people do."

I paused, thought about it for a full minute, and then said "Got you!" as soon as I could utter the phrase. For her, not me, it did belong to the essay.

Of the many events that happened in my first year of teaching in a community college, these three incidents seem to stand out in my memory, and I can't tell if they were really separate cases or all in the same boat. In retrospect, I remain amazed at how worlds are different and how apparently it is so, especially between the teacher and the student. In fact, one might begin to probe the difference in terms of socioeconomic status, race and ethnicity, and the making of knowledge. Effective communication truly demands an open mind.

* * *

I tell this story of three tales, or one tale after the other, to my composition students whenever I get a chance. When told early in the term, these narratives not only introduce me alternatively but also set a storytelling tone for the course.

Like the student characters in the story, my first-time listeners tend to be silent immediately after the telling. In a talkative class, I get to respond to my own story by following a discussion they will have begun; in a reserved group, I'll have to lead a discussion. Most students like to respond to the monk story, the Katie story, and the Jennifer story individually, while I am more interested in their reactions regarding any perceivable relationships among the mini–tales or regarding the larger story as a whole. The session always continues with my soliciting more stories from my students of turning points or simply thought-provoking experiences. They also get a chance to write their responses down *informally* either before or after the telling.

* * *

Telling "Now I Get It" has a twofold purpose: it presents a metaphor for communication, teaching, and learning and it encourages the class to *reconsider* the conventional, teacher-centered classroom. More interestingly, the story set solicits a further discussion on the intricate relationship, among social classes, teacher and student, writer and reader. The telling part draws immediate attention by countering any preconceived notions about how a writing class should be conducted. To me, then, storytelling offers an engaging scenario that is essential to every good class.

Based on this early engagement, perhaps we, as teachers or students, consider how a class could function, literally, as a close-knit group of people who have more common goals than different ones. The class is actually *a writerly community.* That is, as college writers, we begin our community experience as *storytellers* who work together. Gradually, we will tell or write not only stories but also essays, which benefit from peer or communal review—community support. So we confess. We enjoy stories, especially personal ones. We crave details. And then we turn the oral stories into written ones. Eventually, we write papers with stories in them. We anticipate constructive feedback and will not be intimidated by it, because we listen, write, and revise together. As a writerly community bound by stories, we also speculate on how storytelling becomes relevant across the university curriculum and beyond. Hoping you will do the same in your classroom, I would like to share a few more stories with you, together with a few specific assignments as entry points into traditional academia.

Community Bonding:
Telling, Listening, and Writing Informally

Many teachers believe that developing drafts—usually of formal expository essays—helps all of us to rethink, rework, and reevaluate our writing. The class benefits from discussions about process and product, collaborative learning, assessment, and reflection. Nonetheless, a gap exists between most students and their instructors in terms of finding an effective process leading to final drafts. In order to bring people together for a common goal—that is, in order for all of us, teachers and students, to look forward to the next draft (or the next class as workshop)—we need to understand the dynamics of a writerly community and to establish such a community by *storying:* telling the stories, writing them down, and eventually writing them academically into the university.

I always remember how attentive people are when they first listen to "Now I Get It," even when they barely know me at the time of telling. I call it a turning-point kind of story. First, by looking for turning points, we access experiences that are personal but not necessarily painful or psychologically traumatic. Second, turning points suggest moments that are telling us something meaningful, indicators of epiphanies or insights, something worth attending to within a class period and following up more fully after class. Third, turning-point stories are reasonably public, available for sharing, such as what we might find in a like-titled section in *Reader's Digest,* the popular magazine. (I always begin with spoken stories, influenced by such oral traditions established by my home culture, Mark Twain, and Native American tribes.)

Let's sample a student story that followed "Now I Get It" in a different composition class during the same quarter.

Cheri, in her thirties, told us a story about the need for humor in raising special kids; this excerpt of her oral story would become a paper for an assignment, and eventually a manuscript for *Parenting* magazine:

"The Quality of Laughter" by Cheri Kowitz

Often as parents of children with disabilities we read article after article filled with technical jargon on new therapy regimes and programs designed to improve our children's quality of life. In reading I sometimes turn things around: How has Seth improved "my" quality of life as his parent? I need look no further than his sense of humor.

Seth, my eleven-year-old son, is autistic (high-functioning) and has Tourett's Syndrome. The blend of these two disorders excludes him from many communicative interactions in daily life. . . .

Despite his physical and emotional malfunctions, Seth has been a source of purposeful comic relief. . . . We were ready to go shopping with two other children (ages 2 and 4). . . . I had asked Seth repeatedly to go to the basement to get his boots. . . . He could see my anxiety level was rising and meekly offered "I just can't." "And why not?" I shot back in exasperation! "I have furnace-o-phobia." Having caught me off-guard I couldn't help but laugh heartily, with which he joined in. (The boots were stored close to the furnace.)

He carries this wit into the world with him. Recently I was summoned to school after a "hitting incident" on the bus one morning. . . . Seth stuttered pitifully and persevered on it being "her" fault a minute or two longer. Glancing at the Principal, his teacher, and me, noticing the "it-won't-work" look on our faces, he then said, "Sometimes I think an agent of Satan is disguised as my sister." Needless to say, we cracked up and Seth was quite happy with himself, having broken the tension. . . .

Everyday life with a child with a disability can be difficult at best. Choosing to look at their strengths and allowing them to improve the quality of "our" lives as care-givers, develops a positive, healthy attitude that can increase the reserves needed to sustain the hard times.

Cheri's story inspired a few more stories about parenting, especially those involving special children. The class was moved by her string of personal narratives. Among many observations, we noted that life continues to surprise us, no matter who we are and what we plan. As another surprise, too, Cheri's story related to mine in its interest in constructing different perspectives in a world otherwise occupied by chores, with mine in teaching writing and hers in raising a family of differently abled children.

The ancient Greeks developed an important trio of terms to describe effective rhetoric or persuasion: *logos* (reason), *ethos* (persona), and *pathos* (empathy). These are things that we could all consider in personal stories. Being Asian American, I tell stories in order to create my membership in the emerging writerly community.

"Now I Get It," for example, constructs an ethos, or persona, already familiar to most American listeners: my personality projection of an Asian person who knows and does something philosophical, all in the practice of orally telling a story about something in the historic past. Second, by telling my audience how I once worked with different kinds of student writers, I also indirectly tell them how I have taught and continue to teach. Third, by reflecting on the incidents, which is the bulk of the story itself, I appear to be patient, open, even democratic. And fourth, the persona of a teller seems to solicit more telling, hence leading to the potential for or actual sharing of class stories, especially early in the academic term.

Logos, or reasoning, is achieved through the actual events described in "Now I Get It." Despite the philosophical overtone, most students, when asked, see related dynamics among the events and draw provisional conclusions about what each could mean. Even though I try to discourage analyzing the story too much (at least until students tell some of their stories), I have noticed that many tend to deconstruct my story, thus giving attention to what is not told as much as to what is told. (Some, for instance, have asked if I made it up or if it came from Confucius.) The logos—the complex relationship between knowledge and perspective—exists in every class. Through the subtle messages or implicit morals, my students and I begin a needed relationship by getting to know one another as learning partners mutually seeking truth.

Pathos, finally, is the most important benefit I hope to achieve when I tell my story. The first weeks of the term are trying times, especially for composition. Most students hope to pry open the standard set forth by the instructor and expect to write only to meet that standard. Most instructors, by contrast, aim at engaging students, hoping to help them develop their voices without having them worry too much about specific criteria or standards as they begin to write. All of this guessing and negotiating, then, is further complicated by the simple but essential need for committing students to *writing a lot,* for practice's sake. Hearing "Now I Get It," according to my students, makes them feel invited into an open-minded classroom in which all members have voices.

Given any writing class, my storytelling is a surprise to begin with; and, following my story, their storytelling and sharing usually makes for another surprise. The class, having heard its stories about turning points, is now moving along, ready to make the transition to writing formally.

Community Writing: Writing Formally About Ourselves

In her 1987 story of no more than 250 words, author Patricia Grace (1992) highlights the crucial connection between knowledge and perspectives for her readers. "Butterflies" is a simple narrative in which a girl's first day at school becomes an eye-opening experience. In essence, she is challenged by her teacher regarding her drawing—which depicts herself killing butterflies—as something *wrong,* therefore *unacceptable* in the class. The concerned grandmother, after picking up the girl after school, asks:

> "What your teacher say?"
>
> "She said butterflies are beautiful creatures. They hatch out and fly in the sun. The butterflies visit all the pretty flowers, she said. They lay their eggs and then they die. You don't kill butterflies, that's what she said."
>
> The grandmother and the grandfather were quiet for a long time, and their granddaughter, holding the book, stood quite still in the warm garden.
>
> "Because you see," the grandfather said, "your teacher, she buy all her cabbage from the supermarket and that's why." (13)

This particular story usually solicits a rather lively discussion, first on the puzzle about the why, and second about how the grandfather may have to revise his original educational advice to the daughter, which was "Go to school. Listen to the teacher. Do what she say" (12). Students growing up in farming communities realize the importance of killing the butterflies (which hatch in cabbage leaves) as a good act; this realization is especially powerful on two levels. On one, the realization critiques an educational system based on passive learning, arguing that hands-on experiences importantly contribute to the knowledge-making process. On another, the realization points out that a teacher too could be a lifetime learner who needs to develop perspectives beyond the classroom. As a springboard for more writing, this story works best for discussion at the first-draft workshop for the Personal Experience Essay (see Hint Sheet C).

For another formal writing assignment, we may develop expositive/informative essays discussing the importance of language, language as a changing element, and the exploration of language based on our personal narratives as *experiences with language* (see Hint Sheet C). In the following excerpted sections, we will see how two students, a nonnative speaker and a native speaker of English, have adapted their stories in order to inform their papers critically, in a turning-point sort of way. In the spirit of storying, let's first listen to them:

"Linguistic Walls: The Difficulty of English for Japanese" by Makiko Yamamoto

It is no exaggeration that the biggest interest for Japanese people is English. To master English is like a ticket to success in the Japanese society; you are likely to enter a big name company or to expect promotion and raises in pay. . . .

I remember that when I was an elementary schoolchild, I boasted to my friends that I just saw a foreigner in my city. My hometown is a suburb of Tokyo, yet seeing foreigners was unusual at that time, so foreigners were like TV talents. . . . It is sure that Japanese people are not used to real English. For example, if my family receives English letters or telephone calls from Americans, they cannot react properly: they either ignore them or agitate too much. . . . In these two years, I have been trying to use English everywhere struggling with my shyness. I believe that shyness is one of Japanese specific characters, since Japanese society is based on collectivism. . . .

English involves many consonants, yet every Japanese sound has a vowel; as a result, it is difficult that Japanese people's ears catch consonant-only sounds. . . . Whenever I stay in my room, I try to listen to the radio, even while I am in bed. Besides that, I often watch movies and TV news with mumbling what they said. . . . Now, I am feeling that English speaking is like a song, and English conversation is like a duet. It has much rhythm, many accents, and major musical scales. . . .

While I am talking in English, I have little birds that talk to me all the time, "Is that right English?" "That grammar is too bad!" English is not our native language, so it is impossible to think in English, I think. . . . It is undeniable that English's high speed is one of the reasons why Japanese cannot catch up with English conversation. Japanese need to do too many things . . . in short time, so we are often confused and panicky in English. English is the bridge to the world . . . I am dreaming of mastering English.

"Man-speak" by Frank Campbell

"Man, I'd like to get some of that." This is, on the face of it, a perfectly innocuous statement. And if a person were talking about ice cream, or fill dirt, or the fresh fish he saw in the market, it would be. But this sentence was uttered to me by a buddy, a smart educated liberal and mature man, about a woman who was passing us on the street minding her own business; business which certainly did not include us. . . . This subtle language of discrimination and dominance towards women is so ingrained in our culture we indulge in it without giving thought to its true meaning. . . .

I first started to become aware of this language, and the concept of male sexual license it supports, when I was in third grade. I would hear older boys that I looked up to talk about girls; girls who would "do it," girls with "big ones," girls they "did." I would listen to the stories (lies of course) about their many sexual escapades and I could hardly wait for the time to come, when I too, would boast of my conquests. . . . The consequences of this were disastrous. . . .

I heard the term "bitch slap" on a TV sitcom recently, "You do that again and I'm gonna 'bitch slap' you into next week," there is canned laughter, it's all good, and the asinine show rolls on. But, what does this say to us? It says, "It's OK to slap a bitch." And in today's America, even women sometimes refer to each other as bitches. What does this language say to young people, male or female? What does this language say about us as a culture? . . . Man-speak tells them what a good woman is; passive, obedient, faithful. . . . Of course after a period of time, the fact that this other person is someone with a mind of her own may very well become apparent. Maybe she will want to go to school or get a new job; any change he might feel threatened by. . . .

Of course young girls and women are not unaware of this language, and it works its way into their psyches as well. "Man-speak" not only allows men to perceive women as property; it also encourages women to accept that role. . . . It is said, "If one among you is not free, then none among you are free." If that is true, we are all slaves of man-speak.

Based on these two student papers, we can see how narratives of events, as personal turning-point experiences, might inform the many expository papers we write as formal class assignments. Makiko and Frank have meaningfully adapted their personal experiences into their expository papers, which could be further informed by secondary sources and developed into research papers. These students do two important things: they summarize the gist of the personal stories and further reflect on them in order to support specific propositions in their papers. In addition, they have benefited from their storytelling early in the quarter and the many workshops in which we worked collaboratively. Much of the feedback we made at workshops was a direct response to readers asking for details of personal experiences. Technically, the papers have moved from the personal to the public and have indeed become more elaborate and interesting as a result.

Storying Beyond Composition

Communities Within the University Community:
Writing in the Academic Disciplines

As composition students, we seldom imagine how writing might function outside the general education sequence. As college writers, however, we may consider how and why writing is required beyond composition and what type of writing is required in a specific academic field. We can learn much from the process of real-world publication.

For example, imagine how different academic majors have to communicate differently and how their papers may need to address readerships within their fields. Writing in our academic majors requires insiders' talk, writing tailored for different academic or professional fields, or manuscripts shaped for different publications.

Based on an assignment titled Feature Article (see Hint Sheet C), my students learn to develop their thought-provoking stories into writings relevant to their areas of expertise or majors, which, in turn, become manuscripts tailored for potential publication. The two excerpted pieces that follow, written by Laura Doerr and Jodi Gurnoe, were published within a year after they completed their composition courses. Consider how their individual stories are showcased for their intended forums or publications.

"A Song of Happiness" by Laura Doerr
(published in *Around the River Region:*
A Newsletter About the Members of River Region Health Services)

When my grandfather died, no one knew that grandma was dying also. At first we rationalized her confusion and despondence as extended grief. Married for 58 years, grandma was lost without grandpa. She was elderly and grandpa's sudden death had been a shock. It was understandable that it would require time and patience for grandma to return to a "normal" life.

My mom and I visited grandma daily. Initially our visits were social. We talked, shared rolls and coffee and extended love and companionship. Within a few weeks, it was evident that grandma was not doing as well as she claimed. Thyroid medication was not being taken, meals were not eaten, and bills were not paid. . . .

Alzheimer's Disease is the leading cause of severe mental impairment in older people. It is an organic brain disease that destroys the brain cells. . . .

The decision for nursing home placement was made with many years. We had fought hard to keep grandma at home and to admit we could no longer continue to do so left us feeling like failures. Had we betrayed grandma?

Our visits to grandma are once again enjoyable. She lives in the Alzheimer's Unit at the Seminary Home. Knowing that she is well cared for and safe brings us peace of mind. She has gained weight, wanders about with her new friends and enjoys the scheduled activities. The proof of contentment is her smile and song. My mom and I did not betray grandma. We recognized our own limitations. We found the courage to seek help and admit we could no longer manage grandma's life. Grandma was changing and we had to let go.

With Alzheimer's there is no return to a "normal" life. Learning to accept the progression of the disease continues to be a lesson for us. Grandma is who she is now. Unable to call me by name, she smiles and her eyes twinkle at the sight of me. She maintains her sense of humor, although there are times I have no idea what we are laughing about. We hold hands and together sing all the songs she can remember. These treasured visits are highlights of my life.

I love you Grandma!

Laura's story was particularly memorable to me for interesting reasons. I remember telling her how I thought that we had done a similar paper for the Turning-Point assignment, and how, for the Feature Article, she might tell less of a story and invest more in the expository form. She submitted a draft that both surprised and pleased me. My response to her draft had affected her much, she said, where I described my experience of having a mother dying of cervical cancer my first semester away from home (another one of my personal stories); as a result, she wanted to write about caring for her grandmother and could foresee a readership in *Around the River Region*. When I was handed the published article the quarter *after* the class. I was simply elated to see it in print.

In another class, "The Fine Blue Line" by Jodi Gurnoe presented a different subject matter (published in *Show-Up: Official Publication of the Police Officers Federation of Minneapolis*).

Imagine a world without police. "Great!" You say while smiling. "No more speeding tickets!" Not just that, but no one to call for help. No one to mediate the problems we humans usually find ourselves embroiled in. No one to protect us from those who will break into our homes, steal our cars, rape our women, beat up our men, and sell our children crack. Do we, as a society, realize how much we really need police?

No. Most people distrust police. Some truly hate them. Few really like them, or at least appreciate them. Why? Because they have always been there. They are easy to take for granted. . . . Now what is a day in the life of a cop like? I had the privilege of spending a day with Officer Wells of the Minneapolis Police force. As a silent observer, I saw some of the most startling aspects of human nature. . . .

This morning, the first call was an "unwant." Officer Wells uses his radio to talk to the dispatcher regarding this call. . . . The woman explained that she was through partying and she wanted to go to bed but the men wouldn't get out. We looked at the men and Wells asked if they would now be willing to leave, or if they had to be physically removed. They didn't answer. Glazed eyes stared back at us, while spittle dripped from their mouths. Silver iridescent paint was stuck to their faces. He asked again. Finally one of them answered. "Yeah," he said but failed to move. I turned to look at another cop who had come to assist. . . .

The following call was to go to a shelter to take a report about abuse that one of their residents had suffered at the hands of her boyfriend. The woman had a puffy eye, lip, and nose. . . . The woman said she would identify him if she saw him but she was obvious about not wanting to press charges. . . . Wells explained to me later that most women don't want to press charges; they just want to be left alone; or in some cases, to return to the abusive man. Usually, however, the victim wants to talk to someone; they want to know that someone cares. Officer Wells was sensitive and showed her some much needed compassion. We left to go look for the goon anyway so that he could spend a much needed night in jail. . . .

Later on that day he handled assaults, burglaries, shopliftings, and personal injury calls. . . . I watched him struggle with a man armed with a knife, and I saw him comfort a child that had gotten separated from his mother. . . .

I wondered what the world would be like if we did not have police, someone to call when we need help. Pure chaos. Cops are the fine blue line between anarchy and a semblance of order. . . . Yet people take them for granted. But who do they call for help? Cops. Cops who would lay down their life for them if necessary.

Like "A Song of Happiness," "A Fine Blue Line" was published unchanged from its final draft. I had, for instance, discussed with Jodi the word choices (such as *goon*) and the purpose of the expository piece, but we both agreed that the language was appropriate and in fact the final draft was "audience-based."

For the Feature Article assignments, Laura and Jodi began with their personal experiences with something they knew about firsthand, or as experts within their professional contexts. In class we talked about our experiences and explored the connections between experience and our academic majors or intended majors. (Laura was a major in nursing and Jodi in law enforcement.) As both student writers came up with their first drafts, we talked about audience as target readership and how different majors or professions communicate differently. We adopted an Audience Analysis Worksheet (see Hint Sheet C) that really helped class members further revise their papers for certain publications as writers, directly and indirectly, showed us what and how academic or professional fields communicated in terms of topical issues, language convention, and types of experience or knowledge. We finalized the process by getting feedback from student review boards, which were composed of class members role-playing different editors representing the selected publications we brought to class.

Certainly the writing experience itself asks all writers to consider the worlds outside the class and beyond composition. I, too, as their instructor, have learned much about my students' interests in relation to their majors and acknowledged the genuine need to assess their writing more contextually and flexibly with a real-world interest. (See how I got it now?)

Writing for Publication: Academics Begin with Stories

Several of my publications begin with actual classroom stories, which are teaching scenarios leading to the research interests in my articles. Here is one story I can hardly forget that concerns student resistance.

Scene: In a suburban community college, Kate remains silent throughout the evening while the class discusses Langston Hughes' poetry, including his "Nightmare Boogie" and "I, Too." Instead of submitting a regular class journal explicating the poems, she submits her own poem:

Can You Tell Me How We'll Ever Be Free?

Dear Mr. Hughes, O brilliant Man—
I am struggling to understand,
Why on me, you lay this weight;
Why in words you seal my fate—
While you sing that hate breeds hate?

I was born color blind—
But your words burn in my mind,
telling me about my kind.
Do you think we all look alike,
All of us, nightmarish white?

I, too am American, and proud to be,
But can you tell me how we'll ever be free—
If all I see of you and all you see of me,
Is what is left for dead?

I, too—am ashamed
I, too—cry at night
I, too—have had struggles,
Although I am white.

The Universe knows of the change to come—
A band of Strong Darkness will circle the sun,
Will all injustice then be undone—
Or will it just turn to two wrongs from one?

And what if that is all?

I struggled to know you,
To feel your acceptance too—
But when all is through and through—
I'll only know me and—
You'll only know you—

What a loss it will be to the world.

After the poem, she writes: "'Nightmare Boogie' defeats its own purpose. Today's America has made great strides in racial equality. . . . How can we ever achieve this if we both view each other as evils to our society? How can we become a one race society (human race) if everything is color coded?"

Surprised by her sounding off in this note, I had the hunch I needed to reflect on the situation. So I only responded briefly and encouraged Kate to incorporate this view into a critique paper for the semester.

On the surface, Kate simply deviated from the class agenda, became a nonparticipant; yet, by writing her poem as a response to Hughes', she seemed to resist the assignment or retreat to herself rather meaningfully. Reflecting further on her writing and her writing occasion, I wrote an essay titled "Engaging Students in the Literature Classroom: Reflections of a Compositionist," focusing on the connection between imaginative literature and students' lives, between teaching literature and teaching writing, and between reading and writing. Quite technically, sharing student stories helps connect me back to composition research, which is further informed by my teaching and learning experiences. I've learned much about teaching and about writing this way.

Storying for Learning's Sake

In the summer of 1996, my wife and I moved from St. Paul, Minnesota, to Portsmouth, Ohio, so that I could start a new job in a four-year college. That same year I shared with my students a local experience as a part of my draft for the Turning-Point assignment I wrote *with* them. The following narrative recaptures the climax of an otherwise typical house-hunting trip:

> A lady answered the door, quickly recognizing me as we had talked on the phone; she was in her late forties or early fifties, dressed as if she had just returned home from work or gotten ready to leave. Like many in town we had just met, she seemed rather courteous or even apologetic in every way, explaining the physical status of the property and why it was better than it looked. But, all for sixty-two thousand dollars we thought—what a deal.
>
> "A quiet neighborhood," she reassured us, "my aunt really has no idea that she is sitting on a gold mine." She began, "She's been here for thirty years and if she were not moving to the nursing home she'd be quite happy here."
>
> We inquired about her own background; she replied, "I've just moved back here after twelve years in Texas; I am a nurse. . . . Yes, everybody is nice here. Mrs. Smith took good care of her house . . . ," pointing her finger to the neighbor on the left. "And Mr. and Mrs. Warnock used to work for the city government, and that is the house to the right. . . . People are rather decent here, you know what I mean?"
>
> I nodded without thinking about it much. As she looked across the street, she continued, "You see that house with a brown door? That is a black family over there. We don't interact with them much. But they seem nice too. You know how you don't see them as black people sometimes? Well, you know what I mean."
>
> "Well," I tried to continue, "I don't know what you mean. . . . I mean, isn't that true in every race? Do you see us as Asian?"

The conversation sort of ended there. . . . We did not buy the house. The year was 1996 and the town seemed peaceful. Apparently there were stories perhaps not as noticeable as the town's old structures. . . . Education should be the single most important thing in the world.

Because this story is usually told in the context of a first-paper workshop, most students tend to comment on the technique of storytelling (such as the use of dialogue, subtle characterization, and other narrative technicalities). A few students gradually expand on the racial theme (which is as subtle as the discrimination practiced in our twenty-first century).

Stories like this one always live with me, because they seem to teach me about people and places. Reflectively, they give me ideas about who I am and how I grow as a human being. The house-hunting story seems to grow in effect as well; since I used it again this past September in an inservice seminar, many new writing teachers working with me have been writing and trading personal stories of their own.

In this chapter, we have heard several personal stories, examined their contexts, and explored many possible applications in the university contexts and beyond. We have also become familiar, I hope, with the idea of a writerly community in which we bond ourselves by telling, listening, and writing down stories. These stories have helped me grow as an academic writer, a teacher, and a language user at the same time. Perhaps more importantly, I have come to know the author-tellers behind these stories, my students, their peers, and some of their lives after class. Storying, after all, is learning about ourselves and others.

* * *

Note: The author would like to thank Iris Gribble-Neal for sharing her version of the assignment on language experience.

Works Cited

Doerr, Laura. 1994. "A Song of Happiness." *Around the River Region: A Newsletter About the Members of River Region Health Services* 3 (1): 5.

Grace, Patricia. 1992. "Butterflies." In *Responding to Literature*, 12–13. Edited by Judith A. Stanford. Mountain View, CA: Mayfield.

Gurnoe, Jodi. 1994. "The Fine Blue Line." *Show-Up: Official Publication of the Police Officers Federation of Minneapolis.* 9 (12): 7–8.

11

Ancient Tradition and Contemporary Storytelling

Gayle W. Duskin

They came from their homeland to the New World. Bound in shackles and loaded onto ships by slave traders, the Africans huddled together, bemoaning their state and their forced departure from all they knew that was safe and secure—their villages, their tribes, their families, their sense of community. Nevertheless, even in the horrid condition in which they found themselves, stripped of their dignity and selfhood, there was a solemn and unshakable commitment to use whatever means necessary to retain their traditions, customs, and values.

In Africa, orality, in the form of the spoken word, music, and dance, was at the center of a communal and profoundly religious way of life. To the African people religion was not something apart from life; it was life itself and they reflected this belief in the creation of various forms of lore, which became embedded in their folk culture. These elements of their culture—the proverbs, folk cries, hollers, shouts, work songs, spirituals, and folktales—were retained by the slaves and served as temporary respite from the master class. After a day of work spent laboring on cotton, rice, and tobacco plantations, the slaves gathered in their quarters, where they would, in these clandestine, secret, and forbidden enclaves, exchange stories about African life, create new lore about their American experiences, and express these reflections in dance, song, and tale.

Unlettered and forbidden by their masters to learn how to read and write, most slaves depended on their knowledge of African oral tradition to create narratives that embodied reflections upon their state in particular and the human condition in general. One striking example of their narrative technique can be found in African American spirituals, which reflect the African heroic epic in form, content, and style. The African oral epic consists of long narrative recitations and songs interwoven with praise poems, chants, sermons, hymns, prayers, and improvisations. Likewise, the African American spirituals

111

are epic narratives, praise poems, sermons and prayers, lyrical songs and poetry, and frequent improvisations, including African antiphony, or overlapping call and response.

Consequently, these original and beautiful expressions of human life have emerged to become one of the most expressive achievements of African American literature and culture. An amalgam of African and biblical tradition, these spirituals are folk poetry; they are in the oral epic tradition, the cultural and historical record of African American people in their struggles for survival, freedom, and equality.

Initially shaped for group singing and performance, the songs reflect the slaves' daily experiences—their sorrows, troubles, weariness, dreams, and aspirations for release from bondage—and their strong, but coded, antislavery messages. They are what W. E. B. DuBois calls "sorrow songs," such as the deeply moving pieces "I Been 'Buked and I Been Scorned," "Nobody Knows de Trouble I Seen," and "Motherless Child." Yet, as can be seen in the words of the first two songs, feelings of despair are counteracted by a sense of hope and affirmation. These sorrow songs are powerful calls for deliverance from collective, communal oppression and exile and for redemption from individual hardship.

Continuing the lyrical forms transmitted by the African griot, these anonymous folk spoke of the experiences of capture, forced transportation, and enslavement with its wrenching away from homeland, family, friends, and the past. They wove thematic threads into a recurring motif of being lost, homeless, and motherless—of a search for liberation, community, and identity. It is a worldview of African Americans that has survived through the creation of a tradition that lives on and transforms itself in a variety of ways.

In this chapter I will briefly address how these threads from the African past have been transmitted into a modern art form, rap music, and discuss how African American rap artists have written the lyrics that tell their stories grounded in a cultural tradition. In using rap artists and their narrative lyrics as the tool to drive this essay, I wish to demonstrate how, in a larger scope, the storytelling traditions of the past underpin the new forms and structures of the stories told today.

Tradition and the Search for Liberation Theme

For years African Americans have wrestled with the debate regarding the purpose of art and have aimed questions to the norm of the day regarding art. Is art created for art's sake or for people's sake? Their response has come in a variety of forms where, as Johanna Grimes has stated, "they have defined and/or expanded conventional form, technique, and content; and have generally struggled for freedom, dignity, and self-definition through art" (1998, 15). They have, in sum, followed an unwritten definition of creativity and through their own inventiveness reconformed the traditional definition of art and simultaneously declared empowerment and liberation.

The framing question here, then, is how does the writing of African American storytellers conform to the traditional definition of art and simultaneously declare liberation? In large part, many such writers have relied on unrecorded definitions of creativity and have achieved success in their aims to illustrate that issues relative to defining art are recurring and are reflective of an attempt to challenge what African American art is and should be. On the other hand, there are others who perceive these writers to be the manufacturers of a tradition within an already established tradition. For example, Henry Louis Gates has observed, perhaps rather shortsightedly, "Literary works configure into a tradition not because of some mystical collective unconscious determined by the biology of race or gender, but because writers read other writers and *ground* their representations of experience in models of language provided largely by other writers to whom they feel akin. It is through this mode of literary revision, amply evident in the texts themselves—in formal echoes, recast metaphors, even in parody—that a 'tradition' emerges and identifies itself" (1988, 71).

While Gates' point about literary forms is well taken, we are reminded that not all texts in the literary tradition of African Americans were written down. Often, as Joanne Braxton states, "It was the memories of the ancestors handed down through their descendants that kept the community together. The mother tongue is not just words or even the array of cultural symbols available to a people to resist its tormentors. The mother tongue *is* the oral tradition" (1989). Indeed, this "unwritten literature" and the juxtaposition of literary and oral forms create a linguistic vitality that informs written literature on many levels.

The quest for liberation has taken a variety of forms involving exploration and discovery of the evolving shape of artistic creativity, but it continues to be embedded in the call and response tradition. The call, founded in African oral tradition, comprised the proverbs, work songs, shouts, spirituals, and folktales, features representing a centrality of oral expression in African society that has encouraged the continued vitality of such forms among the African American slaves and beyond. And, still using the verbal artistry of the ancient African griots, African American artists have retained these cultural traditions and responded in myriad ways in the creation of an evolving artistry (particularly in music) in the forms of blues, jazz, rhythm and blues, and on to modern-day rap.

Blues, the most significant of these new forms, originated at the beginning of the twentieth century. This music borrowed harmonic and structural devices and vocal techniques from earlier work songs and spirituals, but, unlike these other forms, this music was usually sung not by a chorus but by a single voice accompanied by one or more instruments. Like the earlier forms, however, blues involved a compellingly rhythmical sound that relied on patterns of call and response between singer and audience, and at times between singer and instrument, too. And retaining the touchstones of old African American slave narratives, which told of despair and misery, the blues emerged as a stylized complaint of earthly trials and troubles, yet a complaint countered by the liberating promise of a future good time and perhaps a loving companion.

Worth noting here is how this powerful form has inspired writers and artists throughout the twentieth century. Albert Murray elaborated on this notion by stating, "We all learn from Mann, Joyce, Hemingway, Eliot, and the rest, but I'm also trying to write in terms of the tradition I grew up in, the Negro tradition of blues, stomps, hollers, and swing. After all, very few writers have done so much with the American experience as Jellyroll Morton, Count Basie, and Duke Ellington" (1974, 33). Ralph Ellison also penned the following compelling definition of this form:

> The blues is an impulse to keep the painful detail and episodes of a brutal existence alive in one's aching consciousness, to finger its jazzed grain, and to transcend it, not by the consolation of philosophy but by squeezing from it a near-tragic, near-comic lyricism. As a form, the blues is an autobiographical chronicle of personal catastrophe expressed lyrically. (1948, 1964)

Jazz, on the other hand, emerged sometime during the first decades of the twentieth century out of an artistic meeting of elements including ragtime, spirituals, works songs, and especially the blues. Its haven was New Orleans, where, in spite of racial segregation, musicians could tap into the city's broad range of musical influences, which were extraordinarily plentiful.

It was from the beginning primarily an instrumental music that was strongly influenced by the sound of the African American voice. Scored as band music, it is an African American voice with all of black talk's flair for storytelling as well as signifying, understatement as well as braggadocio, whispering love calls as well as loud talk menacing—the exalted eloquence of a Martin Luther King Jr. to the no-holds-barred oration of a Malcolm X. All that "talkin' and testifyin'" and "speaking and speechifying" boldly make their way into this music, giving it great force and flavor.

Yet, even with the blue, tragic sense of life that underlies the music, there is within an overwhelming impulse to celebrate the human experience, for jazz is, in a larger sense, a music of rejuvenation—and liberation. This is so because like blues-idiom music, jazz proclaims the human will to persevere in spite of troubles. Jazz, in other words, suggests empowerment, the desire to take the frailties of life, shake them off, and rise once again.

Then, somewhere during the decade of the 1950s, rhythm and blues came forth as another musical art form. Although, as a descriptive term, R & B has never had one clear single meaning, it has basically come to be seen as an African American musical art revved up with jazz rhythm and vocals reflecting the blues. With its impulse to feature rhythmical musical sections backed up by solo blues progressions, R & B displayed retentions of traditional call and response patterns.

In the beginning R & B was somewhat ambiguous because it seemed to change and become whatever musical style it was attached to, but it became, in the 1970s, a recognizable force with the appearance of Marvin Gaye. It was Gaye, one of the most influential and popular rhythm and blues singers of his time, who introduced the notion of recording rhythm and blues "concept" albums. One of his most important albums, for example, *What's Going On* (1971), deals with such serious themes as civil rights and the Vietnam War and laid the foundation for other performers to infuse tales of social protest in their music.

Finally, born in the mid-1970s in New York City, rap emerged as the latest in a reconfiguration of the African American musical art form. It has been defined as a form of music that is generally spoken or chanted at a fast pace and performed over musical accompaniment that emphasizes rhythm rather than melody. It draws from storytelling traditions as competitive trickster toasts and badman boasts such as those of Staggerlee and Shine; the scat singing of jazz musicians like Ella Fitzgerald and Cab Calloway; the patter of radio disc jockeys; and the poetry of such artists as Nikki Giovanni and Amiri Baraka. Most notable are the African retentions in the music where the spoken or chanted words simulate the ancient, spirit-driven drums and chants that prevailed on the continent.

The first rap hit, *Rapper's Delight* (1979), was recorded by the Sugar Hill Gang, and, like all the other later artists who performed the music, it remained true to its parents, rhythm and blues and jazz, as an in-group ritual, a performance music, and a dance music. However, it also diverges into a more radical mode with its raucous tone and bawdy language that speaks of sexual and imagined conquests, along with fantasies of power, mobility, and money. Yet, the retention of the trickster figure, a feature in African and African American folktales, is evident in pieces of rap music, where artists like NWA. (Niggahs Wid Attitude) use lyrics that broadcast the will to meet a violent world with alluring fast talk, and, if necessary, with hard fists.

Nevertheless, despite rap's controversy, rappers seem to tap into the African American prophetic tradition in its urging to audiences, using virtuoso-rhyming language, of the need to not only address the serious matters of disempowerment and spiritual drift but also to celebrate the empowering and liberating effect of fundamental change.

In sum, these constantly evolving patterns of musical art suggest there is no *one* definition of African American creativity and inventiveness, or the African American artist, and, operating out of this conviction, African American rappers have declared their independence by reconforming the format of their stories while at the same time defining themselves within the community.

Modern-Day Voices of Creativity

Two young men I recently met, Dwayne and Carl,[1] are clear examples of this inventiveness and independence. Both of these young men were students in one of the sophomore-level literature classes that I taught. Dwayne, aka Lil Redd, a business major, writes the lyrics and performs with a local rap group, Ushake. Carl, aka Brass, a mass communications major, also writes lyrics but is a solo performer. Their writings show evidence of their response to a challenge: to write both within and beyond a tradition. Their response is to use all the tools necessary to frame the human condition. It is this departure from the norm that reforms the rapper artist as liberator who is himself liberated. Moreover, the rappers' acts of inventiveness and creativity and the liberating results resonate for other writers who seek to also create new forms that are individual, personal, and empowering.

Tradition and the Theme of Community

Even in the African homeland, a sense of community was integral to the structure of a culture. It was a sense embedded in the ideals and promises inherent in tribes to view themselves as part of a greater whole. As the slaves huddled together on ships during the Middle Passage and then departed to be dispersed to various parts of this country, they took with them a communal spirit that continued to weave its way through the spoken and written literature. Posed in the form of various idioms, the African tradition of embracing a sense of community can be seen in the writings of many African American artists. It is particularly noteworthy how this theme has been formed and reformed down through the years.

For example, there is the *Narrative of the Life of Frederick Douglass: An American Slave Written by Himself* (Douglass 1967), in which the writer forms the narrative written in a political idiom where he shows how the American effort to break the spirit of the slave only worked to increase the slave's yearning for physical freedom and a return to the companionship of his people. On the other hand, in *Incidents in the Life of a Slave Girl*, Harriet Jacobs (1973) frames a feminist idiom in a text that illustrates the ways in which black women subvert societal conventions, how one can achieve black female empowerment despite the limitations of slavery and still retain one's place in the black community.

In this modern era the rap idiom has emerged to take its place beside the other idioms that were formed in the past. Carl's "Ghetto Visions" is an example. Here, the call for a return to a communal spirit is extended through the raucous voice of a rap songster.

---

1. Names changed throughout.

My Ghetto Visions I made moves with precision
I learned as a youngster to listen
My Ghetto Vision makes moves to keep liven'
Give back what I been given'
I learned as a youngster 2 listen

Here viewed through the lens of a vision formed and underpinned by the neighborhood into which he was born and grew, the rapper expounds upon the lessons he learned as a child—to listen and obey. Characteristic of the African oral tradition, which is to tell and perform tales that both instruct and entertain, the rapper speaks not only of the lessons he has learned but also for the necessity to practice this instruction in his interactions with his community.

In a social commentary the voice of rap here encompasses the despair and rawness of life, a condition expressed by the slaves in their tales, music, and dance. However, in spite of a worldview that is sometimes nihilistic, there is below the surface a power or hope, or both. This is rap's link to the tradition of the past (its sampling of messages, form, and formulas), and it too calls for a sense of community.

Tradition and the Theme of Identity

While questions of identity and the definition of self have been a preoccupation of the American psyche since the colonists strove to divest themselves of their British roots, it is also "undeniable that the question of identity has added dimensions and a particular edge when seen within the context of the African American experience—given the uniqueness of that experience on the American landscape" (Grimes 1998, 35). Multiple fictive works portray characters who embark on deliberate journeys toward self-discovery, awareness, and identity; the search is generally conducted within the context of several motifs that recur across genres.

One of the common recurring motifs associated with identity and the creation of self is the idea of masking. Masking as an African American tradition reaches back to the oral tales of Brer Rabbit and the John and Old Marster narratives but also resurfaces in poems such as Dunbar's "We Wear the Mask" (1968) and short stories such as Chestnutt's "The Wife of His Youth" (1992). In each case the theme of identity highlights an uncertainty of self, and one's place in society.

For contemporary artists the masking motif is an obvious choice, given that in many rap lyrics there is the penchant for promoting oneself in a personal and individual frame. The journey toward selfhood portrays the wearing of the mask as a denial of the past in the creation of a new self, as seen in the following lyrics:

I grew up in the hood, movin', makin'
Crack. Dogs everywhere, Bein' on attack . . .

Takes its toll, Can't produce
Blame it on the brain, cockiness, and game
Am transcending my domain

—(Dwayne, aka Lil Redd)

Here we see an aspect of identity and the mask motif like the figure of Uncle Julius in Chestnutt's "The Goophered Grapevine" (1992), where the wearing of the mask is representative of a denial of the past of slavery in the creation of a new self. The rapper speaks of a past filled with violence and degradation but also of a brainpower that leads him to assume another self, the inference being that he must assume the mask to disown this past in order to effect the creation of another identity to "transcend his domain."

The rapper's message thus is one that conveys an impulse to present a deliberate journey toward self-actualization and transcendence. This motif is one that has its basis in a storytelling tradition where the characters seem to be at the mercy of a hostile environment, one that is tinged with tension and violence over which they have no control and where the only recourse is to engage in flight as a means of achieving a whole new self. The theme of identity can thus be viewed through several prisms, each of which can be traced to both African and African American literary traditions, and new rap artists are an extension of this tradition.

A Final Note

The two students whom I have mentioned in this essay have suggested in personal conferences with me that their participation in my literature class has influenced their desire to write and perform their lyrics from several perspectives. Most importantly, there was the matter of issues that surfaced during class discussions, particularly those of identity faced by the characters of particular works, such as those in the works of Richard Wright, who are at the mercy of a hostile environment, one that is tinged with tension and violence over which they have no control. Many of Wright's characters, like Bigger Thomas in *Native Son*, engage in flight as a means of achieving a whole self. This perspective can be seen in Dwayne's lyrics.

Then there is the matter of finding one's own voice to articulate from a black male's perspective in a very personal way one's vision of empowerment and authority, to create, like Olauduh Equiano and Frederick Douglass, an individual and communal self. This perspective is featured in Carl's lyrics.

In sum, the collective voice of the African folk has enduringly hovered over the storytelling techniques of their descendants, and the subsequent narrative works of these artists prominently bear the threads of tradition. Just as contemporary artists continue the lyrical forms evident in the African narrative, the promise and reality remain there for writers from other cultures to also find ways to return to their past ancestry and utilize the traditions, customs, and values of their cultures, to produce stories that will live again in multiple ways that impart the sustaining values and complexity of the storytelling tradition.

Topics for Further Consideration

In connection with a course you are taking or on your own, you may want to think, talk, and/or write about the following topics, improvising upon them if need be:

1. What is the purpose, or purposes, of art, in your view? Link your answer to an art form with which you are familiar—anything from popular music to graphic design, sketching to dancing, painting to acting. To what extent do you believe you need art or a certain art form? Why? What do groups, communities, and nations get out of art? What is the purpose of an art form like the Hollywood blockbuster movie? And finally, what is the purpose of one form of storytelling with which you are familiar?

2. Consider a creative or intellectual *product* you often produce. It could be an essay, a cartoon, a poem, a song, a landscape design, a detailed automobile, a mural, an arrangement of photos and posters on a wall. Think and write about how you invented this product. How would you describe your process of invention, creation, production? To what extent do others understand your process? Why do you think you create and produce the way you do? Would you change anything about the way you work? Why or why not? What is the most satisfying part of such invention, creation, and production? In a journal entry, perhaps, tell the story of one particular invention.

3. Try to put your own journey of self-discovery into the form of a story. The story could take the form of several journal entries, an autobiographical essay, a story in which you refer to yourself in the third person, a fictionalized story (in which you change *some* of the facts), a short video documentary, a parable, a folktale or fairy tale ("Once upon a time, . . ."), a song, or a performance piece, such as a monologue enhanced by a few props.

4. Assuming you tell stories to family and friends, how would you describe your storytelling style? (Here *storytelling* can mean just telling someone something happened to you one day.) What are the most recognizable elements of this storytelling mode? In your view, from whom did you acquire your storytelling style? Do you tell stories like your father, mother, sister, brother, or another relative? To what degree do you think your storytelling ways spring from your ethnic background? To what extent do you think people your age in your community tell stories the same way? Among your family and friends, who is, in your view, a great storyteller and why?

Works Cited

Braxton, Joanne M. 1989. *Black Women Writing Autobiography: A Tradition Within a Tradition.* Philadelphia, PA: Temple University Press.

Carl aka Brass. 2001. "Ghetto Visions."

Chestnutt, Charles. 1992. "The Goophered Grapevine." In *Collected Stories of Charles W. Chestnutt,* 118–141. Edited by William L. Andrews. New York: Penguin.

———. 1992. "The Wife of His Youth." In *Collected Stories of Charles W. Chestnutt,* 1–17. Edited by William L. Andrews. New York: Penguin.

Douglass, Frederick. 1967. *The Narrative of the Life of Frederick Douglass: An American Slave Written by Himself.* Edited by Benjamin Quarles. Cambridge: Belknap Press.

Dunbar, Paul Laurence. 1968. "We Wear the Mask." *In Dark Symphony: Negro Literature in America,* 41. Edited by James A. Emanuel and Theodore L. Gross. New York: The Free Press.

Dwayne aka Lil Redd. 2001. "Intro to Life."

Ellison, Ralph. 1964. "Blues People." In *Shadow and Act,* 189–198. By Ralph Ellison. New York: Random House.

———. 1994. "Chapter 1" ["Battle Royal"]. In *Invisible Man: Commemorative Edition,*15–33. By Ralph Ellison. New York: Modern Library.

Gates, Henry Louis, Jr. 1998. *The Signifying Monkey: A Theory of Afro-American Literary Criticism.* New York: Oxford University Press.

Grimes, Johanna. 1998. *Instructor's Resource Manual: Call and Response.* Boston: Houghton-Mifflin.

Jacobs, Harriet. 1973. *Incidents in the Life of a Slave Girl.* By Linda Brent. Edited by L. Marie Child. New York: Harcourt, Brace, Jovanovich.

Murray, Albert. 1974, 1989. *Train Whistle Guitar.* Boston: Northeastern University Press.

Sharing Ideas

1. The essay by Robert Brooke, Rochelle Harris, and Jeannine Nyangira stresses the *responsibility* of the storyteller. Think of a story that you have told or might tell about an experience involving a friend or a family member. What responsibility do you owe the friend or the family member? In your opinion, is it all right to add details that "make for a better story"? Why or why not? Should you ask the friend or the family member for permission to tell the story? Why or why not? If the tables were turned and the story were being told about you, what responsibilities would you want the storyteller to fulfill? Write about one or more of these questions. An alternative: Write about a story you told that, during or after the telling,

made you feel guilty for some reason. What was the source of your self-doubt concerning having told this story? Explain. Another alternative: Write about an instance when you were tempted to tell a story about someone but decided not to do so. Why were you tempted to tell the story? Why did you choose not to do so? What do you think now about your decision? To what extent was the decision driven by a sense of responsibility?

2. According to Carolyn Alessio, writer Eudora Welty believes that almost all people are driven to tell stories by three chief emotions: love, pity, and fear. Make a list of stories—perhaps in three categories—that you might like to tell and that seem to be driven by one of these emotions. The stories might be directly from your own experience, or they may concern other people. Alessio also suggests that stories based on these emotions often contain clichés or are unsuccessful for other reasons. Consider a couple of stories on the list you made; think and write about what would be especially difficult about writing or telling these stories. What cliché traps might be waiting for you? What other problems might arise?

3. Think of some pieces of writing (essay, autobiography, short story, poem, novel) that (a) you found to be especially moving, memorable, and effective, and (b) concerned love, pity, or fear. From the list, select one and write a critical essay about it that analyzes the work and tries to explain its apparent power.

4. In several dictionaries and glossaries of terms, look up the words *catharsis* and *cathartic*. Find out the origins of these words and arrive at a definition you believe to be satisfactory and useful. Then write about a work of art—painting, musical piece, play, film, novel, poem—that seems, according to your definition, to be cathartic for you. Describe the work and explain why your experience with it was cathartic in some way.

5. Let us assume you want to or have been asked to write an autobiography—the story of your life (so far). Write at least three different first pages of this autobiography. Try to make these beginnings as different from one another as you can. Then think and write about the strengths and weaknesses of each initial page. Is there one version that makes you feel as if you must continue writing? Show the pages to a couple of people and get their responses to these different first pages.

6. To what extent do you see yourself connected to an ancient tradition of storytelling, myths, and other cultural frameworks? As you consider this question, think of ties that your family might have to cultures in Africa, Asia, Australia or New Zealand, Europe, Latin America, the Middle East, Native America, the Pacific Islands, Russia, or Scandinavia. Make a list of stories, rituals, words, myths, recipes, or values that you believe came from or were at least influenced by an ancient tradition or by a culture different from the one you live in now. Think and write about your connection or lack thereof to this tradition or culture.

7. Write a short narrative in which you retell, perhaps even radically revise, a folktale, a fairy tale, a myth, an urban legend, a fable, or a religious parable.

8. Try to identify a folktale, fairy tale, myth, urban legend, fable, or religious parable that you believe somehow exemplifies your personality, your life so far, or your sense of yourself. Write about the connection between yourself and this story.

Part IV
Persuasion, Product, Process, and Story

Logic is a wonderful invention. It is so wonderful, people often mistake it for reason. Reason, however, requires sense. Logic requires only consistency.

—Orania Papazoglou

12

Cognitive Travelogue: The Essay as Travel Narrative

Paul Heilker

My style and my mind alike go wandering.

—Montaigne (1957, 761)

In my experience, even the most struggling students understand a basic yet profound truth about writing: that writing *moves* (or at least is *supposed* to move). Even those of you who find writing desperately difficult can recognize which texts flow and appreciate how these are better than texts that are choppy. Likewise, you realize that while it may be hard to get going in your writing, once you do, things just seem to roll along, and the words just seem to pour out. The problem for me as a writer and teacher of writing is that analytical nonfiction is almost always presented as a narrow, one-way street. The directions in which our thoughts are allowed to move in analytical nonfiction are few indeed; the paths we are allowed to travel are deeply rutted, worn-out, and lined with fences and "no trespassing" signs. You have undoubtedly heard the traffic cops by now: "Don't use *I*. Narrow and focus your topic. Construct an assertive, argumentative thesis statement; place it at the end of your first paragraph. Employ an obvious structure to organize your thoughts. Use clear, coherent, logical transitions to link one paragraph to the next. Begin each paragraph with a topic sentence that explicitly states the singular main idea of that paragraph. Support each claim with specific details and concrete evidence. Maintain unity and order: don't stray from your thesis. Maintain a singular point of view on your topic. Use a voice that speaks with authority, certainty, and objectivity about the subject at hand."

If you are like me, you have probably experienced a range of responses to these well-known rules of the road. If you have been unsure what a teacher wants from you in your academic writing, for instance, their simplicity and straightforwardness may have come as a welcome relief. At other times, you may have found them a useful set of tools for gaining control over difficult material or your own confused ideas. At still others, they have probably proven to be an intellectual challenge, a intriguing puzzle ("OK, how can I get what I want to say into that form?"). But you may have also found them disconcerting and frustrating at times, since they require you to lop off large chunks of your thinking that don't fit ("Why *can't* I talk about my feelings?") or to narrow your topic to the point of obviousness and inconsequentiality. You may have even found yourself having to lie to follow the rules, having to fake a certainty and assertiveness about your subject matter that you didn't really possess, your true feelings on the issue being far more ambivalent and indecisive than you were allowed to admit. And you may have even come to rage at the constraints, flailing and squirming in an effort to get the straightjacket off but not knowing how to do so.

This felt need to color outside the lines, to think outside the box, to take off the blinders (we have many, many metaphors to express this common desire to stretch out as thinkers and writers) is what originally drew me (and still draws me) to the *exploratory essay,* a genre of analytical nonfiction with a venerable history and a long pedigree of remarkable writers working in it. Exploratory essays are wonderful and challenging pieces to write, but they are also notoriously slippery things. They refuse to stand still long enough for us to pin them down, and they run counter to just about every expectation we have been taught to have for analytical nonfiction. You may find it helpful, therefore, to think of yourself, the essayist, as a traveler and to conceive of the exploratory essay as a cognitive travelogue—as the story of where your thinking starts, where it goes in its explorations of the unknown (including all the digressions, wrong turns, and dead ends), where it finally ends up, and how and why it ends up where it does.

To begin with, there is a long line of metaphors and analogies, stretching all the way to Montaigne, the sixteenth-century originator of the genre, which consistently figures essayists as travelers and the essay as some kind of journey into the unknown, as "a literary vehicle for the act of exploration," as Zeiger puts it (1985, 464). Graham Good, for instance, describes the essay as "a foray, physical or intellectual, into an open world where almost anything can be encountered" (1988, 10) and notes that the word *essayer* embodies "a feeling of venturing outside the paths of conventional methods" (29). Kauffman agrees: "Entering the road laid down by tradition," he says, "the essayist is not content to pursue faithfully the prescribed itinerary. Instinctively, he (or she) swerves to explore the surrounding terrain, to track a stray detail or anomaly, even at the risk of wrong turns, dead ends, and charges of trespassing" (1989, 238). This movement away from the traditional, conventional itinerary necessarily entails a movement into the unknown. As Howarth suggests, essays "open doors, take to the road, launch a stream of discourse. Their authors begin and move out, heading for uncertain destinations" (1988, 633). In like manner, Fakundiny contends that in writing an essay,

> the route is not planned beforehand, or if planned, then only in a general way. There is room for being dilatory, time for digression. There is the prospect, too, of the occasional sally: a spirited little foray to some appealing spot ahead or sideways, some object or sight that calls for a closer look. The route is mapped in the going. And except for a general familiarity with the terrain to be walked, there's no anticipating what will come your way; you set out to see what is out there to be seen. (1991, 16)

Similarly, Sanders suggests that

> The writing of an essay is like finding one's way through a forest without being quite sure what game you are chasing, what landmark you are seeking. You sniff down one path until some heady smell tugs you in a new direction, and then off you go, dodging and circling, lured on by the songs of unfamiliar birds, puzzled by the tracks of strange beasts, leaping from stone to stone across rivers, barking up one tree after another. Much of the pleasure in writing an essay—and, when the writing is any good, the pleasure in reading it— comes from this dodging and leaping, this movement in the mind. (1988, 662)

This "dodging, leaping movement in the mind," as Sanders puts it, brings us to a second useful concept for those trying to come to grips with the exploratory essay: not only are essayists travelers and essays journeys into the unknown, but *thought itself* moves. Montaigne, for instance, insists that his "conceptions and . . . judgment move only by groping, staggering, stumbling" (1957, 107), that his "understanding does not always go forward, it goes backward too . . . a drunkard's motion, staggering, dizzy, wobbling" (736). In like manner, Howarth writes that essays "chart the mind's motion" (1988, 640); Newkirk suggests they "track movements of the mind" (1989, 28); Sanders says they follow "the zigzag motions of the inquisitive mind" (1988, 661); and Chapman contends they embody "the twists and turns of [their authors'] thought" (1985, 95). Pebworth similarly argues that the essay "is the record of a mind apparently roaming freely" (1977, 18), while Core maintains that the essay is a transcription of "a ramble through the basement or the attic of the essayist's mind" (1989, 219). Finally, Hall notes that early essayists tried "to portray in language the actual process of the mind seeking truth . . . in a style which reflected the movements of the author's mind" (1989, 79).

If an essay tracks and follows the movements of its author's thought, if it is the record, the transcription of her mental roaming, the representation of her sometimes rambling search for truth, then an essay is the *story* of the author's mental journey into the unknown. An essay is a travel narrative of the mind, a cognitive travelogue.

Indeed, it is remarkable how closely the critical accounts of travel writing and the essay line up in this regard. A quick survey reveals that scholars use the very same terms to talk about both travel writing and the essay, describing them both as

- hybrid literary forms that borrow freely from a wide range of genres and combine a variety of academic disciplines;[1]
- texts that push toward the subjective and the objective, toward personal intimacy, universalizing abstraction, and factual objectivity, all at the same time;[2]
- records of what happens in the writer's mind, foregrounding his or her uncertainty as he or she crosses borders, both literal and figurative, and encounters new and unfamiliar data;[3] and
- subversive textual forms that challenge the authorities, assumptions, conventions, and stereotypes at work in the writer's own society in his effort to jolt readers out of complacency.[4]

Thinking of yourself as a traveler and conceiving of your essay as the story of your intellectual journey toward some understanding of a topic can help put you in the proper mind-set, can help give you the proper attitude and stance to be used in writing an exploratory text. For instance, Paul Fussell (1980) argues that there are three kinds of people making journeys: explorers, travelers, and tourists. As a writer of analytical nonfiction, you should want to be an explorer or a traveler at least some of the time; you should not want to be a tourist, at least not always. The "explorer seeks the undiscovered," Fussell notes, and thus "the explorer moves toward the risks of the formless and the unknown, [whereas] the tourist moves toward the security of pure cliché." The traveler, he says, mediates "between these two poles" (39). On the one hand, then, are *writers,* the explorers who can muster "a variety of means and an independence of arrangements" (41), "people willing to travail to earn illumination" (45), whose rewards are "adventures . . . [and the] high hopes of misadventures" (40). On the other hand, though, are *student writers,* the tourists who seek safety and familiarity and guidance at every step of the way. Sadly, Fussell contends, "the tourist is assumed to know nothing" (42). Thus, "tourists are set down not in places, but in pseudo-places [like Disney World]" (43), he says, "and the tourist's rewards, much like the dutiful student writer's

1. Korte 2000, 9; Chadbourne 1983, 133; Kowalewski 1992, 7; Cherica 1982, 209, Holland and Huggan 1998, ix; Kauffman 1989, 227.

2. Kowalewski 1992, 8; Huxley 1959, v; Holland and Huggan 1998, 11; Comprone 1989, 123.

3. Fussell 1980, 39; Sanders 1988, 665; Kowalewski 1992, 7; Kauffman 1989, 231; Fussell 203; Lopate 1984, 47; Holland and Huggan 1998, 13; Recchio 1989, 272.

4. Holland and Huggan 1998, 4; Spellmeyer 1989, 271; Krist, qtd. in Caesar 1995, 14; Hall 86, Holland and Huggan 3; Newkirk 1989, 11; Duncan and Gregory 1999, 5; Kauffman 1989, 231–232.

rewards, are not adventures, but rather a "calculated isolation from the actual" (44) and a "sense that he is being swindled and patronized, or that important information is being withheld from him" (45). If you've ever bristled at being forced to work in a palpably unreal rhetorical situation as a student writer— struggled with an *imagined* audience, a *hypothetical* purpose, or yet another exercise *simulating* an actual writing task—then you know the frustrations and limitations of writing as a tourist.

Moreover, in a scheme much like Fussell's, Paul Theroux (1985) maintains that there are "two sorts of travelers": travelers and mock travelers. As a writer of analytical nonfiction, you should want to be a traveler/writer, at least some of the time; you should want to avoid mock travel/student writing, at least some of the time. In the first category, we find those people who are "clinging to the traditional virtues of travel, the people who endure a kind of alienation and panic in foreign parts for the after-taste of having sampled new scenes," those who understand that "travel is at its best rather comfortless," that

> travel is never easy: you get very tired, you get lost, you get your feet wet, you get little co-operation, and—if it is to have any value at all—you go alone. Homesickness is part of this kind of travel. In these circumstances, it is possible to make interesting discoveries about oneself and one's surroundings. (131)

That's what writing an exploratory essay, telling the story of your thinking, should feel like. When your analytical nonfiction does feel this alien and thrilling, you will know you are truly traveling and that your cognitive travelogue is especially worth recounting. If, as Theroux says, "travel is very unsettling, and it can be quite hazardous and worrying" (132), then the stories we tell of that travel should be as well. If writing your exploratory essay feels weird—unsettling, worrying, or even hazardous—then you are probably on the right track.

In the second category, however, we find the mock travelers/student writers. As Theroux says, "For these people travel, paradoxically, is an experience of familiar things; it is travel that carries with it the illusion of immobility. It is the going to a familiar airport and being strapped into a seat and held captive for a number of hours—immobile." Once you arrive, you realize that "the hotel and food here are identical to the hotel and the food in the city one has just left," that "there is nothing new." As Theroux notes, "This is all tremendously reassuring and effortless" (131), but "it is wrong to mistake [this] as the sort of travel which allows a person to make discoveries" (133). If you've ever felt like you had to crank out one more paper for school, if you've ever groaned at the prospect of having to once again fill in that same static and stagnant but familiar textual form, then you know the experience of mock travel. To some degree, mock travel is inescapable, of course. As Theroux notes, "It is not possible for people to travel in large numbers and have it any other way. In order to process and package travelers in great numbers, a system has to be arrived at. This system, in an orderly way, defeats the traditional methods of travel and has made true travel almost obsolete" (133). In this light, it is easy to see the ubiquitous five-paragraph theme that still dominates academic writing instruction in this country as a quintessential process and package of cognitive mock travel, one that results in an orderly system capable of processing great numbers of students but which also results in a system of familiar, nearly identical, and immobile stories of thinking that never really goes anywhere, never discovers anything new.

Let us pause here for a moment to acknowledge that while these clear-cut categories (these neat distinctions between adventurers and tourists, travel and mock travel, writers and student writers, and exploratory essays and five-paragraph themes) lay out conceptually pure extremes that can help clarify our thinking, these absolutes do not hold in the real world. Real travel, real analytical nonfiction, and real writers are almost always a mixed bag, a complex, variegated, and fascinating combination of these pure essences and polar opposites. As a writer, it is not a case of your choosing between an either/or—either you are an adventurer or you are a tourist, either you write exploratory essays or you write five-paragraph themes—but rather a case of understanding that these are the opposing extremes on a continuum of possibilities and choices, the infrared and ultraviolet at the far ends of the spectrum, and that most of us live and work in the visible light between them. As Fussell (1980) says, *travelers* mediate between the poles of explorer and tourist. You, too, will live and write and travel in that great middle ground, and each task of analytical nonfiction you undertake will give you the opportunity to relocate yourself and your work along the continua between exploratory essay and five-paragraph theme, total risk and utter safety, complete formlessness and pure cliché as you compose your own amalgams by combining well-tested and reliable modes of production with a relentless push to engage with the unknown.

In addition to helping you develop the stance and attitude necessary to avoid becoming stuck at the mock traveling, cognitive tourist end of the spectrum, thinking of yourself as a traveler and conceiving of your essay as the story of your intellectual journey toward some understanding of a topic can help you reenvision what it means to develop your material. When working in this mind-set, commonplace remarks about writing like "I don't know where I want to go with this," or "this doesn't seem to be going anywhere," or "you seem to be going in circles here," or "you lose me in this section," for instance, suddenly take on whole new realms of nearly literal meaning. Similarly, conceiving of the essay as a travel narrative reinvigorates the classical rhetorical topoi, the standard methods speakers and writers have relied on to discover and develop topics for the past twenty-five hundred years, changing them from common places into topographical entities, into particular places, mental-geographical localities where we might go for or go with our thinking during our mental-discursive journeys. As Corbett (1971) explains, "*Topics* is the

English translation of the Greek word *topoi* . . . Literally, *topos* meant 'place' or 'region,'" hence our word *topography*. According to Corbett, "a topic was a place . . . to which one resorted in order to find something to say on a given subject" (35). Later, he writes that the topoi "were the 'regions,' the 'haunts,' the 'places' where certain categories of arguments resided" (108). As reliable destinations for our mental travel, the topoi "help to overcome inertia," as Corbett puts it. By calling us toward them, he says, the topoi "initiate a line of thought, which then moves forward on its own momentum" (109). In other words, while a truly exploratory essay will eventually tell the story of thinking that moves beyond well-worn paths and reliable destinations, the topoi offer us places to go at the outset to get the journey started, to get us beyond that nervous paralysis that so often precedes a leap into the unknown. When you think of yourself as a traveler and your essay as the story of your mental travels, then all those standard-issue modes and strategies of development embalmed in your writing textbook—like definition, classification, division, description, comparison and contrast, cause and effect, process analysis, testimony from authority, famous quotations, and so on—change from being deadening things you *have to do* into invigorating places you might actually *want to go*.

If you are still with me, if you have made it this far, then you are surely saying, "OK, I get it. I'm game. Now, how do I get started?" I think the easiest way into writing exploratory essays would be to first write a literal travel narrative, to tell the story of an actual, physical trip you made to a new, exotic location, including the surprises and uncertainties that this journey involved. Since your first visit to *any* place constitutes an exploration of the unknown, a visit to a new and exotic location, you do not need to have traveled great distances or visited foreign countries or flown overseas for this exercise to work. Think back to your first visit to any particular place on your college campus, for instance. You could tell the story of what you experienced and how it affected you the first time you crossed the border into the unknown and encountered the strangers inhabiting such strange places as your English classroom, or your history lecture hall, or your chemistry lab, or the library, or a professor's office, or the central administration building, or the game room in the student union, or the fitness center, or your dorm room, or the laundromat, or the dining hall. If you imagine yourself as an anthropologist from Mars for a moment, as an alien looking at these places and people for the very first time, you may be able recapture that initial sense of just how odd and wondrous they were when you first encountered them, even though they now seem so normal and unspectacular. Or you might prefer to work with fresher information, in which case you could purposefully set out to explore some place on campus or in town that you have never been before. You could, for example, venture into some small, unusual shop near campus, like the tattoo parlor, the health food store, the head shop, the photocopy center, the international market, the all-night coffeehouse, the pawn shop, or the used book store, then tell the story of your experience of this new place and the people in it and how this experience affected your thoughts and emotions. Similarly, you could go to some event on or near campus that you have never witnessed, like a keg party, or a college football game, or a poetry reading, or a classical music concert, or a zoning board meeting, or a court case, or a religious service, then tell the story of your experience of that event and how it affected your ideas and feelings. In short, remember that the new and exotic places you explore for this exercise need not be on the other side of the planet; they can be just outside your door.

Telling the story of a physical journey first will allow you to grapple with the difficulties of how to render *concrete* phenomena and experiences effectively, and while this process is hardly an easy one, it will give you good practice before you try to work with the *abstract* phenomena and experiences of a mental journey. Working to tell the story of a physical journey first will give you a context, a basis, a model, a springboard by which to understand better all the slippery oddities exploratory essays share with travel narratives. For example, it will help you get comfortable with producing writing that is an interdisciplinary hodgepodge as you ask yourself "What is the sociological, architectural, economic, historical, psychological, biological, theological, cultural significance of what I am witnessing and experiencing?" In like manner, it will give you practice in melding different genres as your writing moves toward the personal, the factual, and the universal, all at the same time. For instance, you may find you need to weave strands of poetry (to render your emotional responses and idiosyncratic perceptions) with techniques from short fiction (to describe the people you encounter and reproduce their dialogue effectively), elements of hard news reporting (to represent the concrete facts of who, what, when, where, why, and how), and stretches of philosophical speculation (to consider the abstract and universal significances of what you are experiencing). Working to tell the story of a physical journey first will help you warm up to the intense, introspective reflection—to the deep analysis of your own mental and emotional processes—you will need to describe and explain how and why your border-crossing encounter with the unknown is subversively affecting your mind and imagination, altering your understanding of yourself and the cultures from which you come, and challenging the assumptions upon which all of these things rest.

Writing about physical travel first will also give you good practice in trying to find a home for these odd but lovable texts. As I am sure you've realized by now, exploratory essays don't get a particularly warm reception in academic circles, mostly because they are "inefficient": the ambling (if not rambling), digressive, uncertain paths they cut require quantities of time and patience on the parts of their readers that most busy teachers just cannot afford. They can simply process the tightly controlled, straightforward movements and certainties of the typical academic paper faster and more easily than those of an essay. When you are assigned papers in your classes, then, you would be wise to play the game of *academic* analytical nonfiction by the rules. Not every teacher has ultra–rigid guidelines for student writing, of course, but don't try to force an exploratory essay in where it is not welcome.

Instead, find a place where this kind of analytical nonfiction *is* welcome. Since writers don't just write, since they also work to *publish* their writing, look around for an audience that will appreciate this kind of text. You can start small by sending your exploratory essays as letters and e-mail to friends and family living somewhere else. Ask them what they think, and use their feedback to revise your pieces. When you are ready, present your essays to a slightly wider audience: remember, campus publications are always starving for material. The editors of the student newspaper and literary magazine at my school, for example, regularly complain about their having to churn out material themselves in order to fill the pages of their publications. Exploratory essays can make excellent newspaper feature articles and engaging reviews of concerts, theatre productions, art exhibits, and restaurants. Student literary magazines crave creative nonfiction to help leaven the overabundance of poetry and short fiction they typically receive. And when you are ready, you can present your essays to an even wider audience, trying to get them published in local newspapers or regional magazines, for example. And don't forget that you can always take matters into your own hands at any point and reach a worldwide audience instantaneously by publishing your exploratory essays as a weblog or part of your personal homepage.

From my last couple of paragraphs, it may seem as if I think exploratory essays have no place at all in your academic writing. That is not exactly the case, though. While exploratory essays are typically inappropriate as *final products* for your academic writing, they can yet make for wonderfully deep, elaborated, and fecund *prewriting* for academic assignments. From the moment you get a writing assignment from your teacher, you could start writing your cognitive travelogue on the topic, telling the story of where your thinking begins on the subject matter at hand; where it goes as you do your research, talk to others, and think your way through the issues involved (including all the wrong turns, dead ends, and changes of direction); and where, finally, it ends up—all the while trying to take a step back to analyze *why* your thoughts are moving in these ways, don't forget. The resulting highly detailed, conceptually complex, and carefully nuanced record of your developing understanding can make for exceptionally rich prewriting, providing you with a wide variety of perspectives you might take on the subject matter and any number of ways you might choose to focus toward an effective topic. Moreover, this prewriting could and should pull double duty: once you reconfigure and deploy the material in your cognitive travelogue so that it functions as effective *academic* nonfiction (in other words, once you turn in the paper for that assignment), you can then return to that same prewriting and hone it for possible publication as *exploratory* nonfiction, once again looking to reach an appreciative audience by way of the student newspaper and literary magazine, local newspapers, regional magazines, and/or the Internet.

In the end (and this may come as a hard blow if you are like me and like to think of yourself as a swashbuckling intellectual bushwhacker), the sad fact is that you can't always be an adventurer. Sometimes you will just be too exhausted or frightened to leave the beaten path and will seek comfort in the safety of following a proven route, one that is clearly mapped out for you ahead of time and that you have walked countless times before. Sometimes you will want to have an adventure, but the places you would like to journey to will have already been completely overrun by previous travelers/writers. And sometimes you may want to have an adventure, but the journey itself will have other ideas. For example, I tried to write this piece as a performative text, as an exploratory essay/travel narrative about the exploratory essay as a travel narrative. I nearly tied myself up in knots trying to stay true to that original itinerary. The piece itself, though, made it quite clear early on that it wanted to go in a very different direction, a safer and more familiar path. The journey has been less thrilling than I first imagined it might be, but we have arrived at a satisfying destination nonetheless, I think. Given the unpredictability of our journeys, it is a good idea, then, to have a range of travel/writing options available to us and to be comfortable with them all, because we never know where we will end up and what we will need along the way. As Virginia Woolf famously said of essay writing, "We should start without any fixed idea where we are going to spend the night, or when we propose to come back; the journey is everything" (1948, 97). Bon Voyage!

Works Cited

Caesar, Terry. 1995. *Forgiving the Boundaries: Home as Abroad in American Travel Writing.* Athens: University of Georgia Press.

Chadbourne, Richard M. 1983. "A Puzzling Literary Genre: Comparative Views of the Essay." *Comparative Literature Studies* 20: 133–153.

Chapman, David W. 1985. "The Essay as a Literary Form." Dissertation. Texas Christian University.

Cherica, J. C. Guy. 1982. "A Literary Perspective of the Essay: A Study of Its Genetic Principles and Their Bearing on Hermeneutic Theory." Dissertation. University of South Carolina. May.

Comprone, Joseph J. 1989. "Textual Perspectives on Collaborative Learning: Dialogic Literacy and Written Texts in Composition Classrooms." *The Writing Instructor* 8: 119–128.

Corbett, Edward P. J. 1971. *Classical Rhetoric for the Modern Student.* 2nd ed. New York: Oxford University Press.

Core, George. 1989. "Stretching the Limits of the Essay." In *Essays on the Essay: Redefining the Genre,* 107–220. Edited by Alexander J. Butrym. Athens: University of Georgia Press.

Duncan, James, and Derek Gregory. 1999. Introduction. In *Writes of Passage: Reading Travel Writing,* 1–13. By James Duncan and Derek Gregory. London: Routledge.

Fakundiny, Lydia. 1991. "On Approaching the Essay." In *The Art of the Essay*, 3–19. Edited by Lydia Fakundiny. Boston: Houghton-Mifflin.

Fussell, Paul. 1980. *Abroad: British Travel Writing Between the Wars.* Oxford: Oxford University Press.

Good, Graham. 1988. *The Observing Self: Rediscovering the Essay.* London: Routledge.

Hall, Michael L. "The Emergence of the Essay and the Idea of Discovery." In *Essays on the Essay: Redefining the Genre*, 73–91. Edited by Alexander J. Butrym. Athens: University of Georgia Press.

Holland, Patrick, and Graham Huggan. 1998. Preface and Introduction. In *Tourists with Typewriters: Critical Reflections on Contemporary Travel Writing*, vii–xiv; 1–25. By Patrick Holland and Graham Huggan. Ann Arbor: University of Michigan Press.

Howarth, William. 1988. "Itinerant Passages: Recent American Essays." *The Sewanee Review* 96 633–643.

Huxley, Aldous. 1959. Preface. In *Collected Essays*, v–ix. By Aldous Huxley. New York: Harper and Brothers.

Kauffman, R. Lane. 1989. "The Skewed Path: Essaying as Unmethodical Method." In *Essays on the Essay: Redefining the Genre*, 221–240. Edited by Alexander J. Butrym. Athens: University of Georgia Press.

Korte, Barbara. 2000. *English Travel Writing from Pilgrimages to Postcolonial Explorations.* Translated by Catherine Matthias. New York: St. Martin's.

Kowalewski, Michael. 1992. "Introduction: The Modern Literature of Travel." *Temperamental Journeys: Essays on the Modern Literature of Travel*, 1–18. Edited by Michael Kowalewski. Athens: University of Georgia Press.

Lopate, Phillip. 1984. "The Essay Lives—In Disguise." *The New York Times Book Review.* 18 Nov. (1): 47–49.

Montaigne, Michel Eyquemde. 1957. *The Complete Works of Montaigne.* Translated by Donald M. Frame. Stanford, CA: Stanford University Press.

Newkirk, Thomas. 1989. *Critical Thinking and Writing: Reclaiming the Essay.* Monographs on Teaching Critical Thinking 3. Urbana, IL: ERIC/NCTE.

Pebworth, Ted-Larry. 1977. "Not Being, But Passing: Defining the Early English Essay." *Studies in the Literary Imagination* 10: 17–27.

Recchio, Thomas E. 1989. "A Dialogic Approach to the Essay." *Essays on the Essay: Redefining the Genre*, 271–278. Edited by Alexander J. Butrym. Athens: University of Georgia Press.

Sanders, Scott Russell. 1988. "The Singular First Person." *The Sewanee Review* 96: 658–672.

Spellmeyer, Kurt. 1989. "A Common Ground: The Essay in the Academy." *College English* 51: 262–276.

Theroux, Paul. 1985. "Stranger on a Train." In *Sunrise with Seamonsters: Travels and Discoveries, 1964–1984*, 126–135. By Paul Theroux. Boston: Houghton-Mifflin.

Woolf, Virginia. 1948. "Montaigne." In *The Common Reader,* I. 87–100. By Virginia Woolf. New York: Harcourt, Brace and Company.

Zeiger, William. 1985. "The Exploratory Essay: Enfranchising the Spirit of Inquiry in College Composition." *College English* 47: 454–466.

13

Suasive Narrative and the Habit of Reflection

Stephanie Dyer and Dana C. Elder

Change of Heart

Often in writing, especially narrative assignments, writers neglect to reflect upon what they are writing. During the years he has guided writing teachers, Dana learned to discourage narrative assignments. Experience, conversations with many other teachers, and professional literature taught him that narrative assignments came with the danger of inappropriate personal disclosure. Writers would write papers that clergypersons, psychological counselors, or psychiatrists might want to read, but not what a teacher would choose to know or attempt to deal with.

The primary reason for minimizing or excluding narrative assignments was experience. Most writers can handle chronological order and include multisensory details, but when asked "What is the meaning of the story?" or "This happened when you were nine years old, why do you remember it?" answers were few, long in coming, and often upon arrival turned out to be well-worn aphorisms only loosely related to the stories told. What seemed to be lacking was the habit of reflection. Perhaps this was part of the price of our prepackaged culture, of media that digest our news and entertainments for us before we get the chance, that tell us what things mean before we even think to ask ourselves.

On the other hand, in a time and place where reflection is so little practiced, should teachers limit reflection further or, instead, provide assignments and offer writing practices that encourage the habit of reflection? Dana invited Stephanie, a next-generation scholar and perhaps future teacher interested in pursuing ways of writing with reflection, to join him in addressing this question. The result is the suasive narrative, a specific way writers can practice and perhaps enhance the habit of reflection and further incorporate reflection in their writing. Before we look at the suasive narrative, however, we need to first shift gears for a moment to introduce and clarify a couple of terms.

Kinds of Persuasion

In ancient Greece and Rome, students were taught writing to help them learn to become effective public speakers. Members of numerous communities made decisions that would govern or otherwise impact each citizen, so all citizens were trained to be effective public speakers. What they learned was called rhetoric, what we today normally call persuasion. Persuasion can take many forms, and it is useful to divide these forms into two separate clusters based on the purpose of the speaker or author. These are the argumentative (or eristic) and the suasive, and the idea has always been to match the type of persuasion used to the audience and the situation.

Argumentative (eristic) forms are employed when people disagree, when individuals or groups have different opinions, interests, or agendas. Western culture is very rich in argumentation. The English word *eristic* comes from an ancient Greek word meaning "eager for combat or strife," and argumentation can be a kind of verbal warfare. Think about two candidates for the same elected position arguing before voters in a public debate; both candidates want to win in a war of words and votes. Law courts are also sites of argumentation. Two sides argue their own perceived best interest before a judge and jury. In addition, and some think unfortunately, this kind of persuasion is used in workplaces and families as well. The problem is that somebody wins and somebody loses.

An alternative is suasive persuasion. Persuasion is suasive when it is based on already shared opinions and values. Elsewhere Dana has called suasive essays "join-me essays" in the sense of inviting others who share one's values to act with one upon them (Elder 2000). The purpose of this kind of persuasion is not to change someone else's mind but to encourage joint action on already held beliefs. Examples of suasive persuasion can be seen all the way from students calling upon other students to join them on a Saturday to clean and beautify the school grounds to the president of the United States calling upon all citizens to renew our commitment to and act upon the founding principles of our nation. Suasive persuasion reinforces the values of the community for the benefit of the community.

The Suasive Narrative

Speeches and essays can be suasive, and so can stories, or narratives. The notion of a suasive narrative is older than ancient Greece and mixed in, one suspects, with the origins of language. Fables, for example, can be seen as narratives with suasive intent. One suspects that telling stories to teach and reinforce cultural values is intrinsic to human nature, as can be seen in the following fable:

The Bundle of Sticks

An old man on the point of death summoned his sons around him to give them some parting advice. He ordered his servants to bring in a bundle of sticks, and said to his eldest son: "Break it." The son strained and strained, but with all his efforts was unable to break the bundle. The other sons also tried, but none of them was successful. "Untie the bundle," said the father, "and each of you take a stick." When they had done so, he called out to them: "Now, break," and each stick was easily broken. "You see my meaning," said their father.

—Aesop

The special type of suasive narrative we advocate asks writers to

1. mix narrative with suasion,
2. base the narrative on actual events, and
3. call upon or invite readers to be and act upon their better selves.

Basically, this writing should apply lessons from personal experience to the growth and well-being of a community. Unlike many personal narratives in which a situation yields a life lesson mostly or exclusively for the writer, the suasive narrative reaches beyond the self. Consider the following example:

I Know

Back in 1977 I was teaching in a High-School-Equivalency Program in a small town in Eastern Washington. While most of the students were "catching-up" academically, especially in terms of reading comprehension and vocabulary development, one particular and very young student needed far more catching-up than her peers. She often and loudly shared comments that were off topic or, just as frequently, several minutes or even days behind the rest of the class and me.

During a vocabulary lesson we approached the word "amorphous." She asked what it meant. "Without shape, formless," I responded.

"Oh," she said through her sweetest little-girl smile. "You mean like I think."

"No," I countered through my own weary grin, "I think the word 'incoherent' better describes your thought process." And I knew that instant that I had spoken to cause pain, to hurt, to offend, abusing my own power and position, and I wished right then I could have unsaid those words.

"Well," she replied, and there was fire behind her clear, brown eyes, "you can insult me if you want, but you really should use words I understand when you do."

And I knew she was right. And I know it today.

—Dana C. Elder, October 16, 2001

This suasive narrative is addressed to other present and future educators. The lesson is implied rather than stated and applies equally to writer and reader. It is a snapshot rather than a documentary and attempts to make meaning from the ordinary, the incidental. Consider the following suasive narrative by Ann, an undergraduate:

Parable of the Talents

"So, are you going to be there?" There is no mistaking the high-pitched voice on the other end of the line. Linda wants to know if I am going to the church ladies' midweek group.

"I'm sorry, Linda, but I'm going to be busy," I lie. The truth is, my youngest child just started school and I'm bored. I am ready for something different. Even though I'm not exactly sure what I want, I do know what I don't want. I just can't get over the fear that if I join the group I will turn into my mother, or, worse yet, become a rusty link in the gossip chain. Nevertheless, I really do appreciate her efforts to help me make friends in my new community. With all the moving around as my husband climbs the career ladder, and the time commitment of having a house full of preschoolers, it has been hard to make and maintain friendships. However, my fears still hold me back.

So, where do I go from here? I've always dreamed of going back to school and pursuing my passion for writing. Oh, to get a work published! But school is out of the question while living in this small, isolated community nestled in the mountains of Montana. I suppose I could just forge through the writing/publishing process on my own and see what happens, but where do I start? What would I ever write about? Do I really have anything worthwhile to say?

Over the next few months, Linda invites me over and over to the ladies' group. I continue to come up with excuses. Meanwhile, my not knowing what to do with myself has gotten me down, and I frequently find myself hosting a pity party to which I am the only guest. I guess I'm waiting for a burning bush and a voice to tell me what I want to do with the rest of my life.

Then one day there is a knock at my door. It's Linda. All four feet and eleven inches of her is standing there smiling. "Here, I made this for you," she smiles as she hands me a wrapped package. I tear open the paper and there is a beautiful, counted cross-stitched picture that contains the words, "Friendships like flowers need tending to bloom."

"Oh, Linda, it's beautiful. Where did you ever learn how to make something so lovely?" I really am touched. I know it took her hours and hours.

"At the ladies' group. We set goals and help and encourage each other to achieve them. This is something I always wanted to do, and I found someone to teach me how." Her answer surprises me, and my opinion of the ladies' group goes up a whole notch. But the real kicker is when Linda shows up on my doorstep waving a copy of a poem she has written and a certificate. The certificate is naming her as a winner in a poetry contest. Her poem will be published, and she has been invited to a public reading of her composition in California. Now she has my attention. She set a goal, wrote the poem and the ladies in the group helped her submit it to the contest.

To complete the story, I must confess there is an element that I have left out. I have neglected to inform the reader that fearless, little Linda with the toothless grin functions on a fourth-grade level. She is a mentally disabled adult who continues to be an inspiration to me to pull my talents out from under the bushel whence they have been so carefully tucked away and use them in positive and productive ways. Next time, Linda, I will be there.

—Ann Reed, October 13, 2001

Here Ann moves from the familiar and incidental to remind readers of shared positive values, and she does so beautifully. An even more reflective example is the following by Stephanie:

The Benjamin Tree

"Hello, Oma," I greet this frail and gentle-faced lady. "Do you know what your name means in Dutch?"

"Why yes, 'grandmother,'" she answers. I tell her my grandmother lived in Holland and was known as "Oma" to me. "What's your name?" she asks. I tell her. She asks me to spell it. I do.

She asks for the spelling again. This time I present each letter as though I am handing her cookies from a tray, "s–t–e–p–h–a–n–i–e."

"That's a lovely name," she says. "Have you been here before?"

This is my first time volunteering at the Senior Care Center. We talk for a few minutes. She repeats that she is tired, and then she says she's embarrassed.

I ask her why she feels embarrassed. "Because I am so tired," she says. "Would you rather I come back another time?" I ask.

"Yes, yes I'd like that." Her eyelids flutter shut. I reach for my bag.

"You needn't hurry off," she adds suddenly. I put my bag back down. Again her eyelids flutter.

"I used to dream when I was young. I would dream of having children. I wanted one boy and one girl." She looks over at me. Pushing her cotton nightcap away from her forehead, she continues. "I kept having girls." Her voice goes to a whisper. "I had a baby that died. I had a fever. The baby was stillborn. They told me the baby was a boy." Oma glances away sadly and then she smiles, "Then I had my boy."

She announces this in a way that I feel like I should say 'Congratulations.' But I don't; I just smile back.

Oma tells me all about her Teddy. He lives in Pullman and has his own business. He was recently married, and she is so pleased that he's found "the right girl."

"While Teddy was growing up, the neighbor girl was after him. She had always liked my Teddy. Her mother called me once and got mad at me for not buying her daughter new shoes. Can you believe it? This girl was an only child. I had four children, and that mother was mad I didn't buy her daughter shoes. I didn't say much then. Maybe I should have said more." She tells me this as though it happened yesterday. She's still upset by it. Strange, what we decide to remember and repeat, after all those years.

I ask if her son has any children. "Oh, no," she laughs, "he's nearly 60."

She looks at me anew. "What's your name?" she asks. I tell her. "That's a lovely name," she says. "Have you been here before?"

* * *

Why volunteer? Why do we do service projects, found non-profit organizations, and give money away through foundations? What is it in us that drives the desire to help, share, and perhaps love?

Have you been here before?

Yes. I am you. You are me. We cycle through this life—completely unique yet strikingly similar. I see myself in her and wonder if she sees herself in me. I glimpse what I will be someday in this elderly, smoothly wrinkled body. Will my face hold soft wrinkles or dry, tight wrinkles? Will I be free to remember and roam, or will I be ever forgetting and frozen in my motions?

Will I end up in a care center with a cockatoo as my friend?

* * *

"What kind of tree is that?" Fern asks me.

"I don't know. It looks like a tree I once bought. It was called a Benjamin tree," I tell her. "It's nice for you to look at."

"Yes, I like that tree," she says.

"I don't think it will go anywhere. It looks rather heavy to move." I think this might reassure her that the tree will be a permanent neighbor for her.

"Yes, I think its heavy," she says. Looking at the tree, she continues in a low voice, I'm not sure if she is talking to me or to herself, "I have got to be going along. I just need to get out that door."

I talk with her about the weather, about the town, and about family. Her eyes remain on the door to her room. After a few minutes she dismisses any further conversation. "Well, I must get going. I have to get out that door if I want to make it home."

I wonder now if she meant her bedroom door or the exit door just behind the Benjamin tree.

Will people come visit with me, just to talk for a while? Will I have cards on my side table and pictures on my wall like Oma has? Or will my walls be blank like Fern's?

* * *

When Betty doesn't smile, her face looks distant: somewhere else. When she smiles, her eyes stand out a brilliant light green.

Betty doesn't talk. She can say 'yes,' 'no,' and 'okay.' She says, "I don't know" for everything else she would like to articulate but can't. These few words make up her side of the conversation for almost an hour.

I entered a game of trying to guess her favorite flower. After listing tulips, roses, daisies, daffodils, and bluebells, I realized I was in trouble of causing frustration for both of us. Luckily I came up with iris, which she said "Yes" to, either because it is her favorite flower or she wanted to save me from further floundering for flower names.

When I told her I would come back and visit again, next time bringing one of my children, she turned onto her side, looked at me, smiled and said, "That'd be great."

* * *

Why volunteer? I look at her face, hold her hand, and feel a sense of awe, a sense of direction, a renewal, like I feel when I look at a fall tree or breathe in the wind. Does holding this hand aged with life, smooth loose skin warming my own, help her or me?

—Stephanie Dyer, October 2, 2001

The following suasive narrative may serve to reinforce the notion of a community's values to the form. Here a teacher is writing primarily to the community of other teachers.

Just a Thought

So I'm talking with a student, a pensive, twenty-some-year-old, healthy, handsome, white male. His teeth are straight; his writing and speaking language is Standard American English. He's grown up here in a part of the country where minorities remain occasional curiosities, where "other" humans hope not to be noticed but always are.

He's using the word "anomie," which is decodable as a combination of the Classical Greek "a," meaning "without," as in apolitical, amoral, etc., and "nomos"—"cultural tradition, custom, or law"—so that "anomie" is literally "without cultural forms/boundaries." A college dictionary defines it as "lawlessness." He explains that for him and for the authors he's read the term identifies a state of high anxiety caused by finding oneself in a cultural setting/situation completely foreign to one's own, what an Asian student might experience while studying in the U.S. or the culture shock faced by a student-athlete coming here to the Inland Northwest after having lived all her or his life in a distant, less prosperous, and less orderly urban neighborhood.

So far, so good. But then he asserts that since he's felt anomie—out of place, isolated, unsure of himself and cultural boundaries and forms (although he's never been outside of the Pacific Northwest), he can empathize with the international and minority students whom he tutors in English. "I know what they're going through," he says in all sincerity.

"Now wait one arrogant, naive, and racist minute," I want to shout. Instead I say, "Dan, I'm going to tell you a story and then give you an analogy upon which to reflect."

"Okay," he responds, presenting an expression of earnest attention.

"Back in the fall term of 1969 I was a first-quarter freshman at the University of Washington. I'd grown up in a de-facto segregated town, and Seattle itself was a diverse and large city. One Friday night a buddy and I found ourselves in the lobby of a large campus dormitory at about midnight. We may have been," I admit, "slightly 'under the influence.'

"In the lobby, just hanging out, were six large, fit, young black men dressed in university sweatsuits. My buddy, just to greet them, asks 'How are you boys tonight?' In a nano-second they're on us. In retrospect, the beating they gave us wasn't much—a chipped tooth, a split lip, a black eye, and some scrapes and bruises. But imagine if you will the feeling of being completely under the control of others whose casual violence you believed you'd neither invited nor earned, and whose boundaries for violence were a complete mystery. Imagine the fear." I take a deep breath and pause in my own reflection; I hadn't realized how hard it would be to speak of this incident.

"And here's what I'd like you to ponder. That night we took a dunking, but there's a big difference between taking a dunking and living under water. That other guy and I suffered about eight minutes of right-now displacement, but those young men—not 'boys'—may have known a great deal more about 'anomie.' Just a thought."

—Dana C. Elder, September 20, 2001

Taxonomy Choices for the Suasive Narrative

As seen in the previous sample suasive narratives, there are different ways to set up and present the writing piece. Although they differ, they all contain personal experience, reflection, and a call or invitation to renew a commitment to a shared value or to initiate action based upon one.

Each of the following taxonomies is made up of several numbered steps. Each step represents a part of the suasive narrative. The parts should be balanced in approximate length. For example, the first and last steps could be single paragraphs of similar length. The intermediate steps may have one to three paragraphs each, again with each step being similar in length.

By writing these parts similar in length, not only does the completed paper have a better sense of balance and become more reader-friendly, but the writer avoids the trap of putting too much emphasis onto one aspect of the paper and, therefore, overwriting one part and underrepresenting the other parts of his paper.

The following taxonomies offer a selection of ways to approach and organize suasive narratives.

Taxonomy 1

1. Begin with a recent personal experience, A.
2. Contrast or connect this with another personal experience from the past, B.
3. Return to the recent experience A and present another aspect or continue the story.
4. Return to the past experience B to connect or contrast with the recent experience.
5. Reflect on the two experiences, ending with this reflection and a call, either stated or implied, to recommitment or action on a shared value.

Dana uses Taxonomy 1 in "Just a Thought." He begins with a recent experience, connects it to a personal experience from his past, and concludes in a reflection that connects these experiences, inviting the reader to reflect beyond the self and to renew a commitment to this shared value.

"I Know" is a snapshot of Taxonomy 1, providing the parts of a suasive narrative in a single past experience and concluding with reflection and an implied reminder of a shared value. The "Parable of the Talents" may be considered an extended snapshot; Ann has several paragraphs on a past personal experience, intermingled with reflection. She concludes by sharing information that not only causes the reader further reflection but also invites the reader to go beyond just "pulling out" his or her talents, a call that extends beyond the self.

Taxonomy 2

1. Begin with a personal experience that has meaning for you. This may be a family memory, a trip, a service project, a walk in the woods, and so on.
2. Reflect on the experience. Write regarding those reflections or ask questions regarding them.
3. Return to the experience and continue or introduce another aspect of that experience.
4. Reflect on the new aspect or next part of the experience. (Steps 3 and 4 may be repeated.)
5. End with a final reflection and a call to action or a question based on a shared value, and somehow suggest to the reader that he or she recommit to or act upon that value.

Stephanie uses Taxonomy 2 in "The Benjamin Tree." She begins with a personal experience, reflects on that, returns to another aspect of that personal experience, reflects on that aspect, repeats this, and closes with a final reflection and call to action in the form of a question.

Taxonomy 3
1. Begin with a topic such as nature. This may be a simple observation concerning any facet of nature.
2. Write about a personal experience having some correlation or relation to the topic.
3. Reflect about the connection between the topic and the personal experience.
4. Return to the topic with additional observations.
5. Return to the personal experience. Move beyond the personal to the general.
6. Reflect on the topic and experience and call for or invite action.

Dana uses Taxonomy 3 in "Bear Kin," included in Hint Sheet D at the end of this book. There are published suasive narratives of all lengths. A good book-length example is Derrick Jensen's *Language Older Than Words* (2000).

The Writer and the Suasive Narrative

Perhaps the biggest obstacle the writer will face in approaching the suasive narrative is overcoming the desire to write the dramatic. If coming up with a topic is approached from the "Think of a personal experience that had an effect on your life" angle, then the result will be papers that need to go to counselors, therapists, and confessionals, but not, however, suasive narratives.

Many flounder under the misconception that meaning can only be found in a loss, a birth, or a death. They think "an effect on your life" must be something earthshaking, so they reach toward the dramatic and find all the meaning within the drama itself.

This is natural enough considering the dramatic stimuli by which we are surrounded. The dramatic provides headlines. The extreme is television programming. Lust for the dramatic has given name to such things as extreme sports and spawned a spectrum of daytime talk shows. Unless something is fantastic, many viewers do not choose to look at, listen to, or read about it. Switching this mind-set can be challenging. Yet, in approaching the suasive narrative, this switch is crucial.

Change of Mind

The personal experience wanted for the suasive narrative is the everyday, the ordinary. The discourse form requires taking the everyday, reflecting, and extracting the meaning from it—extraordinary insights from ordinary life. Writers should, as Emerson said, "be surprised to find that things near are not less beautiful and wondrous than things remote. The near explains the far. The drop is a small ocean" (1996, 69).

The change of mind required is a switch from the usual surface thinking to reflection. Think *reflection* rather than *thought,* and *personal experience* rather than *event.* It is reflecting beyond the *I like* and *I don't like,* beyond the *exciting* and *boring* to *what does this mean?* Questioning the meaning puts the writer on the path of reflection, which may lead to a remembering, or an unforgetting, of her true self or values (anamnesis). Plato taught anamnesis as the soul's need to recall its true essence. Anamnesis strikes a chord of resonance not only within the writer but also within the reader.

One needs to ask, "What does this mean to me?" Then one goes a step further and reflects, "What does this mean to others?" This kind of reflection in writing leaves the microscopic view and recovers the larger human value.

We all know that exercise is not an event but a habit. One visit to the gym or health club does not make one fit. Exercise should be a regular part of our lives. The same can be said of writing and of reflection. Habits are acquired through repetition. Stephanie and Dana believe that repeated opportunities to read and write suasive narratives encourage the habits of writing and reflection. The appeal of the suasive is characterized very well by St. Augustine in late antiquity; its purpose for the audience is "not that they may know what is to be done, but that they may do what they already know should be done" (1958, 137). It is a worthy goal.

Works Cited

Elder, Dana C. 2000. "Expanding the Scope of Personal Writing in the Classroom." *Teaching English in the Two-Year College* 27 (4): 425–433.

Emerson, Ralph Waldo. 1996. *Essays and Poems.* New York: Penguin.

Jensen, Derrick. 2000. *A Language Older Than Words.* New York: Context Books.

Saint Augustine. 1958. *On Christian Doctrine.* Translated by D. W. Robertson Jr. Upper Saddle River, NJ: Prentice Hall.

14

Telling Process Stories, Drawing Product Lessons

Wendy Bishop

As you read Rachel's observations, think about where your story might agree with or diverge from hers. About what are you passionate as a writer?

> We sat in a circle and had a discussion about what gets us going and keeps us going as writers. I found this to be very interesting since our class seems to be very diverse in interests. I really liked listening to what others had to say, and I pretty much remained quiet for some time because I was thinking about what I feel passionate about when I write. I think there are several things that I like to write about; I like to write about things I know. When I do so, I always have a lot to say. I do have to admit though that I do not do much writing in my free time unless it is in my own personal journal, but I do enjoy writing for classes where I know my writing is going to be read and that I will receive some positive feedback on what I have to offer as a writer.
>
> ——Rachel

I'm a pushover for the writing story. As another writing teacher, Richard Miller, puts it, "I am as interested in the expectations that we bring to the activity of writing as I am in the writing we produce to meet those expectations" (2002, 50). Like Miller, I'm fascinated with the "how" and the "why" of writing even as I get ready to read the "whats," the written products produced by classroom authors. When I read others' writing narratives, I get to rethink my own life in writing. When I read Rachel's journal observations, for instance, I'm reminded that writers need to care about their texts, have competing interests for their writing time, and respond well to success—writers like to have readers. Seems like common sense, of course, but sometimes the most obvious of lessons can get lost in the complexity of our everyday lives, lives that often seem too busy for writing and reflecting on writing.

Because I ask them to explore who they are as writers at every turn, my students get tired of telling me process stories. So, term by term, I use different writing triggers, several of which I'll discuss in this chapter, including the literacy narrative; the "How I Write" essay; the sharing of metaphors, beliefs, habits, and rituals; and a letter to a future writing self. For instance, in one class period we may begin by discussing what compels us to write; during another class period we complete initial self-inventories, answering What do you write? When do you write? How do you write? and Why do you write? Across a term, we regularly share the stories of how we composed a particular draft and analyze those stories for commonalities and differences.

> It's past two in the morning now; the hall is quiet. My roommate isn't here; he's out partying as usual. It's better this way, no distractions. I sit down. My computer's word processor is already running. I scoot my chair back from the screen, set the keyboard on my lap, and prop my feet on top of the desk. I stare at the screen, type a few words, delete a few words, and get up. It's not right.
>
> —Ben

> One thing I realized was that many people do not do much drafting, or brainstorming. They just begin to write. And, many people do not write their paper long hand. They stick to the computer and they have their reasons for doing so.
>
> —Rachel

My students get pretty tired of telling me stories about how they write because this is contrary to many of their earlier classroom experiences where they were told what to write and the final product was the primary class focus. To some degree, it's new and potentially stressful to tell writing process stories, simply because they represent a new genre of writing. The emphasis in other classes was writing success or failure more than the interesting paths that lead to successes and failures (which are of inherent writerly interest, too).

My students get tired at first and then later in the term they get more interested when they discover for themselves how writing (process) narratives can lead to better self-understanding and how literacy narratives of any kind can help them rethink the worlds they are writing themselves into. For instance, Ben's story, above, is individual, yet the particulars here gesture toward the universal. Ben writes in the very early morning hours, but these early morning hours come at the end of his day. My story is similar but different. I compose in the early morning hours, too, getting up at 5 A.M. fairly regularly in order to work on writing projects like this one. While I start my day with writing, Ben, like many of the writers in my classes, ends his day that way, composing while other dorm residents are still out or when he comes back from evening excursions. We both write during the darkness of early morning hours, but how different are the worlds of his 2 to 4 A.M. and my 5 to 7 A.M.! When we meet in the writing class at 2 P.M. that day, we're comparing apples and oranges, different writing worlds. Still, I once inhabited Ben's world—not surprisingly, I was in college then and worked until 10 P.M. in a music library and came home to write poetry for classes late into the night. It wasn't until I had children, and different work and life demands, that I found my desire to write made me rise early, hoping to tap my most energy-filled and quiet work hours.

Rachel, too, learned her classmates' habits varied from her own. A planner, she found others didn't plan to the same degree. A brainstormer, she found others sat down and pounded out a draft (often that 2 A.M. draft) and worked under the pressures and pleasures of a very different process. While Ben tended to stop and start at the word level and Rachel did a lot of brainstorming, both, as we learned through their class writings, were comfortable drafting and returning to a draft. Contrast their composing stories with this portion of Rob's:

> If I can get started then I don't have any problem. Its when I start the paper, stop and wait until later, and then start working on it again that I get confused as to what I was trying to say. It's just like trying to verbally tell a story, stopping until later, then trying to pick up where you left off. I just can't seem to get back into the same voice or style to finish the essay. That's what made the revising of this essay so incredibly difficult. I'd add in some new sections and they'd just appear to stick out, or not flow with the rest of the story.

There is no single best writing process. There are many writing processes with instructive commonalities. Each of these writers faces different challenges, and each might learn from the others' preferences and practices. Ben likes not to have the distractions of a roommate but in some ways appears to be creating his own distractions by stopping and starting (perhaps he's actually unproductively weary when he finally out-waits his roommate and finds a quiet writing moment in the normally cacophonous dorm?). Rachel writes in longhand and might find computing could help her capture more of her brainstorming. Rob relies on his storytelling voice to propel his work and he might find that organizing brainstorming of the sort that that Rachel practices could help him block out a text's direction. If he did this preplanning, Rob might feel less dependent on single-breath drafting and might be able to leave a composing screen and return renewed and ready to make his text more complex.

Process narratives, then, let us ask useful questions about writers and writing. When should you write, how should you write, what do you write, and how do you learn to write better? The more thoroughly you detail your activities, the more detailed can be your discoveries. As he continues, Ben identifies for himself some of the problems inherent in late-night work:

> The fourth song of the album . . . it's been fifteen minutes. My mind flies while my fingers on the keyboard try to keep up. I've found my angle. . . . Just when it seems I'm gonna get to bed before three thirty, I hit a wall. As usual, I didn't prewrite or even gather all my thoughts for the paper, just

wanted to get something down and see where it took me. Well, it took me right into a dead end. Words have stopped coming to me. At first I panic— start thinking about how I don't have time to stop. I try to force myself to write something, but keep deleting it. My head begins to throb. My panic slowly recedes and I realize I've only lost five or ten minutes. I go back and read what I've got. It seems all right, a little interesting. . . . Getting past the mind block took me three songs. The eighth song [on the CD] is over. It's been just under forty minutes. Now there's almost a page. . . . After two minutes without typing, I've got it. I start my final paragraph. My words are sincere, albeit cheesy. Conclusions are not my forte. They take as much time as three paragraphs of the body would take, and I always hate them anyway. By the time the next song, the twelfth and final song, is done, I too have finished. I have two pages; it's been about an hour.

With relief I select all the text and change it from single spacing to double spacing. A two-page paper has become a four-page paper. I love computers. I print the pages and begin to read them. It's good that the album has finished now so when I read the paper in my head I can find the weak spots. I make corrections, move some sentences, delete a lot of words, save, and go to bed. I sleep well even though I know I'm going to hate what I wrote when I read it the next morning. I'll butcher it, especially the overly emotional parts, and still hate it. That's why no paper of mine is ever finished. It just ends.

As writing advisors—and that's how I envision the role of peers in a writing workshop classroom—reading Ben's narrative allows us to identify several places where we could offer him sympathy *and* suggestions. He already knows a lot about his writing, but he could use what he knows to change his process, to experiment with it, to improve the odds that he'll have a productive writing session. In telling process stories, writers both recount and rehearse. They try out versions, examine options, and propose futures. After reading several process narratives of this sort, Katie shared this observation in her journal; she was revising her own "How I Write" essay draft at the time:

> I haven't really investigated the routine that my writing life takes on and maybe by not investigating it I have ignored the fact that in the large span of time between blank page and finished product there is something going on that I should remember so that the next time I am writing I can skip the amount of time it takes me to just get started. Maybe here, in my discussion of how I write, I will unlock the hidden secrets and truths that take place in that long process, enabling me to shorten the process in the future and discover how it actually is that I write.

Katie is interested in using what she learns to change, in creating a new story of writing that can reposition her with regard to her work.

While composing "How I Write" essays, class authors shared drafting narratives filled with roommate interruptions, idea block, last-minute scrambles, senioritis, and pure writing apathy. In their responses to initial drafts of these class essays, Kara and Will quickly noted this surprising negativity, surprising to them given that most first-day "self-introduction" stories in our class had been about how much each class member loved to write. The procrastination theme continued to demand our attention as class drafts were revised and discussed during our first month together.

> I noticed that the majority of the "How I Write" essays concentrated on procrastination, an enormous obstacle in the writing life of college students anywhere. I think that work, school activities, and other social events seem to take away from the time and the discipline that is needed to sit down with a piece of paper and pen, or at a computer, and actually concentrate on writing, whether it be for an assignment or for creative expression. I know that this obstacle is something that almost every student in this class can relate to.
> —Katie

> Everyone procrastinated, everyone basically hated to rewrite. What I really enjoyed about the "How I Write" essays was the fact that some people were exactly like me. Every time I have to write, my major ordeal is concentration and trying to focus on writing my assignment. It was funny how everyone went through this.
> —Genie

> Procrastination was repeatedly deemed a force stronger than gravity. Each of us feels its effects. My essay alone may be titled procrastination, as it is a half-baked product whose absence of content testifies more to procrastination than to what actually is there.
> —Anna

By examining stories of procrastination, class members began to consider the number of times they relied on procrastination as a major part of their actual writing repertoire.

> I think I am like most people in that anything can distract me. If my room is messy I feel like I *have* to get that cleaned up before I can *possibly* write. If I have reading to do, I will reason with myself that writing is easier than reading a book I don't want to read, so I make myself read first. It takes me a long time to get myself settled at the computer, but once I am set, I am usually good to go.
> —Etta

Some defended their habit and some had alternate habits that others could consider as potential work-arounds. A classroom freewrite and discussion about writing rituals (productive habits versus unproductive blocks) led Kristen to these process observations:

Driving is when I get so many of my thoughts. When I drive, I think constantly. I need the windows down and a long road with no stops—a rural
highway. This gets the ball rolling. I also like to lay on my bed with my head
practically out the window. The window near my bed is always in the sunlight so it is bright and warm and there are vines growing on the screen that
make great shadows. Waking up slowly in the morning puts me in a great
mood and thoughts pour out. Dreams also are a big part of my story-telling
and therefore are sometimes included in my writing. I have a double bed and
I only sleep on one half and books, notebooks, and journals fill up the other
half. I can wake up and find a pen or pencil somewhere in the sheets and
begin writing. Sometimes I fall asleep with the light on and my head on my
journal. My roommate hates this because it "wastes electricity." The time my
habits or fetishes take away from writing is irrelevant because it is some of
the fun within composition.

—Kristen

Some class writers began to realize that certain practices of avoiding writing were part of writing. They began to use "How I Write" narratives to ask
questions about why they wrote. For Kristen, writing requires the pleasures of
desire, dreaming, and reflection.

Another writer, Katie, draws a distinction between school writing and writing for creative expression. This distinction may offer an insight into procrastination. We may all be more likely to put off *assigned* writing. If we can resee
such writing as self-assigned (after all, we are the ones enrolled in class, agreeing to write for a local newspaper, or completing a chapter for a book like this
one), if we can focus on the productive aspects of delay and the pleasures of the
process, we may be more encouraged to take needed time for our composing.

I wanted to know if most of them [classmates] were only writing for assignments for school, or had an insatiable desire to watch the thoughts of their
imaginative minds develop into beautiful language on paper. Overall, I think
this would be an interesting assignment for the entire class to write again
[about "How I Write"] five to ten years down the road. It would be interesting to see how each person's perspective of how they write would change as
they find they hardly ever write (not being students any longer), or those who
continue to write for careers or personal pleasure.

—Katie

By exploring process stories, writers gain insights into their commitment
to writing. Meeting themselves in their writing, they can envision options and
allow the old to interact with the new. Anna, for one, left herself more time to
write her next essay, a literacy narrative (see Hint Sheet E), as a result of cri-
tiquing her own initial, half-baked product, a product she felt obliged to defend
in a full-class workshop when under public scrutiny and then admitted to not
valuing much herself when undertaking private self-analysis later.

There are, of course, two schools of thought on this idea of writing about your writing. The writing product school suggests that to write about your process is a waste of words, self-indulgent, navel gazing, or beside the point. This type of writer believes you either have it or don't—the knack, the art, the ability. If we hear about these writers' processes, it is after they are widely published and when, under controlled conditions, they allow interviewers to ask questions about genre, inspiration, and writing history. At this point, with a reputation to uphold, protect, or create, these writers remember the story they want to tell about their writing, often ignoring and glossing over the inevitable and difficult detours of apprenticeship. We read their narratives and agree to the myth: they have it, we don't. They're writers. We're not.

The writing process school of thought admits that the writer's goal is to invent a strong and effective product but posits that the journey toward an effective text predicts missteps, experiments gone awry, and dark nights of the soul. In fact, that's how one learns, by aspiring to, experimenting with, trying out, and learning from writerly moves. No pain no gain. Not that all writing has to be or should be painful. *Quite the contrary.* Writers work best by tapping the pleasure in their processes, but it's hard sometimes to know where the pleasure lies unless actions are examined.

Certainly the author is as worried as anyone about the plausibility and quality of the final product. So, in search of better products, writers seek improvement through self-analysis, by drawing lessons from previous attempts. In fact, many writers enjoy this journey, a lot: that's what keeps them writing. It's what the phrase "I love language" means to many. As in cooking, they try the genre—the recipe—again. They modify, they taste, they get new ingredients, they go down the engaging paths of trial and error, gaining skill and expertise. These writers consider the steps along the way—salt, now? cool before mixing, or not?—not simply in rose-colored, after-the-fact professional writers' interviews (although they're as willing as any other writer to talk after the fact, too) but throughout the act: they ask themselves productive questions about their work. Because memory is fallible, they keep journals, they discuss drafts with friends, they know that their writing results from action and reflection both. And any writer can learn to incorporate self-questioning and writing narratives into his work life.

In his popular book *Writing Without Teachers,* Peter Elbow (1973) tells the story of learning from his writing problems through careful self-study. Blocked time and again as a writer, and particularly when trying to complete a dissertation, Elbow stuffed his pockets with small notes about each writing problem he encountered. He studied those scraps of paper, noting the habits he developed to work around and through his writing problems, realizing he improved both attitude and aptitude through exercises. Elbow went on to popularize his best exercise, freewriting: writing through blocks and indecision, just writing in timed bouts of ten, twenty, or thirty minutes as a method for warming up, for deflecting self-criticism, and eventually for enlarging and deepening the thinking in a draft anywhere along the way. In some ways, I ask my students to pursue Elbow's method of self-study for a term by writing all manner of process self-audits and self-analyses and keeping records of their composing. You've been reading portions of such freewrites, journal self-analyses, and process narratives in this chapter.

While writers of the product school focus on the "why I write story," writers of the process school find the "how I write" story crucial. I don't want you to take sides but to experience them both. Most of us need both sorts of stories and often learn that we discover the "why" along the highway of the "how." If we simply say why—that I write to please myself, to graduate, to meet that assignment—we give over control, caving in to exigency. We take control when we examine and improve our performance.

Here's another way to think about processes and products, using the distinctions between plot and story offered by E. M. Forester. "The King died and then the Queen died" gives us plot—cause. "The King died and then the Queen died *of grief*" creates a story—cause and effect. To write paper after paper without seeing what these compositions add up to, is to my mind a writing life based on plot. Something caused me to write. Something else caused me to write again. Caught up in plotting—getting from one project to the next, often just barely—writers can only add up, accumulate discrete pieces into a writer's grab bag of variable quality: this piece, that piece, a lot of discrete pieces. Hit and miss, page after page—good or bad pages, we don't know. Far different then to use the learning in one paper to inform the potential of the next:

> My original story idea, the one I am stuck in front of this laptop writing the story about trying to write, was about a man in his eighties steadily deteriorating from excessive alcohol and drug abuse as a younger man and the onset of Alzheimer's disease. The story was to expose the situation from the perspective of his forty-year-old son and how he was dealing with the sad, but also humorous actions of his father. But I am not a forty-year-old man with an eighty-year-old father. I could try to pretend I am in the voice of the character, but the voice would not be honest, not real. This really makes me realize that the best stories would be stories that my audience and I could relate to together. I am a twenty-four-year-old woman. The experiences that I have been through, go through, and may go through, could be used in my stories, fictionalize them a bit, but deep down they would be me, my voice. I could create imaginary events, experiences, characters, but they would all stem from some part of me. I could create one character who is the sympathetic side of me and one who is the hard cold side of me, and I would know those characters, their reactions to events. I could write those stories.

After learning that you *can* learn about your writing life, you may be more inclined to look for such lessons. Systematic disruption in the form of self-analysis and reflection can lead to an enlargement of your writing repertoire. Explaining her own writing education, Nancy Welch discusses the way her academic advisor urged her to take a fiction workshop in order to disrupt Welch's academic writing, which "was a seamless, predictable little package that neatly excised any potential disruption." She feels her advisor was in this way trying to offer her broader knowledge: "Maybe she saw that my understanding of expository and argumentative prose needed the 'sideshadows' of fiction or poetry" (1999, 120). *Sideshadowing* is a term Welch borrows from literary theorist Gary Saul Morson, a Bakhtin scholar. Not foreshadowing, but sideshadowing. Instead of assuming a set future, in sideshadowing, we ask the opposite: What are possible futures? Options? Challenges? Opportunities? We ask, How else might it be on the road(s) traveled by our writing and by our writing life?

In Hint Sheet E, I offer you specific invitations to these journeys—the literacy narrative, writing about "process" metaphors, and writing to your future writing–self. Use exercises like these to sideshadow yourself, to enjoy the possibilities. Since writing is an artistic, recursive, subjective, creative, and complex activity, the more you learn about writing, the more you realize there is to learn (the same can be said of any expert process). As you examine writing process narratives, you develop a sense of your writing life *as story* and have the opportunity to realize you are and will be a writer lifelong. You're a novel with many dramatic chapters ahead of you: read and write on.

Works Cited

Elbow, Peter. 1973. *Writing Without Teachers*. New York: Oxford University Press.

Miller, Richard. 2002. "Why Bother with Writing?" *College English* 64 (1): 49–50.

Welch, Nancy. 1999. "No Apology: Challenging the 'Uselessness' of Creative Writing." *Journal of Advanced Composition* 19 (1): 117–134.

Sharing Ideas

1. The kind of essay Paul Heilker discusses is one, he writes, with "a route not planned beforehand." For several days, carry a notebook (or a laptop) with you wherever you go, and when you get a chance, write in it. Think of this writing as an essay, or as a prelude to an essay, with "a route not planned beforehand." You need not write extensively when you write. For example, you might be waiting in line at a bank or ticket office and have only a moment to write a sentence or two; consider such writing a completely legitimate part of the route and the journey. As Heilker suggests, this kind of writing requires the writer to trust that a route or a subject for the essay will make itself known.

2. Write an essay about one of your travel experiences, and of course the experience need not be a grand safari; it can involve traveling to a nearby

town or city, visiting relatives, going camping, taking a short road trip. Use a couple of the categories mentioned in Heilker's essay: *tourist* versus *explorer.* In this travel experience, when do you think you behaved as or looked at things as a tourist? As an explorer? From your perspective, what is the difference between the two, if any? Perhaps we assume that it's better, or at least more glamorous, to be an explorer than a tourist, but feel free to write *against* this assumption and suggest what is good about being a tourist.

3. Write an essay about an instance in which you experienced homesickness. What, exactly, were you *sick* for? That is, what precisely did you miss about *home*? What specific images, feelings, objects, people, animals, and behavior did you, do you, associate with home?

4. Stephanie Dyer and Dana Elder refer to a *suasive* essay as a kind of "join-in with me" essay, based on some kind of preexisting agreement or bond between the writer and her audience. Write a suasive essay based on a group of which you feel a part. The group could be several friends; a sports team; people who like similar books, films, or music; people your age from the same town or city; people from the same region; your generation; people in what you consider to be your social class; people of your same gender. Although this essay is based on some sense of agreement or commonality, it could, in fact, be somewhat critical of the group, or at least questioning. For example, you might explain why you are worried about your friends, their futures. You might write about what you like and dislike about your hometown. Or you might speculate about what special challenges face your generation. You could even write a humorous piece about how to spot a teenager from your hometown or about how people behave at concerts or clubs you and your friends attend.

5. Wendy Bishop encourages her students to write "How I Write" and "Why I Write" pieces. To continue this work of discovering your writing self, write some pieces about when I write and where you write. For the first piece, you might begin by writing, "When I write, . . ." and then create a long list of what happens when you write, or how you behave physically when you write (do you fidget, slump, pace, eat, drink, fret, sweat?), or what *always* happens to interrupt your writing, and so on. Try to generate a rich, full list. For the "Where I Write" piece, describe your writing place in exacting, vivid detail. Make us see, hear, touch, and even smell (use your judgment here!) your writing place or places.

6. When writers tell us why they write, to what extent should we believe them? Write a persuasive essay that takes a position on this question. The position may lie somewhere between the extremes of "We shouldn't believe a word of what writers write about why they write" and "Of course we should believe them." What will you use as evidence to support your position?

7. Write an essay about why you . . . take photographs, listen to hip-hop, go to college, like working at a café, dislike working for your parents, paint, draw, dance, play guitar, go to bed very late, like English, dislike English, read novels that others consider trashy, like a TV show you feel guilty about liking, are glad to be out of high school, or wear the clothes you wear.

8. Write an essay about how you do math or how you do science.

Part V
Hint Sheets for
Teachers and for Students

Hint Sheet A:
Additional Ancestry
Writing Invitations

Stuart H. D. Ching

(Using Chapter 5, "Remembering Great Ancestors")

* * *

1. You may find that envisioning a specific person generates material for writing. And I have learned from the teaching workshops of Hawaiian poet Eric Chock that a person's humanness—for example, hands, tears, laughter, and eyes—bear a person's memory and that writers can evoke this memory through figurative language such as similes and metaphors. For example, "my mother's eyes are like . . ."; "my father's hands are like . . ."; "my great-aunt's tears are like . . ."; "my great-uncle's laughter is like . . ."; "my mother's hair is like . . . ." Chock uses several versions of the simple simile structure to prompt writers to compose verse. His prompts can also motivate prose. Respond to one of these prompts (or an adapted version) with a list of similes and metaphors and explore where the figurative language takes you. Do any of the similes or metaphors evoke memory of events in your cultural past? Do they reveal the depth and complexity of an elder or ancestor about whom you would like to write? Can you generate stories that emerge from your figurative language and that illustrate this elder's or ancestor's depth and complexity?

2. In *In Search of Our Mothers' Gardens: Womanist Prose* (Harcourt Brace Jovanovich 1983), Alice Walker teaches us that our elders have inscribed their memory into the everyday spaces of our lives: in conversations of women, in quilts, in gardens. Do everyday spaces in your own life bear such stories? Where can you hear, revisit, observe, and seek the voices of the past? Can you locate these spaces, and recount the voices in these locations? Which stories compel you most to write? Will any one story or a combination of narratives sustain an entire essay?

3. I think that a memoir can sometimes function as a prayer or a letter to or for an ancestor. The "Great Ancestor: Ritual" passage at the end of my

chapter functions partly this way—as a prayer for and letter to my grand-mother, Ethel Yuk Hin Ching. If you could write a prayer or letter to or for an ancestor, what would you say? What would you write? What would you recall? What events would you allude to as points of conversation? Explore this genre—the prayer or letter—as a means of generating ideas, a voice, or a form that may initiate and sustain an entire essay. After you generate your preliminary text, identify areas that can be expanded into complete scenes or even entire works. And as you develop these scenes, consider what motivates you to write this letter or prayer—this story. What value, message, resolution, question, idea, or emotion do you hope to convey, complicate, or explore?

4. My elders have taught me lessons through their stories. As I revisit my chapter, I discern the values of filial piety, cultural and communal alle-giance, and sacrifice. Through my writing, I extend these values for my own progeny. Do stories similarly teach lessons in your own family or community? Recall a story from the past and explore the ways in which it teaches you in the present.

5. For much of my childhood, my parents made me perform rituals to please my grandparents, for example, bowing respectfully three times over an ancestor's grave during the Clear and Bright Festival; pouring tea for Popo on Chinese New Year; washing my hands before leaving the ceme-tery. I cannot pinpoint exactly when such rituals took on deeper meaning, but eventually they did. In a large sense, the passage that ends my chapter reflects on this growth in understanding regarding my participation in the tea-pouring tradition. Can you recall a ritual, a duty, or a tradition that you once performed out of duty but now perform with a deeper understand-ing? Write about this experience at different stages of your life and reflect on how your perspective or understanding has transformed.

Many of the prompts here and in my chapter ask you to write about an elder, an ancestor, a place, or an object. Remember that more likely than not, although you initially begin your story with one of these external subjects, your story may really be about you, the writer, the one who remembers and who writes memory into her or his own life. In 1986 during my undergraduate study at the University of Hawaii, in an advanced writing course taught by Professor Suzanne Jacobs, I encountered William E. Coles Jr. and James Vopat's text *What Makes Writing Good: A Multiperspective* (D. C. Heath and Company 1985). In that text, Coles and Vopat provide some writing wisdom that has stayed with me since. They remind the writer that through composing, the author often begins a process of "coming to terms," resolving an issue, complicating an idea, illuminating a condition, or asking a new question (75–76). Similarly, as you recover the lives of great ancestors, you may ini-tially direct your attention away from yourself. Eventually, however, you may need to bring the subject back home. What does the story mean to you? How does it inform or challenge or edify your own life and condition? I predict that through realizing an answer, you will also be able to send the story back out so that it compels your audience the same way.

Hint Sheet B:
On Inviting and Being Invited to Author Your Life

David Wallace

(Using Chapter 7, "The Poems Came Late")

For Students

Authoring your life is a dangerous business. If you take it up, there are no guarantees that you'll get the grades you want, that your family and friends will praise you for your insights, that your teacher will understand what you are trying to accomplish, or even that you'll be able to bring any closure to the process in a single assignment or writing course. Authoring your life can lead to pain, to a long struggle, to hurt feelings. I can't tell you exactly how to do it, but I have a few suggestions.

Start early and revise often. You may have a wonderful emotional breakthrough as you write, but don't fall in love with the first draft. In fact, the first draft often may simply lead you to a critical insight, and you may have to completely revise or rewrite the piece once you get to that understanding. Also, leave yourself time to simply scrap the piece and do something else if the emotional commitment becomes too great.

Size up your teacher. Teachers are people: they are men and women; black, white, red, yellow, brown; gay, lesbian, straight, bisexual, transgendered. They are secure and insecure; supportive, cranky, condescending. They are usually honest, never completely unbiased, and often overworked and underpaid. A good rule of thumb is that it's probably safe to write about things like those that you have discussed in class or like those that the teacher reads from his or her own writing or chooses as course readings. If you're in doubt, first ask yourself how open your teacher seems. What kind of vibe do you get from him or her? Trust your instincts. If you're still unsure, stay after class, show up for office hours, write a journal, or send an e-mail message to pitch a topic. Not only will you show your teacher that you're someone who is taking the class seriously, but you'll also likely get some important hints about what will be valued in the teacher's evaluation of your work.

Write as concretely and honestly as you can. There may be times when you don't want to be too graphic (e.g., describing a scene of physical or sexual violence), but a general rule of thumb is to put what you want to say into nouns and verbs that show what happened or into key dialogue before you explain why those details or dialogue is so important. If you're not willing to connect the general things you want to say with specific instances from life (whether your own life or others' lives), then you may not be ready to write yet. If you aren't getting beyond generalities and if you're trying to impress people, then you probably aren't authoring your life.

For Teachers

Inviting your students to author their lives is a dangerous business. There is no single right way to do so, but I can offer several principles to consider.

You must be willing to risk yourself. If you cannot share your own struggles with your students, then it becomes very hard to create a space in which they will feel safe to move beyond the usual. But making yourself vulnerable to your students is far from risk-free. As a tall, thin, white, male, tenured professor, I can afford to take risks that I would never counsel brand-new teaching assistants to take. Also, as a man who is willing to make himself vulnerable publicly, I often win over the women in my classes quickly. A woman who does the same might find that she has undermined her authority with the men in her class. I make the first attempt during the first or second day of class, but I always choose a relatively safe piece to share. As the semester progresses, I share increasingly personal pieces with some (but not all) classes. Often I out myself in a fairly safe, expository piece, but I also recognize that once I am out, I will exist only as a gay man for a small percentage of my students.

You cannot create a completely safe space for your students. When students author themselves they often examine hard issues for the first time in their lives. You need to be a sympathetic reader, but you also need to know your limitations. When students share experiences of abuse or emotional instability, I always ask whom they've talked to the issues about, and I discuss counseling with them as a normal option that many people choose. When I share my writing with my students, I also talk with them about the risks it entails for me, and I tell them that they are invited (although not required) to take such risks but that they have to be willing to share what they write with me and (in most cases) with at least one other member of the class. They also have to be ready to take constructive criticism about their texts because in a writing class, revision is the norm. Finally, I try to always remember that I am not a safe reader for all my students. Many of my students respond eagerly to my example and my invitations, but others (e.g., homophobic men) find me a hard audience to write for.

Authoring a life can't be limited to single assignments. This sort of approach to teaching writing can't be limited to a single unit or the narrative assignment that precedes the more important expository stuff to come. Nor can you dictate to your students in class discussions, running roughshod over their points, and then expect them to suddenly open up in their writing. Don't take up this challenge unless you are genuinely interested in finding starting places with your students from which you can grow with them in your understandings of how words can be used and genres twisted and reinvented to meet writers' individual needs.

Hint Sheet C:
The Personal Experience Essay; the Expository/ Informative Essay; and the Feature Article

Joseph Eng

(Using Chapter 10, "Necessary Confessions")

The Personal Experience Essay

There are many reasons to write. In college, writing is most often used in a rather formal way to inform and argue. For example, you might write a paper for a history course explaining the causes of World War II or you might write a paper for a business class arguing that Starbucks is a good company in which to invest. In these assignments, you explain and use public information. In a personal essay, a writer shares a personal experience, and he or she tries to make sense of the experience. The personal essay is written in the first person (using *I*). The purpose of this assignment is to enable you to write about a personal experience in a meaningful way, to show you that writing can benefit you personally as well as academically, and to teach you to use description and narration to make a clear point.

Your task is to write a three- to four-page personal essay that shows your peers and instructor (or a target readership) how a specific, one-time event in your life significantly changed the way you think and act. (You may remember how we called them turning points when some of us shared our stories with the class informally.) Writing about your senior year of high school or even a particular class in high school would not work; it's not specific enough. But writing about, say, how you reached out to a shy or unpopular person on a bus trip to a club or a sporting event and started a friendship with him or her would work. Aim for that level of specificity. Although you might involve other people in your essay, you should always choose an event in which your thoughts or actions are emphasized.

Prewriting

Complete two or three sets of prewriting activities from the following list or create your own topics.

- List three to five events you've witnessed that moved or shocked you. (2 minutes)
- Pick one of these and describe what happened and why it is memorable for you. (4 minutes)
- List three to five memorable experiences you've had with your mom, dad, and/or siblings. (2 minutes)
- Pick one of these and describe what happened and why it is memorable for you. (4 minutes)
- List three to five memorable experiences you've had with a close friend or friends. (2 minutes)
- Pick one of these and describe what happened and why it is memorable for you. (4 minutes)
- List three to five experiences that started out intensely uncomfortable or embarrassing for you but that ended up being positive in the end. (2 minutes)
- Pick one of these and describe what happened and why it is memorable for you. (4 minutes)
- List three to five experiences in which you helped someone mentally (i.e., you taught him or her something useful), emotionally, or physically. (2 minutes)
- Pick one of these and describe what happened and why it is memorable for you. (4 minutes)
- List three to five experiences in which someone helped you mentally (i.e., he or she taught you something useful), emotionally, or physically. (2 minutes)
- Pick one of these and describe what happened and why it is memorable for you. (4 minutes)
- List three to five projects, assignments, activities, or specific skills from extracurricular or summer programs (including clubs, sports, or religious programs) that you're proud to have accomplished. (2 minutes)
- Pick one of these and describe what you specifically did or learned and why that accomplishment is memorable for you. (4 minutes)
- List three to five projects, assignments, activities, or specific skills from your formal education that you're proud to have accomplished. (2 minutes)

- Pick one of these and describe what you specifically did or learned and why that accomplishment is memorable for you. (4 minutes)

Expository/Informative Essay: Experience with Language

You will concentrate on language in this essay: the importance of language, language as a changing element, the exploration of language. I want you to think about what definitions mean to you and what they could mean to others. This will enable you to better communicate with others in your writing. You will be expected to write an expository essay whose key elements are to be informative about language and to communicate that information clearly to your chosen audience. As in any paper, discovery of your own knowledge as well as that knowledge gained from reading or researching is of utmost importance.

You may use one of the following suggestions:

- Responding to any of the essays we have read, write a paper discussing your experience with language; how does your experience compare with the examples given in the essay? Be sure to use specific examples from the readings and also from your experience.

- Choose an instance of language that you can compare or contrast, or research and develop a history of.

- Choose a word that has meaning in your life. Discuss the way that word has changed for you over your life, using liberal examples.

The Feature Article

Be a professional writer! For this paper you will write an article explaining a particular issue, topic, consumer product, or process to a specific audience. One way to consider audience is to think of it as a target readership of a certain publication. As a feature article, your essay may inform as well as entertain; but your primary goal is explanatory, which is to be pursued in clear, effective language, supported with good examples appealing to your target readers. You might consider your drafts as manuscripts for potential publication; information about real-world publications can be found in the annual edition of *Writer's Market*. Following are some topics and their target readerships students attempted last quarter:

- "The Fine Blue Line," targeting *Show-Up,* an official publication of the Police Officers Federation of Minneapolis

- "A Song of Happiness," targeting *Around the River Region,* a newsletter about the members of River Region Health Services

- "Building a Home Theatre System Under $300" for *Popular Mechanics,* a consumer magazine

- "Coping with School, Jobs, and Children: Confessions of an Overworked Parent," targeting *Family Life,* a consumer magazine

Your own ideas are just as good as the above, especially when you start thinking about how what you are saying might be particularly meaningful or helpful for a specific audience. When you consider who *should* read your essay, you might want to remember things such as their prior knowledge or attitude toward the subject matter, the technicality of your language, your style of writing in general, and so on. You should also look up a couple of published articles in your target magazine or professional journal. An Audience Analysis sheet follows.

Audience Analysis Worksheet

Your name: _____

Title of your sample article: _____

Instructions: Fill out this form as *completely* as you can by answering the following questions. Cite examples from your sample article to support your observations. (Use additional paper if needed.)

1. Target readership of your sample: Which pop-cultural/academic/ professional field? Who exactly are they? (E.g., academic discipline, profession, expertise level, etc.)

2. What should be their specific knowledge background in order to understand what your sample article is saying? What might be the attitude or assumption this readership has regarding the topic?

3. What is the author's relation (based on your sample) to the reader? Circle one:

   i. expert to expert   ii. peer to equals   iii. expert to novice
   iv. novice to expert

4. What are the target readers' needs? Circle all applicable.

   i. information   ii. understanding   iii. evaluation
   iv. guidance   v. entertainment   vi. other (specify)

5. Does the sample article have a secondary readership? If so, describe them.

6. Discourse/language conventions: Based on your sample article, describe its use of language conventions such as level of vocabulary, language style, and formatting issues.

7. If applicable, describe any editorial/manuscript policies you find. Copy here information you might find on the Manuscript Guidelines/Call for Paper pages from an academic journal, sections soliciting readers'

contributions from a popular magazine, or entries from *Writer's Market*. Based on the sample article's original publication, for instance, what seem to be the kinds of topics/writings acceptable for their consideration?

8. Based on your responses to all of the above, how might you go about tailoring *your own paper* for the same publication in which you found the sample article? *What are the important issues/features your response group should know in order to help you revise your manuscript effectively?*

Hint Sheet D:
Assigning and Responding to the Suasive Narrative

Stephanie Dyer and Dana C. Elder

(Using Chapter 13, "Suasive Narrative and the Habit of Reflection")

Example of Taxonomy 3: "Bear Kin"

My fictive nephew received a shotgun from his parents on his eighteenth birth-day. "Fictive" is a term social workers use for kin relationships that are real but not biological. I am, according to my social-worker friends, a "fictive uncle." Fictive or otherwise, I am lucky we are kin.

Anyway, this strong and good fellow, Joshua, and I climb a mountain, armed, in pursuit of the wiley and tasty forest grouse. We climb this mountain, maybe an 1800-to-3400 foot rise in two-and-a-half miles. He stops at three thousand feet and suggests a rest. It is 80° Fahrenheit. I know the place and ask for another seventy-five-yard pull uphill, where I know there's a flat false sum-mit with a forty-mile view. There we rest. It is noon on Sunday, September 27, 1998; we carry shotguns, ammunition, and water.

* * *

I love the woods and treat them as if they were my yard, my aquifer, a park created for the good of many more than me, and a neighborhood. My kin—Jim, John, Linda, and Lynn—and I have walked hundreds of miles of moun-tains. We walk among them, so we see and talk about the mountain creatures. We share stories and advice; the previous summer in the Bitterroots in Western Montana, Jim and I warned two-day packers that pursuing the moose that had just walked through our sub-alpine camp was a bad idea. Moose, Jim and I had publicly agreed, like their space. So do bears. The other rule about bears that Jimmy taught me is that they are unpredictable. They make their own rules. Jimmy and his family are kin.

* * *

171

So after five-minutes' rest-and-water break, we top the ridge. Now on much flatter ground, we move slowly and quietly, side by side, Josh with his twelve-gauge and I with my sixteen, down an overgrown logging skid. We carry no big-bore handgun, although sometimes I do, but it's a steep mountain and a powerful revolver weighs several pounds. I know it will be hot. In this place one sees bear scat and occasionally large black shadows departing through heavy cover. Grouse, rabbits, deer, chipmunks, two ravens named Ron and Karen, at least four wild turkeys, and many pine squirrels all live there; kinikinick, pine, Oregon grape, and grasshoppers share the space. There are many spiders who rebuild the webs we break going up before we come back down. This is a busy neighborhood, and I try to stay alert.

But I don't see it. As we move shoulder to shoulder onto an old burn, waist-high in dried scrub and mountain grasses, Josh asks quietly, "What's that?"

I see it then. Twenty-five feet, maybe, the forty-pound furball moving ahead of us at a run is like a big dog but rounder, gray-black, and quick. Oops.

"A bear cub," Josh observes; he's right. At once I want to know all the predatory players in this woody world, and every sense opens for all of us.

"And there's Mama," I breathe.

To say Josh has no woods experience would be wrong. He's hunted deer successfully with his people for two years, but at that moment his thick black eyebrows move an inch and a half up onto his forehead. His eyes are forest green and filled with fear and wonder. Suddenly, as though waking up, he starts to turn; his rising knee and dropping shoulder suggest imminent departure.

"Josh," I whisper. "Don't turn around. Watch the Mama. DON'T stare. We are going to walk backwards. Slowly. We are NOT going to trip."

Black. At least three hundred pounds of muscle and fur. Slick and thick and a little bluish. The mid-day sunlight brightens the smeared white diamond on her throat. She is thirty yards away and directly in our path. A second cub, sporting mother's coat and diamond, stands up between us and Mom, and the mature bear's eyes and attention are all ours. Those eyes are black. They have no whites; shining holes in a silk face the size of a basketball, they contain no glint of sympathy or fear. Slower than hunting speed, we walk backwards carefully.

Two baby-steps later, Josh raises his shotgun to his shoulder, pointing it at the bruin. She's leaned toward us. She is impolite enough to stare.

* * *

The marvel of kinship is that it bridges generations. Better still, human culture is rich in positive patterns for relationships. Some of the patterns are dysfunctional, unfortunately, but most include listening, learning, and loving. So I'm telling this story six days later to Art and Pat.

Art is a mature man. His twinkling gray eyes light up his full Santa beard. He and his wife Pat write about the western experience; both are third-generation westerners. She has a glowing life force I only see in women. Their latest book (half of which is a diary from the early part of this century) at this time tells of work, food, and kinship in the West from the nineteen-teens through the Great Depression.

Their bear story is about hunting partners who met a grizzly somewhere around Great Falls. One ran, and survived. The other stood alone and was never seen again. Pieces of his jeans were found in the stomach of a bear killed by kin who went to look for him. The man who lived eventually left town because no one would stand near or talk to him. They take their kinships seriously in Montana, Oregon, Idaho, and Washington. They do everywhere, I suspect. Pat and Art are kin.

* * *

"Wait," I gulp. "Don't shoot until she's six foot off your muzzle. I'll be here, but it will take both of us if she charges. Better for us to leave, if we can."

My only plan, if attacked, is to cut that bear in half or die in the attempt. Her choice. Her choice. Her choice. Not ours.

Josh lowers the gun until it points at the overgrown skid. We walk carefully back the way we came, like running a video slow motion in reverse.

Within four minutes we've lost sight of the bear family. Then I suggest he turn around and walk forward while I continue to watch our backs. We watch each other's backs. Two hundred yards further we chat briefly. We decide to hunt grouse elsewhere on the mountain. "Bearanoid," his eyes dart this way and that, left and right, ahead and behind. Mine do too. My heart is in overdrive; my skin feels strangely cool.

* * *

There are brothers, sisters, aunts, uncles, grandparents, daughters, sons, and parents enough for us all, with or without biology, blood, or genetic code. Our blood holds special places in our hearts, as it should. It teaches and reminds us of "kinship."

* * *

We hunted the rest of the afternoon in a state of heightened sensory awareness. We did OK on the grouse. Later, I thanked Josh for listening to me. He thanked me for "taking charge." I told him he'd shown real courage when courage really mattered, that he'd stood while all his instincts shouted at him to flee. He said he was glad we hadn't hurt the bear family.

Me too.

* * *

To my fictive-brother Johnny, who has successfully hunted bear, I tell the story and ask that he leave these bears alone. His response, and he and I have been to the mountain, was that we should all stay out of there now, that that family, and particularly Mama right now, have their place, and we have others. He shared several stories, but the time he backed off from a black bear sow and two cubs was very much like this one; quietly, he'd posed no threat and watch-fully left. John and I go back a dozen years. Johnny and his people are kin.

* * *

Josh called me on the phone two days later, wondering when I'd be climbing that mountain again and if he could go along. I said "another place" but yes, adding that throughout that day he'd honored the rules of gun safety perfectly, even given up an easy shot on a grouse because he didn't want to shoot in my direction.

* * *

On October 11, 1998, Josh, alone with his shotgun, met another bear. This one was fifty yards out, bigger, and probably male. Quietly, just as we had before, Josh left. He told me about it in my pick-up driving back towards town.

"There was no reason to, but I had to look. Something outside of sight told me to look," he said.

"Yes."

"And the bear was sitting but very much larger than 'Mama.'"

"I don't try to take us to places with bears, Josh, but they live in the woods. Today you did everything right . . . again."

"I saw the sign," he said. "I saw a print in the mud I knew was . . ."

"You did great."

He knew he had, and we drove in manly silence towards town.

* * *

These past few years, especially, the bruins have been mobile, something to do with El Niño and his sister or global warming. It's also true that their numbers are increasing while their neighborhoods shrink. Respect is a feature of kinship.

* * *

We can't choose our relatives—we are lucky to have blood and powerful con-nections to them—but we don't decide when they will move away, or die, and there are other kin. In our offices, worksites, neighborhoods, and places of recreation, we interact with others who define where we live, who we are, and how we feel about it all. Our real kin are those who matter when mattering is essential. In part we choose our kin; they are also our blood—even if some of them are real bears.

—Dana C. Elder, spring 2001

For Teachers

Assigning the Suasive Narrative

When first attempting the suasive narrative form, many writers will produce personal narratives of a confessional nature. The meaning of these stories remains to and for the writer, and it does not reach out to the larger community. However, we have found that much of this writing is quite good and often contains an authentic voice in the sense that the writer is saying something true to a real audience. Furthermore, some of these personal narratives are excellent candidates for additional reflection and revision; often the distance between a personal narrative and a suasive narrative is not great. By providing examples of both, you can help students distinguish differences and make decisions based upon that.

Some writers are not accustomed to the notion of discourse forms nor the idea that discourse forms might be generated and/or analyzed in terms of taxonomies. Our response is to introduce several discourse forms with suggested taxonomies to each group of writers. Most students are familiar with the five-paragraph taxonomy and the business letter taxonomy. Mentioning these may minimize the wariness some writers feel when first faced with other kinds of taxonomies.

Responding to Student Suasive Narratives

We all need to have our writing trusted before we can learn to trust it ourselves. Writers attempting discourse forms new to them need the opportunity to work with those forms several times without fear of negative criticism about content or surface-level correctness.

Publishing Suasive Narratives

Because suasive narratives feature shared positive values, campus and regional newspaper editors will sometimes publish them in the opinion or editorial sections of their papers. Such recognition, obviously, further motivates writers.

Writing with Students

Writing one's own suasive narratives with students validates the form and community-centered writing.

Hint Sheet E:
The Literacy Narrative, Writing Metaphors, and Letter from the Future

Wendy Bishop

(Using Chapter 14, "Telling Process Stories, Drawing Product Lessons")

The Literacy Narrative

Composing your own story of learning to read and write is one way of sideshadowing who you want to become as a writer. Investigate how you learned to read and write and cast those discoveries into a literacy narrative (suggestions for writing one follow). Here are two brief examples:

> I know my mother used to read to me when I was too young to do it myself. I remember her changing the stories so that the main character would appear to be just like me. It was no longer "Little Red Riding Hood" but "Skinny Red Riding Hood" and her grandmother became a lot like mine. At the end of the story, the wolf would spit out the little girl he swallowed because she was too bony and skinny for him to feel full. She also made up stories to match my life or to remind me that I didn't do what she had told me to do that day and somehow that would bring bad consequences into my life. I soon learned how to read so I wouldn't have to listen to the moral of the story every night.
>
> —Rosie

> My mom would take my brother and me to the public library and let us check out tons of books. I really could not read then, I just liked to flip through the pages and look at the pictures. Amelia Bedelia was my favorite. I made my parents read her stories to me over and over. Eventually I learned to read them all by myself. I owe all credit to Amelia Bedelia. Another book that my mother said I enjoyed was *Good-Night Moon*. I still have a copy of it somewhere stored in my closet at home today. My mom says it is a symbol of my childhood and that she will keep it forever. She wants my children to have a copy of it also.
>
> —Sarah

Writing a Literacy Narrative

1. Draw a map of a house, apartment, trailer, or living space from your earliest memories. Number every room in the house, including bathrooms, porches, and so on. For each number, list stories of reading and writing that took place in those rooms. Choose the most forgotten, surprising, provocative room or memory of a location and expand it into a two-page sketch. If you'd like, expand this exercise by drawing a map of the community you grew up in; describe literacy events in selected spots in the neighborhood.

2. Draw a life map of important literacy events in your life from cradle to the present. Expand on one event in story form.

3. Compile a list of fifteen texts you have in your room or house. List each text as a complete traditional bibliography entry and after that entry, write a paragraph that responds to, explores, and narrates your relationship to that text. After you've done all fifteen paragraphs, choose to keep ten and arrange them in an order that creates a sense of narrative.

As you write a literacy narrative, consider the ways race, religion, gender, or social class have influenced you as a language learner; consider, as well, literacy in broader contexts by connecting your own literacy to family, community, or national issues related to literacy. In "Reading Representative Anecdotes of Literacy Practice," educator Shirley Rose came to this conclusion about the way authors shape these sorts of stories:

> The first act the narrator describes is *acquiring literacy skills,* learning the conventions for decoding and encoding written discourse. This act is followed by *practicing literacy,* actually reading and writing. The practice of literacy leads to the third act, *becoming aware of one's own literacy* (or illiteracy). And this awareness leads to the fourth act in the recursive activity, *becoming aware of the uses of literacy. (Rhetoric Review* [8.2] 1990, 249)

Metaphors, Beliefs, Rituals, Practices

To begin thinking about writing processes, draw your typical actions. What does your writing process look like? With other writers, negotiate a drawing that represents the common elements in your processes (for instance, do all of you procrastinate, brainstorm, draft?). Make a drawing that represents your commonalities.

Compose a letter to your muse: the goddess of (or inspiration for) your writing.

Make a list of your writing rituals, habits, fetishes. Share these with others and look for commonalities. For instance, one class member talked about driving and dreaming. Many of us clean before writing, and so on.

Explore writing process metaphors, using the following prompts: "For me, writing is like . . .", For me revising is like . . .", For me reading is like . . ." Some examples:

> Writing is like giving birth, conception of an idea, delivery of the idea onto paper (strain, stress, pain, and anxiety) and the completion (relief and joy), leaving one empty and exhausted yet elated with the product and anxious for its future.

> Writing is like expressing an opinion or viewpoint about life. The story— whether fact or fiction—is told as only I can tell it.

These writers took different metaphoric journeys and have different tales to tell; what are some of their assumptions about writing, encoded in the metaphors or similes they chose? How do our metaphors encode our attitudes? As the next student writers discuss revising and reading, each story of writing plays out quite differently.

> Revising is like diluting an original brew, working on an assembly line for twenty years, going through labor again to bear the same child.

> Revising is like cleaning the house; everything is there in front of you just not in an order you're satisfied with. It takes valuable time and effort to get it just like you want it.

> Revising is like a never-ending story; it's hard for me to leave my work alone. I always find some sort of problem or something I want to change.

> The process of reading my own text is like a Sherlock Holmes mystery, scrutinizing every little detail and finding out what went wrong.

> Reading my own writing is like cleaning my room. I have to make sure nothing is wrong and everything is in the right place.

> Reading your own writing is like watching the same movie over and over again. You really don't want to see it anymore.

Process Narratives

Get more detailed in your process analysis by moving from metaphors, which encode past behaviors and attitudes, to actually studying your drafting processes as they are unfolding. The process narrative is a mini-essay or a short story that reflects on the progress of your development as a writer through multiple drafts of one or more papers and is a key element in many workshop portfolio requirements. You may be writing separate narratives for each course paper or one narrative that comments on all the work that you submit. To help you construct this narrative, keep records of the decisions you make and the conditions under which you write across the entire term. Generally, I ask my students for an early draft, a mid-draft, and a final draft for each course paper, accompanied by a two-page process narrative. Here are three excerpts:

Partial Narrative 1

I compose all of my works on the computer so I just started thinking and typing about my encounters with reading all different types of media as a child. I started by drawing a sketch of the rooms in my house. This was fun for me so I continued and I did the majority of the work in that one sitting. I save my Saturdays for my long papers. I did minor revisions and changes throughout the two weeks that followed.

Partial Narrative 2

The first half of my rough draft came very easily. I was interrupted by a phone call, went to sleep and tried to finish the next day. This was a big mistake. My thoughts weren't flowing anymore and I found myself writing in a different voice than the night before. That aside, I came out with about five pages worth of material.

Our in-class editing workshop was a big help. Readers pointed out a few places that needed work that I had never noticed. They all acknowledged that my stop/restart point was noticeable. However, they couldn't really help me with it. I knew that was my biggest problem. Overall, their reactions were positive and nobody seemed bored.

Partial Narrative 3

Overall, I probably spent about four hours writing the paper without stopping for any breaks. During that time I'd write the original draft and read over it several times making corrections wherever I saw necessary. My revising didn't last nearly as long as the actual writing of the paper. I did spend a good amount of time revising without actually getting anywhere since I'd add something and later decide it just didn't sound right. I'm ready for the first workshop.

Letter to Your Future Writing Self

It's easy to dwell in the past, or to get bogged down in the present, so that sometimes it's worth predicting a new writing future. Looking ahead—five, ten, or fifteen years—can let you see your own writing life as a grand narrative. From an imagined future, you may look back and realize that your writing life has an unrecognized promise—one you might start working to tap today. To do this, compose a letter from the future you to the present you. Here's what Kristen learned: ten years into the future she is still taking writing classes, she still struggles with revision, she is focusing on fiction, and she admonishes her present self to just do it: to get writing.

Dear Kristen:

These days I'm taking classes for fun. The teachers are great but it feels strange to have peers for my teachers. I miss the innocence of your writing but with experience, I've collected many more ideas than I ever had at your age. The actual composition is easier now because of practice so I focus more on content. I am really into revision. I like to take the story or subject and come at it from as many different angles as I can work. I end up with five drafts of the same story or essay. I tend to lean toward fiction writing these days but as your teacher Wendy Bishop said, "Fiction is never pure fiction. There is always a base line of non-fiction."

I want to tell you to write. Write all the time because that will really influence me. I want to say forget your fears as well. The essay will guide you but you have to make the first move—pick up a pen. Good luck and have fun with it.

Love, Kristen

P. S. Even now I fear the ugliness of a first draft but I am steadily working on accepting revision as a necessary part of composing.

Contributors' Notes

Carolyn Alessio, winner of a Pushcart Prize in fiction, has published fiction and nonfiction in *TriQuarterly*, *Boulevard*, and the *Chicago Tribune*, is the prose editor for *Crab Orchard Review*, and teaches at a Spanish-English high school in Chicago.

Wendy Bishop teaches writing at Florida State University. She is the editor or coeditor of three previous books in this series (*The Subject Is Writing, The Subject Is Reading,* and *The Subject Is Research*), and she also likes to write and publish poems, stories, and essays. She lives in Tallahassee and Alligator Point, Florida, with her family.

John Boe teaches English at the University of California, Davis. He is also a writer (author of *Life Itself: Messiness Is Next to Goddessness and Other Essays* and coauthor of *Your Joke Is in the E-Mail: Cyberlaffs from Mousepotatoes*), the editor of *Writing on the Edge*, and a professional storyteller.

Robert Brooke is a professor of English at the University of Nebraska–Lincoln, where he directs the Nebraska Writing Project and edits *Studies in Writing and Rhetoric*. He has written more than thirty articles and three books; his collection *Place Conscious Writing: Writing Instruction for Community Involvement* is forthcoming from Teachers College Press.

Stuart H. D. Ching is an assistant professor of English at Loyola Marymount University. His research and fiction have appeared in various publications, among them, *Language Arts, The New Advocate, Fourteen Landing Zones, The Best of Honolulu Fiction,* and *Growing Up Local: An Anthology of Poetry and Prose from Hawaii.*

Stephanie Dyer is a senior studying rhetoric, literature, and education theory at Eastern Washington University. She lived abroad for many years, which let her see and appreciate other cultures as well as the unique aspects of American culture. She believes learning is found within great books, experience, reflection, informed discussion, and nature.

Gayle W. Duskin is an assistant professor of English at Dillard University in New Orleans, where her special interest is in composition and rhetorical theory. Her research includes articles on the nature of literacy and writing by African American learners in nontraditional contexts.

Dana C. Elder is a professor and department chair of English at Eastern Washington University. He has published articles, personal essays, poems, and textbooks while joining students, peers, and other friends in studying and writing for more than twenty-five years. He believes he serves the greater good.

Joseph Eng is the director of composition at Eastern Washington University, where he teaches writing with dedicated graduate teaching assistants. His published articles include topics in writing pedagogy, literature-writing connection, teacher modeling, and writing program administration. A native of Hong Kong, he considers teaching English his lifetime privilege.

Rochelle Harris is a doctoral student in rhetoric and composition at the University of Nebraska–Lincoln. She just finished a stint as the assistant coordinator of composition and teaches freshman and sophomore writing. She has essays, both personal and academic, forthcoming in *Passages North* and *symplok'*.

Paul Heilker teaches courses in rhetoric, writing, and composition pedagogy at Virginia Tech, where he serves as director of the First-Year Writing Program and associate professor of English. He is the author of *The Essay: Theory and Pedagogy for an Active Form* and coeditor, with Peter Vandenberg, of *Keywords in Composition Studies*.

James A. Herrick is the chair of the Department of Communication at Hope College in Holland, Michigan, where he teaches argumentation and the history of rhetoric. A graduate of the University of California and the University of Wisconsin, Professor Herrick is the author of several books on rhetoric, argument, and religious controversy.

Doug Hesse was born and happily raised in small-town Iowa. He teaches at Illinois State University and is past president of the National Council of Writing Program Administrators. He lives in Normal, Illinois, with his wife, Becky (who's a nonfiction writer), and three kids—at least when two of them are home from college.

Jeannine Nyangira graduated in 2001 from the University of Nebraska–Lincoln with an M.A. in English. A visiting instructor at Doane College (Crete, Nebraska), she is also the daughter of a woman who tells good stories over sauerkraut.

Hans Ostrom is Distinguished Professor of English at the University of Puget Sound in Tacoma, Washington. He and Wendy Bishop have collaborated on many publications, including *Colors of a Different Horse, Metro: Journeys in Creative Writing,* and *Water's Night: Poems.* Hans' recent publications include a book of poems, *Subjects Apprehended,* and *A Langston Hughes Encyclopedia.* At Puget Sound he has taught composition, rhetoric, creative writing, and literature. At the moment, he is most interested in the storytelling powers of a British novelist, Muriel Spark.

Michael Spooner directs the Utah State University Press and occasionally writes or cowrites articles or chapters in composition studies—like this one, say. He comes from shy Nordic stock, so what he won't tell you is that he's also published poems, folktales, and a novel for children.

David L. Wallace teaches writing and rhetoric classes at the University of Central Florida, where he does research about literacy and identity issues. When he's not being a boring academic, he writes poems about his frustrated love life, plays tennis and volleyball, and water-skis.